INFORMATION RESOURCES AND TECHNOLOGY TRANSFER MANAGEMENT IN DEVELOPING COUNTRIES

Information is a resource which needs effective management; the management of resources should reduce costs and improve performance. In less developed countries, proper management of such resources is critical if national development is to continue. Richard Ouma-Onyango argues persuasively that on the micro level, information management will improve the ability of an organization to achieve its goals; on a macro level, he reveals how important information and intelligence are in the planning, negotiations and decision-making which are vital to the productivity of a developing country.

Resource management means understanding the characteristics of that resource: its life cycle and productivity; weighing the costs of acquisition, retrieval and storage against the benefits. Current practice in less developed countries, such as Kenya, is that libraries are organized by ministries separate from those concerned with national productivity or development efforts – this divorce illustrates how this sort of bureaucracy precludes the use of known or existing information, knowledge and expertise.

This book attempts to put information management in the context of technology transfer, industrialization and national development. As well as showing the necessity for the efficient use of information resources, Ouma-Onyango also examines the costs of poor information management in undermining negotiation, the preparation of contingencies and the ability to let go of 'dead projects'. To this end, case studies of two technology transfer projects in Kenya, the National Power Alcohol Programme and National Car Project, are considered over a period of twenty years. This book will be primary reading for information professionals, policy makers, economists and business managers, as well as international development agencies.

Richard Ouma-Onyango is a lecturer in the Department of Library and Information Studies, University of Botswana. He has written extensively on information resources in Africa, particularly in Kenya.

ROUTLEDGE STUDIES IN INFORMATION AND LIBRARY
MANAGEMENT SYSTEMS

INFORMATION RESOURCES AND TECHNOLOGY TRANSFER MANAGEMENT IN DEVELOPING COUNTRIES

Richard Ouma-Onyango

London and New York

First published 1997
by Routledge
11 New Fetter Lane, London EC4P 4EE

Simultaneously published in the USA and Canada
by Routledge
29 West 35th Street, New York, NY 10001

Typeset in Garamond by Keystroke, Jacaranda Lodge, Wolverhampton
Printed and bound in Great Britain by
Mackays of Chatham PLC, Chatham, Kent

British Library Cataloguing in Publication Data
A catalogue record for this book is available from the British Library

Library of Congress Cataloging in Publication Data
Ouma-Onyango, Richard, 1955–
Information resources and technology transfer management in
developing countries / Richard Ouma-Onyango.
p.   cm. — (Routledge studies in information and library
management systems : 2)
Includes bibliographical references and index.
1. Technology transfer—Economic aspects—Kenya. 2. Economic
development projects—Kenya. 3. Technology transfer—Economic
aspects—Developing countries. 4. Developing countries—Economic
policy. 5. Information resources management—Developing countries.
I. Title. II. Series.
HC865.Z9T46   1997
338.96761'06—dc21   97–602
CIP

ISBN 0–415–09156–X

To my children Norbert, Joy, Charles and Clara and to the memory
of their brother, James Ouma Onyango

CONTENTS

CONTENTS

TABLES

PREFACE

Information management is the concept of using information as a resource to improve the performance of an organization and its ability to pursue its goals and objectives competitively and cost-effectively. Managing information as a resource means being conscious of its costs of acquisition, storage, retrieval and use as against the benefits that accrue from it. It means viewing information like all other resources in an organization, such as human, financial, capital and energy resources.

Effective and efficient management of a resource requires awareness of its characteristics and peculiarities, including its life cycle. This is what makes it possible to consciously seek what is required and deploy it effectively while remaining aware that a time comes when resources need to be retired. Only then is it possible to institute appropriate measures to manage all the stages of the resource's productivity. Information management is about applying the same principles to the management of information. But, even more importantly, it is about consciously making information improve performance and reduce costs. This is possible because information enables an organization to make optimum selection of possibilities, options and projections. It makes it possible to note early signals of problems and to bring in the best contingencies. It highlights substitutes and complements to inputs in production. Information management makes flexibility possible, and flexibility is particularly important during times of change.

The area of technology transactions is an area of rapid changes generally. It demands alertness to developments to support the best selections and to negotiate the best terms. For a developing country, this is critical, because such countries are not central participants in the changes. A developing country needs advanced information management abilities to acquire technology, to enhance its productivity and to adapt and develop it further.

This book looks at the role of information management in technology transfer, industrialization and development. Two technology transfer projects are looked at over periods of up to twenty years. The national institutions responsible for managing the projects are evaluated in terms of their information management skills.

Current information management practices in less developed countries revolve around educational, cultural and propaganda purposes. This is reflected in the operations and structures of national institutions. Libraries are an accepted part of education and training. When finances permit, resources are made available for libraries in higher education as a matter of course. National library services are the responsibility of the ministries concerned with culture and social services, not, as one would expect, the ministries of information. (Those ministries instead have responsibility for broadcasting government information.) Information is not used as a resource that can contribute to national productivity and development efforts. This book looks at some of the root causes of that situation.

The book uses two empirical case studies to isolate the information management failures of a developing country's (in this case, Kenya's) institutions responsible for managing technology transfer. It identifies poor preparation procedures before negotiations. It points to failures to document negotiations and the negotiation processes. It identifies the lack of a proactive search for projects and partners, and a tendency to confine responses to proposals received without there being appropriate inputs of information and expertise. It highlights decision processes based on bureaucratized routines rather than national realities. This is the decision-making culture that bewilders the information professionals and has made them irrelevant to national development processes. What is observed is a bureaucratic process that precludes the use of known or existing information, knowledge and expertise.

The book attempts to put information management in the context of national development processes. It emphasizes that a fundamental function of information management in development is raising levels of terrain or landscape transparency. The term 'terrain' is used prevalently because it denotes a specific kind of landscape. Information management is about using information to advance the cause of particular landscapes or terrains.

Raising terrain transparency requires the building of appropriate capability in national environment enabling institutions. These are the organizations responsible for managing the development ambitions of a society. Capacity and capability are used interchangeably in this text. However, there is a preference for 'capability' because it connotes an evolving ability, whereas capacity, in a technical sense, carries the meaning of space and utility and therefore is more limiting. Capacity is, however, a widely used expression in economics and other social sciences, and inevitably creeps into the text.

This is therefore a book about the role of information management in technology transfer, industrialization and national development. It demonstrates the importance of information and intelligence in planning, negotiations, the designing of joint ventures, and decision-making processes. It shows how critical the efficient use of information resources can be in productivity and development enhancement. The book also brings out the costs of poor information management in terms of its undermining the development of capabilities for negotiating, preparation of contingencies, fall-back positions and maximum costs, and the ability to let go lost causes or 'dead projects'.

ACKNOWLEDGEMENTS

My writing of this book has been the result of support from many quarters. Friends and colleagues have given strong encouragement over the years and have contributed time and ideas. My family was particularly supportive towards the end of 1996, when much physical work had to be done. They allowed me to relinquish many of my responsibilities and obligations, for which I am most grateful.

I am grateful to many people who willingly gave their time during the research phase of this work. They went beyond the call of duty, and have remained willing to clarify many issues over the years. I have made many friends from this exercise, and hope to retain them.

This study has its roots in a long history going back to my student days in the Department of Information Science at Strathclyde Business School, Glasgow, in 1986. To the tutelage, encouragement and support of Professor Blaise Cronin I will remain forever indebted.

ABBREVIATIONS

ACFC	Agro-Chemical and Food Corporation
ACP	Africa, Caribbean and Pacific
ADC	Agricultural Development Corporation
Aids	acquired immune deficiency syndrome
ARCT	African Regional Centre for Technology
AVA	Associated Vehicle Assemblers
BNPC	Botswana National Productivity Centre
CAD	computer-aided design
CAF	computer-aided fermentation
CAM	computer-aided manufacturing
CBU	complete built-up unit
CIC	Chemfood Investment Corporation
CID	Centre for Industrial Development
CIM	computer-integrated manufacturing
CMC	Cooper Motor Corporation
EASI	East African Sugar Industry
EIU	Economist Intelligence Unit
EPZ	export processing zone
GM	General Motors
GMK	General Motors (Kenya)
HIV	human immunodeficiency virus
IAA	Institute for Sugar and Alcohol, Brazil
IAD	International Automotive Design
ICDC	Industrial and Commercial Development Corporation
ICO	International Coffee Organisation
ICT	information and communications technology
IDB	Industrial Development Bank
IIC	International Investment Corporation
IMF	International Monetary Fund
IPC	Investment Promotion Centre
ISI	import-substitution industrialization

ISPC	Industrial Survey and Promotion Centre
IT	information technology
ITC	Information Trust Corporation
ITDG	Intermediate Technology Development Group
KAM	Kenya Association of Manufacturers
KBS	Kenya Bureau of Standards
KCFC	Kenya Chemical and Food Corporation
KFC	Kenya Fibre Corporation
KIRDI	Kenya Industrial Research Development Institute
KMI	Kenya Motor Industry Association
KNCCI	Kenya National Chamber of Commerce and Industry
KPC	Kenya Pipeline Company
KSA	Kenya Sugar Authority
KVM	Kenya Vehicle Manufacturers
KVMA	Kenya Vehicle Manufacturers' Association
LDC	less developed country
MIRA	Motor Industry Research Association
MIRU	Motor Industry Research Unit
MMC	Mitsubishi Motors Corporation
MNC	multinational corporation
MORST	Ministry of Research, Science and Technology
MUB	manufacturing under bond
NCP	National Car Project
NCST	National Council for Science and Technology
NGO	non-governmental organization
NIC	newly industrialized country
NPC	New Projects Committee
OAU	Organization of African Unity
OECD	Organisation for Economic Co-operation and Development
OPS	open-pan sulphitation
PADIS	Pan African Documentation and Information System
PCI	per capita income
PEC	Process Engineering Company
PRP	plywood-reinforced plastic
PTA	preferential trade authority
SADC	Southern Africa Development Community
SMME	small, medium and micro enterprises
tcd	tonnes of cane crushed per day
UN	United Nations
UNCTAD	United Nations Conference on Trade and Development
UNECA	United Nations Economic Commission for Africa
UNIDO	United Nations Industrial Development Organization
VEW	Vereinigte Edelstahlwerke GmbH
VP	vacuum pan

ABBREVIATIONS

WMI	Willowvale Motor Industries
WTO	World Trade Organisation
WWW	World Wide Web

Part I
RECONCEPTUALIZING DEVELOPMENT

INTRODUCTION

The development process remains a 'mystery' to development specialists despite a growing body of literature over the decades.[1] The 1980s was a 'lost development decade' for much of the Third World. It was characterized by falling per capita incomes, foreign exchange crises, worsening debts, rising malnutrition, deteriorating health and the disintegration of infrastructures.[2] Gaps in the understanding of the development process are confirmed by the uncertainties of the 1990s. With some effort the 1990s may become the decade of stock-taking in preparation for reconstruction and development.[3] This is necessary if the new millennium is to be entered in hope.

This knowledge deficiency is partly due to the narrow disciplinary specialization of social sciences, which has made it difficult to grasp the full nature of the wider development process. Although a focus of various social science disciplines, the sub-discipline of development economics has given economics a high profile in the generation of intellectual ideas in this area.

The frustrations of underdevelopment are exacerbated by tragedies and disasters caused by natural and human-induced calamities that drain human and infrastructural resource investments in less developed countries.

Part I will argue for an information dimension to development studies that takes into account the electronic-based information economy and recent experiences. It will suggest a flexible, multidisciplinary knowledge- and information-based development paradigm. The new framework conceives development as constituting behavioural and institutional changes in a country. The process of change creates uncertainty. This can be destabilizing and unpredictable. Good national information management helps cope with managing change and uncertainties. A proactive information and knowledge-seeking posture makes it possible to conceive policies that take stock of national capabilities and are able to advance national learning. Alertness to internal and external changes among a country's institutions makes it possible to take advantage of opportunities in an international arena.

NOTES

1 O. Sunkel, *The Development of Development Thinking*, Fourth EADI Conference, 12–16 September 1976, European Association of Development Research and Training Institute (EADI), First Inter-Regional Meeting on Development Research, Communication and Education, p. 15.
2 F. Stewart, 'Walking a tightrope: the global economy in the 1980s', *Third World Quarterly*, vol. 11, no. 2, April 1989, pp. 203–4.
3 R. A. Onyango, 'New technology adaptations, SMMEs and reconstruction and development', paper read at the Science and Technology in Reconstruction and Development (STIRD) conference, University of Natal, Pietermaritzburg, South Africa, 23–26 September 1996, pp. 1–8.

1

THE FRAMEWORK FOR DEVELOPMENT

THE CONCEPTUALIZATION PROBLEM

Development was, for a long time, perceived exclusively in economic terms. There have been recent attempts to improve our perception of it by the use of human development indices, but the framework remains unsatisfactory. Development has implications for social well-being, and includes political and regulatory structures and policies – the infrastructures, organizations and the institutions set up to implement national policies. These are the environmental and economic enabling institutions. Not even the human development indices can yet capture this spectrum.

The institutions are intended to deduce and define the path of change and then to encourage and cajole economic agents and the wider society to pursue the path. These institutions amount to a nation's collective thinking, memory and decision-making facility. They depend on resources generated from economic performance. Because economic, social, political and other intangible aspects of development are so closely interrelated, they have proved difficult to separate and study under existing functional structures of disciplines. Only a holistic, multi-disciplinary approach can address the role, activities and organization of humanity, society, the natural and physical environment,[1] and change over time.[2]

While it is realized that economic and social development is too complex a phenomenon to be competently and comprehensively addressed by any one 'functional discipline', or through the models of specialized sub-disciplines such as development economics,[3] a holistic framework has yet to be established. A factor contributing to delay is the traditional segmentation of the disciplines in the area. The result of this gap is that development models have been drawn up and implemented in less developed countries (LDCs) on the basis of ideology and faith, and are intended to legitimize ideology and faith. Many of these models are imported as 'blueprint' solutions with little consideration being given to the realities of where they are being applied.[4] Efforts at, for instance, localizing macro-economic modelling remain confined to improving local modelling tools and local modelling capability. Even with the advent of information technologies, the emphasis is on appending user-friendlier front-ends to models rather than immersing them in local reality.[5]

5

As a study of the problems of non-industrialized countries, development studies is a product of the 1950s.[6] Shifts in focus, and the accompanying strategies, have reflected changing perceptions caused by identified weaknesses in prevailing thinking. Thus in the 1950s, with most LDCs still colonies linked economically, culturally and politically to an industrial country, prevailing theories legitimized the *status quo*. Export of primary products and surplus, and import of manufactures, human expertise, investments, technology, institutions, ideas, values and culture from one dominating source, were considered inevitable factors in the process of development.[7] The 1960s was a period of political independence and hope, which was reflected in the overly optimistic development models of the time. The 1970s was a period of expansive borrowing and the 1980s was characterized by debts.[8] The 1990s marked the end of Cold War dividends leading to public-sector cutbacks, restructuring and retrenchments, and privatizations and financial discipline that could spell doom for many a nation-state in Africa.[9] This changing scenario is difficult to study from static disciplinary boundaries.

THE CONCEPTUAL SHIFTS

In the 1950s and 1960s, the development process was viewed as a matter of time, 'given appropriate measures'.[10] The gap between the LDCs and other countries was considered a product of the latter's earlier start. The concept of 'stages of development' argued that 'once a country reached the critical level of investment, takeoff would automatically occur'.[11] However, Latin America after two centuries of political sovereignty, Africa's continuing deterioration and the unheralded emergence of the Pacific region economies in less than a generation have weakened the time premise.

The African and Latin American debt scenario in the 1980s led to a loss of confidence in governments.[12] In sub-Saharan Africa, this is evident in the retreat to subsistence agriculture by peasants and the expanding black markets. These sectors are out of the control of such organs of state as marketing boards and banking institutions. But this loss of credibility in governments as 'composers and conductors of economic change'[13] is more widespread. Donor nations and funding agencies are also shifting development resource allocations away from national treasuries and towards non-governmental organizations (NGOs) and the private sector, including small and medium-sized enterprises and micro-enterprises.[14] Whatever the reasons, such acts reflect a failure in the intellectual grasp of the process. Many LDC governments, in fact, claim to have faithfully administered blueprint development solutions advanced by prevailing schools of thought with little to show for their efforts. But many now agree that something has to change,[15] although opinions differ as to what.

While industrialization strategies remain trapped by debates on whether second-hand, or intermediate, equipment is the appropriate technology for LDCs, the emergence of multinational corporations (MNCs), their dominance of many LDC economies and their control of the pervasive electronics and telecommunications technologies has shifted the parameters. Information, knowledge and other intangible inputs have taken centre stage. This has occurred at a time when many LDCs are only getting to grips with the management of physical infrastructures, commodity price mechanisms and the collective arguments for new economic order. Natural endowments like climate and minerals are no longer adequate to fund and sustain economic growth in a future threatened by synthetic substitutes, changing tastes and competition between nations.

Conventional wisdom and tested practices can no longer cope with the pace of change.[16] Continuous learning is now a priority for development. However, institutions such as marketing boards and central banks were not structured for learning and change, and have become obstacles.

Economic models have become irrelevant.[17] But a new consensus on how to manage development has yet to be found. The perplexity is exacerbated by open disagreements, such as that between the World Bank and International Monetary Fund (IMF) on the one hand, and the UN-based Economic Commission for Africa (UNECA) on the other, over the *modus operandi* for restructuring sub-Saharan African economies.[18] The scenario is further complicated by the expected capacity devastation occasioned by the acquired immune deficiency syndrome (Aids) endemic. It is only recently that African planning institutions have acknowledged Aids as a factor to be considered in future planning processes.[19]

CONCEPTUAL REDIAGNOSIS

Onimode[20] considers the conflict between development theories and reality an 'intellectual crisis'. He states that theorists have doctored reality to make it correspond to their assumptions, which has led to flawed conclusions. He blames also a trend in neoclassical economics towards narrow, mathematical and abstract models for 'trivialising studies of development'. Such mathematical models have made comparisons with reality difficult and shrouded the process in mystery. They have led to the implementation of blueprint programmes that are opaque to implementers as well as those whose lives are affected by them. Poor constructions of social reality have led to 'false problems begetting false solutions'. With the models wrapped in ideological packages, rational and objective testing and review have been prevented. As a result, accountability has been lost. This has permitted demagoguery and dogmatism to pass for expertise. In recent World Bank/IMF-backed privatization measures, the emphasis on finance and monetary sides of the economy has led to results that have left many economists bewildered. Governments report positive economic growth rates that are in no way reflected in actual experiences.

Lewis[21] points out that income projection models of development economics failed because actual economic success was determined by intangibles such as 'political security, quality of infrastructures, reliability of skilled workers and contractors, and opening of new market opportunities'. But such intangibles do not fit into models. They are thus hidden under unrealistic assumptions which 'foredoom' the subsequent programmes.

Models that 'blind reality' feature in other development-focused social sciences. For example, the 'ideal type' index, adopted by development sociology, ascribed underdevelopment to national characteristics such as 'role diffusion, ascriptive status, particularism and collectivism'.[22] Therefore, successful development depended on adoption of Western society indices of 'role specificity, achieved status, universalism and individualism'. Exceptions like the extended family systems of South Korea and Taiwan, and the downward spiral of individualist Latin America, were not explained.

In political science, political development has been projected as a 'technical input–output process intended to maximize nebulous variables like structural differentiation, cultural secularization, formal equality of the marketplace (not social equality), and Weberian bureaucracy'.[23] Development psychology suggests inertia, lack of foresight and low need-achievement motivation as underlying the underdevelopment trap. Such models obstruct, rather than aid, understanding of the development process. They 'mystify and distort reality'. Implementers of blueprint plans and participants in the development programmes fail to appreciate what is going on. This prevents them from undergoing perceptual and conceptual change central to the process of learning. They do not benefit from participation because they are unable to apply these experiences independently later.

Development means change in the mental and institutional arrangements of a society based on experience; it means learning, and the absorption of new and improved kinds of economic activity. Implementing opaque blueprints that cannot be reviewed on location prevents such change and therefore obstructs the development process. To reconceptualize development means to advance the understanding of the process in society. It is a shift away from static models.

THE FRAMEWORK FOR RECONCEPTUALIZATION

The crisis in development conceptualization is caused by a mismatch between social and economic structures and institutions and changing realities. It reflects the failure of physical and conceptual institutions and structures to adapt effectively to constant changes in the immediate and international environment.

In order to adapt, the institutions and structures need to work towards enhancing the general transparency of the environment. This would improve national appreciation of reality, and make it possible to utilize socio-cultural differences in the competitive economic arena.[24]

The achievement of such national synergies depends on the organizations, infrastructures and institutions responsible for defining, navigating and reviewing the development path. These organs are the national environment enabling institutions. They need to draw up transparent development models that are openly testable and, if their utility is in doubt, discardable; models which emphasize widened participation and learning. Such models would be in step with current trends towards participative multi-party democracy and good and transparent governance. Sacrosanct models and persistence in error are costly. However, to achieve the desired goals the environment enabling institutions require certain capabilities. Davidson's[25] summation that the African development crisis is a 'crisis of institutions' testifies to the absence of, inaccessibility to, or failure to seek such capabilities.

A central role of institutions as environment enablers is to reduce uncertainty and unpredictability in the economic landscape or terrain; in other words, to reduce opacity. Transparency permits informed interaction with the environment by economic agents and the wider society.

Organizations and institutions are organs for information acquisition, processing, storage and dissemination. Their main role is to cause effective and beneficial information flows within the local environment and with the outside world. In LDCs which are poorly infrastructured, multiethnic, geographically widespread and inaccessible, effective information flows are vital. Information flows can advance closer national integration and facilitate government administration. They have the potential to project an incontrovertible picture of what a country's people have in common and of unity in diversity.[26] Appreciation of information flows can assist in bringing about the necessary conceptual and organizational changes that are an integral part of the development process. Improved information flows also help in creating a better-informed community able to anticipate and adapt to changes.

National institutions need to create terrain transparency because it induces confidence by reducing uncertainty. This inspires participatory and informed decision-making which improves economic activity. But crucial intangibles, such as institutional capability to meet such needs, are difficult to measure. Despite this, the building of such capability needs to be incorporated in development concepts.

Advances in information and communications technologies have tied the destinies of countries more closely, made them more vulnerable to international events, and intensified competition between them. Such advances have brought about the *global village*. With the addition of the growing power of MNCs to this equation, the position of the nation-state unit in development needs review.[27] However, participation in the international arena remains dependent on the capacity of a nation's institutions to select and navigate a suitable development path.[28] Negotiating a consensus between competing and conflicting national goals and international participation requires information and knowledge management capability on the part of the relevant national institutions.[29] Such capability has yet to receive adequate attention in mainstream development thinking, although studies of an anecdotal nature abound.[30] Navigating a consensus between conflicting national, and normally short-term, goals *vis-à-vis* international participation can, at times, present serious problems in times of change.[31]

Development as change and, therefore, subject to unanticipated dislocations and disruptions is still in the periphery of mainstream development thinking. Most development models assume stability or absence of change over unrealistic time spans. This results in inadequate attention being paid to contingencies in programme implementations. There is therefore a need to improve the means to anticipate and cope with disruptions that are an attendant part of change and development.

In a transparent environment, the capacity to anticipate among economic agents is improved because crisis signals can be identified early. This inspires confidence by minimizing uncertainty and unpredictability, which is vital to the management of change – and change is integral to development. It is, therefore, institutional capability-building, founded on information management, and how this determines the management of change that are to be the new ingredients in the reconceptualized development framework.

CONCEPTUALIZING THE PROCESS

Economic growth and development are not the same thing. Trends in LDCs have shown that it is possible for economic growth to take place without development in the sense of social, institutional, political and regulatory changes. Growth indicators can be raised even by sudden rises in the value of commodity exports while institutions remain at unchanged levels of operation.

Kuznets,[32] however, defined economic growth as a country's 'long-term rise in its capacity to supply increasingly diverse economic goods to its population'. The growing capacity should be based on advancing technology, institutional demands and ideological demands. This definition excludes countries possessing a resource exploitable by more developed countries and which appropriate the large margins in economic rent, as is the case with developing countries rich in oil or rare minerals. Kuznets focuses on growth founded on efficient and wide employment of technology, on institutional and ideological adjustments and on effective use of innovations generated by the global stock of advancing human knowledge. The fact that the oil-rich Middle East had to turn to ageing Texas oil fire fighters after the Gulf War indicates this is not a natural progression. It must be deliberately worked at. Kuznets's view of economic growth is broader than that which has been pursued in LDCs. An effective use of global knowledge stock requires a national orientation to strive and learn; experiences, information and knowledge thus acquired can be disseminated among and adapted by local institutions.[33] It remains to be seen whether the fire-fighting skills brought to the region by Red Adair and his team have remained in the Gulf. It is not sufficient if the newly acquired and expensive information and knowledge are used circumspectly. In any case, this would reduce the impact of change and, therefore, the rate of development.

10

This view does not regard increases in the number of production plants as effective development, or an increase in the number of wage-earners in technological enclaves whose operations have little contact with the mainstream economic and social activities of a country. Similarly excluded are LDCs which become rich through fortuitous discovery of a resource, like petroleum, whose production costs are small relative to value. The subsequent large economic rents boost economic growth indicators despite limited local participation in the creation and consumption of the wealth.

As referred to earlier, windfalls also follow international commodity price booms. This was the case with the copper prices in the 1970s (with favourable effects on the Zambian economy) and the coffee boom in the mid-1970s following the destruction of the Brazilian coffee harvest by freak weather (which helped the Kenyan, Ugandan and Tanzanian economies). Rimmer[34] has argued that such windfalls can undermine development through 'anaesthetizing national thinking' and financing the maintenance of old institutions, regulations and organizations that obstruct social learning and change. Such obstructive institutions are what Schumpeter describes as prime candidates for 'gales of creative destruction'.[35]

Khalek's[36] concept of development is a 'process of comprehensive social change that releases latent energies for creative behaviour'. This implies the causing of optimal interaction of individual and societal capabilities. But such a synergistic arrangement requires consideration of historical, cultural and material conditions. These vary between countries. Khalek emphasizes the importance of the experience of particular societies as input in their development process. This makes the process historically and socially specific.

Universal models are seen as ahistorical and asocial. Hyden[37] pinpoints such models as the source of widely institutionalized 'blueprint planning in Africa'. Here, the wishes, knowledge, experiences and involvement of local people likely to be affected by the imported blueprints are disregarded in preference for the assumptions about reality made in the pre-packaged solutions or models. The result is that neither the 'solutions', the authors nor the implementers can be subjected to transparent assessment or held accountable for subsequent failures. This has nurtured unaccountability in African bureaucracies and alienated them from the aspirations of the societies they are meant to serve.

Hyden has concluded that Africa's institutions are not bureaucratized and depersonalized enough. This is because the institutions do not depend sufficiently on impersonal rules, procedures and information in decision-making. In many African countries, rules and procedures were downgraded soon after independence as colonial legacies that would delay decisions and actions.[38] The result has been highly personalized systems of operations. Instincts and personal contacts define the quality of decisions made by institutions, and, by inference, the country.[39] When individuals move, many of their skills are lost to organizations. This lack of institutionalized learning and decision-making processes affects the implementation of projects and programmes.

There is, therefore, a search for new conceptualizations that focus on creating a self-sustaining development process, based on cumulative learning in the institutions of an economy. The institutions do this by searching for, identifying and using the advancing stock of human knowledge and technological innovation. This orientation needs to be introduced in those institutions responsible for conceiving, planning, implementing and managing change. Because institutions are essentially information management organs, their ability to manage information has implications for the pace of national development. Failure to consider the information element in the development equation contributes to failures in development programmes. This is the search that brings the promises of new information technologies into the development process. It is also what is required if natural or human-induced distractions to development such as Aids, drought, floods and the internecine conflicts of the 1990s and beyond are to be managed.[40]

NOTES

1   D. Conyers and P. Hills, *An Introduction to Development Planning in the Third World*, 3rd ed., John Wiley, New York, 1984, p. 28.
2   A. W. Lewis, 'The state of development theory: an essay', *Economic Impact* no. 49, 1985/1, p. 82.
3   G. F. Papanek, 'Economic development theory: the earnest search for a mirage', in M. P. Todaro (ed.) *The Struggle for Economic Development: Readings in Problems and Policies*, Longman, London, 1983, p. 10.
4   D. Conyers and P. Hills, op. cit., p. 26.
5   BIDPA, *Annual Report 1995/96*, Botswana Institute of Development Policy Analysis, Gaborone, 1996.
6   O. Sunkel, *The Development of Development Thinking*, Fourth EADI Conference, 12–16 September 1976, European Association of Development Research and Training Institute (EADI), First Inter-Regional Meeting on Development Research, Communication and Education, p. 9.
7   Ibid., p. 10.
8   G. F. Papanek, op. cit., p. 17.
9   R. A. Onyango, 'Information, the nation-state and democracy: an African perspective', in C. Chen (ed.) *NIT '96: Proceedings of the 9th International Conference on New Information Technology*, MicroUse Information, West Newton, MA, 1996, pp. 187–97.
10 R. Lagos, *The Old Model and Its Abandonment*, Fourth EADI Conference, 12–16 September 1976, op. cit., p. 27.
11 W. W. Rostow, *The Stages of Economic Growth: A Non-Communist Manifesto*, Cambridge University Press, Cambridge, 1962. Referred to in R. Lagos, op. cit.
12 R. Lagos, op. cit., p. 29.
13 D. Rimmer, 'Africa's economic future', *African Affairs*, vol. 88, no. 351, April 1989, p. 179.
14 R. A. Onyango, 'New technology adaptations', op. cit., p. 2.
15 'US envoy spells out new agenda', *Daily Nation*, 30 October 1996, p. 1.
16 R. Lagos, op. cit., p. 29.
17 A. W. Lewis, op. cit., p. 80.
18 UNECA, *Africa's Alternative Framework to Structural Adjustment Programme for*

Socio-economic Recovery and Transformation, United Nations Economic Commission for Africa, Addis Ababa, 1989. This publication argued an alternative approach to the World Bank's Structural Adjustment Programme for African countries and questioned the Bank's theoretical basis.

19 FHI/Aidscap, *Aids in Kenya: Socioeconomic Impact and Policy Implications*, Family Health International/Aidscap, Arlington, VA, 1996.

20 B. Onimode, *A Political Economy of the African Crisis*, Zed Books, London, 1988.

21 A. W. Lewis, op. cit., p. 82.

22 B. Onimode, op. cit., p. 34.

23 B. Onimode, op. cit.

24 M. Godet, 'From the technological mirage to the social breakthrough', *Futures*, vol. 18, no. 3, June 1986, p. 373.

25 B. Davidson, *Can Africa Survive? Arguments against Growth without Development*, Little, Brown, Toronto, 1974. Quoted in B. Onimode, op. cit., p. 2.

26 R. A. Onyango, 'Information, the nation-state and democracy', op. cit., p. 188.

27 O. Sunkel, op. cit., p. 15.

28 R. A. Onyango, 'Information, the nation-state and democracy', op. cit., p. 193.

29 E. O. F. Reid, 'Internet developments and government diffusion: case of Singapore', in C. Chen, (ed.), op. cit., pp. 219–30.

30 T. Forester, *Silicon Samurai: How Japan Conquered the World's IT Industry*, Blackwell Business, Cambridge, MA, 1993.

31 O. Obayiuwana, 'Nigerian authorities determined to block Internet access', Available e-mail: *Owner-Kenya-net@Africaonline.com*, 20 December 1996.

32 S. Kuznets, 'Modern economic growth: findings and reflections', in M. P. Todaro (ed.), op. cit., p. 56.

33 S. Dedijer and N. Jequier (eds) *Intelligence for Economic Development: An Inquiry into the Role of the Knowledge Industry*, Berg Publishers, Oxford, 1987, p. xiii.

34 D. Rimmer, op. cit., p. 175.

35 J. A. Schumpeter, *The Theory of Economic Development*, Harvard University Press, Cambridge, MA, 1934; and R. A. Onyango, 'Information, the nation-state and democracy', op. cit., p. 191.

36 G. A. Khalek, 'Egypt's recent aid experiences: 1974–1983', in Fourth European Association of Development Research and Training Institute (EADI) General Conference, 12–16 September, 1976, First Inter-regional Meeting on Development, Communication and Education, p. 3.

37 G. Hyden, *No Shortcuts to Progress: African Development Management in Perspective*, Heinemann, Nairobi, 1983.

38 R. A. Onyango, 'Global information and Africa: on the crest of a mirage?', in 'The Impact of Global Information on Africa', Online debate, Available e-mail: *Conference@mcb.co.uk* or *HTTP:http//www.mcb.co.uk/services/conferen/apr96/global_information/conhome.htm*, April–October 1996, pp. 1–12.

39 K. J. Mchombu, 'The cultural and political dimensions of information resources management in Africa, in N. M. Adeyemi (ed.) *Reader on Information Management Strategies for Africa's Development*, UNECA/PADIS, Addis Ababa, 1995, pp. 103–24.

40 R. A. Onyango, 'Information, the nation-state and democracy', op. cit., p. 188.

2

THE COST OF MISCONCEPTIONS

FLAWED PRESCRIPTIONS FOR DEVELOPMENT

Much of the intellectual input in development studies originates from international agencies such as the UN and the World Bank, and from academics in the developed world. However, recent instability in the field has origins in the realities faced by LDCs. The state of underdevelopment was first made acute by heightened political awareness kindled during the fight for self-determination. It was worsened by increasing international transparency arising from improving communication and information flows, which expose privileged life in rich countries.[1] The post-Cold-War multi-party democracy has now intensified conflicts occasioned by dwindling resources and the articulations of diversity and differences in ethnicity, religion and race. This resources limitation is the result of failed development policies.

Prescriptions that emphasized the export of commodities to finance investment in production and the export of manufactured consumption goods were underpinned by growth and modernization paradigms.[2] The prescriptions did not give adequate attention to mechanisms for widening participation in productivity. The export of manufactured goods thus remains elusive.

The result has been dual and unintegrated economies in which the large, rural, subsistence or traditional sectors remain unlinked to the smaller, urban or export production-focused sectors.[3] The modern/export sector consumes most imports including imported technological improvements and packages for economic reorganization.[4] The rural/traditional sector remains dependent on age-old, relatively inefficient production technologies, outmoded economic organizations and few resources even in times of economic growth. Programmes for change consider this sector and its populace to be obstacles to progress.

The industrialization programmes of the 1970s emphasized the import-substitution industrialization (ISI) strategy. But the industries depended on automated or semi-automated imported machinery in spite of the excessively underutilized local labour. This intensified the deintegration process with much unemployment and underemployment concealed in the subsistence and informal sectors. The raw-material needs of the imported machines were such that they

14

could not be supplied locally. The result was little interdependence or integration between industrial, primary and skills/manpower production sectors of these economies. No substitution took place, only replication. Indigenous initiative, entrepreneurial instincts and capacities were sidelined and stultified.

The enclave ISI industries were recorded as growth and credited to the country as development. But ISI programmes actually converted LDCs into locations for assembly of foreign consumer goods, some machines and a little technical know-how in return for some employment and a few static skills. Wilford and Lochhead[5] find flawed the ISI premise that a country could, by distorting its internal price structure, achieve independence from commodity exports through subsidies and taxation. It led to internal misallocation of resources. Attempts later to shift to export-oriented industrialization (EOI) exposed the structural flaws. Adequate capability was never cultivated for this phase. Institutions nurtured on ISI continue to demand protection measures such as import bans and tariffs.[6]

Because the programmes have been implemented as opaque blueprints, conflicting objectives have been pursued and main goals undermined. The strategies did not take stock of, and therefore did not address the enhancement of, a country's capabilities or base comparative advantages in terms of special cultural traits or skills. No attempts were made to unpackage the blueprints and to relate them to local realities. Pursued as total packages, they have served to undermine confidence in all that is indigenous, and subverted long-term national aspirations of LDCs.

Failure to define and match blueprint goals to long-term national aspirations has prevented negotiations for internal compromises and consensus. This is important in removal of potential conflicts between long-term internationalist national objectives and short-term local needs. Some of the countries that managed this continue with the trend.[7] But many have missed the formula. Negotiating an organic and participative compromise is important for the pursuit of change and development. The Japanese economic miracle and the Pacific Rim follow-up are characterized by an organic compromise between Eastern cultural nuances and Western competitive technology and work habits. Internal conflicts and attendant instabilities, overt or undercurrent, do not augur well for development.[8]

THE CRISIS OF INSTITUTIONS

Sub-optimal compromises, based on ill-defined goals, create conflicts that undermine the wider pursuit of change. In Africa particularly, lack of a consensus has led to pursuit of goals unclear even to national experts. As a result, the performance of expert institutions, responsible for implementing the goals, cannot be evaluated. The accountability of these institutions thus cannot be guaranteed. Such situations permit pursuit of short-term personal gains that have been attributed variously to excessive bureaucracy, a lack of bureaucracy, cultural traits and corruption. But there may be more to it than that.[9]

Ventura[10] points to much effort, guile, entrepreneurial talent and time expended in pursuit of corrupt practices that could be harnessed for positive social ends. He also points to information being used to subvert, rather than enhance, local control and management systems. The lack of accountability in national institutions nurtures this. The development packages based on Western belief systems, values, social modes, economic and political organization[11] have created alienated institutions. Their lack of accountability nurtures corruption and undermines pursuit of excellence.[12] The lack of negotiated compromise between economic sectors permits pursuit of conflicting agendas and this encourages corruption further.

The result is two unrelated cultures that feed conflict. One culture looks externally for nurturing and identification, which prevents local evaluation of its performance. The other is stultified and sidelined, but is too rooted in history to eradicate. The unreconciled cultures each proffer a menu of values and standards that undermines the evolution of a common transparent system of performance standards or a national conscience.

Without such transparency the 'new rules of the economic growth game' are liberally interpreted. It is this personalized interpretation of procedures that Hyden[13] attributed to a lack of bureaucratization. It is Africa's crisis of institutions.

ISI supported this situation. Potential local industrial inputs are dismissed because the criteria for excellence among national modernizing institutions are externally defined. Local control of the definition of excellence and good practice is central to the management of change. In sub-Saharan Africa, local control has been surrendered. The result has been described as prevalent 'mediocrity and fawning mimicry'[14] in the institutions responsible for creating new ideas and change. This has been particularly evident when faced with potentially complex challenges such as the Aids endemic. Many LDCs have, typically, surrendered the responsibility for social engineering methods to contain the spread of Aids infections to Western research institutions and bilateral and multilateral agencies.

In Kenya, ISI strategy led to local cloning of goods previously imported.[15] But the technology required for cloning and much of the input must be identical to that employed abroad. High-precision, machine-intensive production techniques were thus adopted that had no use for Kenya's abundant craft/artisan skills. The technology and programmes failed to marry local capability to the imported, mass-production precision machinery industry. The modern sector did not permit credit to be transferred from such indigenous craftsmanship as metal melting and moulding. Recent studies show that ISI cannot productively employ manpower skills from Kenya's modern training systems either. Kenya's ISI strategy has not addressed unemployment, balance of payments constraints, existing skills or the process of learning. The industrial sector emphasizes consumer goods at the expense of capital goods and has failed to generate a sustainable process of economic growth.[16] ISI's foreign legitimization processes prevent local assessment and do not allow participating corporations and individuals to be held accountable for their undertakings. It gives a country rows of factories run on technologies beyond the comprehension of its people. Such 'black-box' technologies are chosen for the final products, and little attention is given to the evolution of national skills and learning. The responsible national institutions are not encouraged to unpackage the blueprint programmes and 'black-box' technologies that clone previous imports. The institutional curiosity required for learning and re-engineering and the pursuit of excellence is smothered.[17]

Blueprint plans and 'black-box' technology solutions carry an air of mystery that mesmerizes ordinary people and their enabling institutions. Institutionalized decision-making and management processes thus lose objectivity. Informed decision-making, crucial in accountable organizations, becomes unnecessary. This explains why information is not sought in decision-making, and even when available is ignored or suppressed.[18] Underdevelopment is therefore more than a state of physical want. It is a state of institutional, societal or national surrender to ignorance.

This surrender is aided by packaged solutions administered according to the 'slogans and ideologies of distant lands'.[19] Performance is then assessed on the way these packages are put together.

Opaque performance standards permit the few local participants and project managers, and the largely foreign corporations involved in projects, to invest themselves with capacities they may not possess but over which they cannot be held to account. By adopting blueprint plans and black-box technologies, LDCs obstruct their learning opportunities and undermine their autonomous decision-making capacity. The underdevelopment cycle is perpetuated; their institutions are prevented from participating in, appreciating and negotiating the compromises necessary for the management of change. Change is what real development is about. But the management of change is dependent on efficient information management among a nation's environment enabling institutions.

Blue-print planning has contributed to skewed urbanization in LDCs[20] that starves the rural sectors of resources. The results are congestion in cities, social tension, rising poverty and massive foreign borrowing. In sub-Saharan Africa, these tensions are threatening the very existence of states. In Europe, the deskilling of rural craftsmen and peasants, which accompanied industrialization and urbanization, was complemented by the reskilling of factory workers, artisans and industrial-age entrepreneurs. Improved communications led to better-integrated economies. The transfer of resources from the primary (rural) sector to the modern (urban) sector had some logic: the industrial sector produced inputs for agriculture such as fertilizers and machines, which raised output and released labour for the cities. The developments in agriculture were an integral part of the process of change. Changes also took place in institutional frameworks, production processes and organization to meet the needs of the growing urban industrial sector. Certainly there was social dislocation, and

Europe off-loaded many of its surplus people on the rest of the world. But there were a logic and complementarity which are lacking in urbanization in LDCs.

In LDCs, increasing landlessness, environmental deterioration and poverty in rural areas are forcing migration to cities. But also contributing to this is the concentration of industrial activities in and around cities. Urbanization is due more to 'rural push' than 'urban pull' factors. Most notable is the lack of regulatory and institutional adaptations, forged from local peculiarities and intended to manage the change. The result has been the high opportunity cost of the sidelining of 80 per cent of LDCs' people from mainstream economic activity[21] with the result that they are regarded as obstacles to development. Such large-scale departicipation is costly.[22] Recent bloody internecine conflicts are testimony to the high opportunity cost that may still have to be paid.[23]

In Africa, only residual interest has been paid to the institutionalizing of wider participation. The need to address wider participation in the development process and the distribution of the benefits has become urgent. This requires institutional changes.

PUTTING THE PACIFIC RIM IN CONTEXT

The emergence of Hong Kong, Taiwan, South Korea and Singapore was not foreseen by mainstream development theory because the countries lacked natural resources and did not fit commodity-based growth models posited on international division of labour. Although now a focus for studies, these are largely empirical. The model remains elusive. This is possibly due to the inability of existing models to accommodate the information element. The 'miracle' of this region was founded on proactive national institutions that emphasized efficient operations, informed decision-making and consensus. They conceived the destiny of their countries as attainable within an international competitive framework. This ensured high attainment practices in institutions and is evident in the regard accorded public-sector organizations and institutions. It contrasts with what is found in other LDCs, and even developed countries, where perceptions of, for instance, the civil service are unflattering.

The Pacific Rim's success formula was first forged in Japan. Japan is credited with achieving an organic integration of Western technology, production methods and organization with oriental cultural nuances of cooperation, patience and endurance. Confucian values predominate in the region. This has made it possible for other countries to transfer from Japan a tested consensus which is steeped in shared traditions.[24] In Africa, the need for such a consensus bridge has not even been recognized.

Sigurdson[25] points out that Japan acknowledged its lack of natural resources early. It was therefore always eager to collect and process information about the external world in order to acquire negotiating advantages. Japanese organizations have thus worked on the assumption that 'information is their critical resource', as they have little else.[26] This is evident in the orientation of government agencies, commercial companies and academia, which scour the world for relevant information. It has enabled them to make timely, informed and competitive decisions. Sigurdson's conclusion is that the purposive, proactive and dynamic pursuit of information and knowledge is at the core of the proven Japanese ability to adapt to and manage change.

Ventura[27] identified the success of Taiwan, Singapore and South Korea as being based on an opportunistic use of abundant cheap labour and good information, described as 'powerful social intelligence networks'. This permitted full use of new opportunities.

Sigurdson[28] argues that although information and knowledge management is identified as contributing immensely to the success of this region, no attempts have been made to measure or evaluate its real contribution to development. Thus, Japanese national characteristics receive attention but few researchers have focused on how information-processing helped shape the economic success story. Sigurdson sees a 'group-directed quest for knowledge' as forcing leaders to identify information and knowledge that their organizations may need, and forcing them to remain accountable. This results in their sending out observation teams and inviting experts to give advice, to which they give due consideration. Transparent performance and accountability are thus embedded in this internationally driven arrangement.

Enos and Park[29] state that, in addition to geographical propinquity and shared recent experiences, South Korea chose 'the Japanese development path' because it recognized that 'the Japanese had already adapted Western technology to Eastern social and political mores'. In sub-Saharan Africa this need to identify, smooth over and compromise local and imported mores has received little intellectual attention in organizational, management or sociological studies. Irreconcilable but wasteful conflicts and duplications have been the result. On a tangible plane, planners have emphasized and invested in physical infrastructures, but not adequately in the procedural, regulatory and institutional infrastructures.[30]

Henriot[31] traces three stages in the Pacific Rim's evolution:

1 First came the radical redistribution of land and the imposition of minimum curbs on its use in the further accumulation of financial capital. This stage involved negative growth rates, but was seen as necessary to set the economic and political conditions that prevented highly unequal economic growth based on land accumulation and speculation. Land accumulation predominates in the development routes chosen in Latin America and sub-Saharan Africa. Setting aside large tracts of land for commodity production creates static, self-perpetuating institutions that obstruct change. Land ownership in itself takes on a perceptual value totally unrelated to its productive capacity. The institutions that are spun off weaken the national capacity to respond to opportunities created by alternatives that recognize international realities.

2 The next stage involved the massive accumulation of human capital in excess

of immediate demand for skills. In this stage, ownership of human capital was redistributed, the human resource base greatly enlarged, and both economic opportunities and political pressures for the next stage were generated. In the Pacific Rim, this stage was accompanied by relatively slow rates of economic growth, political instability and social tension which forced institutional changes.

3 Rapid and intensive growth occurred after the investment in human resources had been made. An aware human resource base demands the formulation of transparent economic policies that encourage participation in economic activity. In the Pacific Rim, production strategy focused on export markets. These are competitive and transparent markets because of the limited ability of any single country to manipulate them fully. This strategy was accompanied by transparent and accountable planning and government development plans which have been implemented, adhered to and reviewed objectively. These factors enforce a culture of attainment/achievement, accountability and objective evaluation in national environment enabling institutions. In addition, a well-documented landscape permitted the formulation of clear goals and rules of operation.

The experiences of the Pacific Rim region indicate that intelligently formulated and flexibly administered policies can break the underdevelopment cycle. They also emphasize widened participation, without which 'growth in an economy can only reach a certain level and then be stymied'.[32] The experiences point to a comprehensive and holistic approach to the management of change and development, accomplished by informed institutions which are ready to learn, and a large supply of skilled labour.

Smith et al.[33] also identify three ingredients in the success of the Pacific Rim countries:

1 An emphasis is placed on mass and higher education, as exemplified by South Korea's and Singapore's pursuit of 'graduate-crammed populations to create the wealth of the future'. Their investments in universities aim at both specific demands for technical skills and the production of multidisciplinary graduates capable of handling the kaleidoscopic shifts of information-based economies, while avoiding the pitfalls of the rich and poor classes of the Western world as well as the dual economies (modern and traditional) found in South America and sub-Saharan Africa.

2 Consensus and compromise are employed as a means by which to achieve progress for the benefit of all, as opposed to confrontation and adversarial, or obstructive, management styles. Negotiated consensuses have produced 'a rare breed of competitive capitalism and one-party socialism' in which governments set the strategy and invest public money in infrastructures such as housing, education, transport and telecommunications. Business then builds national wealth on that foundation.

3 The successful Pacific Rim nations show an ability to manage constant

change in government institutions and social attitudes which enables the countries to cope with accelerating technological change better than do similar economies elsewhere. The economic advantages of adaptability are likely to increase as international communications continue to expand, putting countries under growing pressure for change.

This last prediction is confirmed by Reid's[34] recent study of Singapore's cautious but determined approach to taming and exploiting the Internet in order to position itself strategically for the information millennium. It contrasts sharply with, for instance, the Nigerian government's attempts to obstruct access to the Internet for reasons of national security even after the nationals have privately syndicated a consortium to fund the project.[35] Singapore fears the decadent inputs accessible in the Internet; Nigeria fears the uncontrolled global documentation that includes records of its human rights abuses. One country sees the greater benefits, the other chooses to be blindfolded. Many countries use subtler devices, such as imposing tough conditions for potential Internet service providers, delaying the upgrading of telecommunications infrastructures, imposing forbidding telephone rates or placing high tariffs on equipment. These acts can only further disable such economies as the world enters the next millennium. The threats to national security will, however, originate from internal conflicts occasioned by poverty and the failure to exploit the ready and technologically accessible pools of global experiences in conflict resolution and productivity.

NOTES

1 U. V. Reddi, 'Leapfrogging the Industrial Revolution', in M. Traber (ed.) *The Myth of the Post-industrial Revolution*, Sage, London, 1986, p. 87.
2 A. L. Mabogunje, *The Development Process: A Spatial Perspective*, 2nd ed., Unwin and Hyman, London, 1989, p. 37.
3 O. Sunkel, *The Development of Development Thinking*, Fourth EADI Conference, 12–16 September 1976, European Association of Development Research and Training Institute (EADI), First Inter-Regional Meeting on Development Research, Communication and Education, p. 10.
4 A. L. Mabogunje, op. cit.
5 D. S. Wilford and C. Lochhead, 'The development decades: a road to recovery', *Futures*, vol. 18, no. 5, October 1986, p. 622.
6 M. wa Ngai, 'Proposed boost to CKD is two decades overdue', *Daily Nation*, 10 November 1996, p. 7.
7 E. O. F. Reid, 'Internet developments and government diffusion: case of Singapore', in C. Chen (ed.) *NIT '96: Proceedings of the 9th International Conference on New Information Technology*, MicroUse Information, West Newton, MA, 1996, pp. 219–30.
8 R. A. Onyango, 'Information, the nation-state and democracy: an African perspective', in C. Chen (ed.), op. cit., p. 188.
9 K. J. Mchombu, 'The cultural and political dimensions of information resources management in Africa', in N. M. Adeyemi (ed.) *Reader on Information Management Strategies for Africa's Development*, UNECA/PADIS, Addis Ababa, 1995, pp.

103–24; F. Diouf, 'Information technology and development in Senegal: the importance of culture', in C. Chen (ed.), op. cit., pp. 81–4.

10 A. Ventura, 'Social intelligence: prerequisite for management of science and technology', in J. Annerstedt and A. Jamison (eds) *From Research Policy to Social Intelligence: Essays for Stefan Dedijer*, Macmillan, London, 1988, p. 172.

11 A. L. Mabogunje, op. cit., p. 38.

12 A. Ventura, op. cit., p. 171.

13 G. Hyden, *No Shortcuts to Progress: African Development Management in Perspective*, Heinemann, Nairobi, 1983.

14 A. Ventura, op. cit.

15 R. Matthews, 'The development of a local machinery industry in Kenya', *Journal of Modern African Studies*, vol. 25, no. 1, 1987, p. 80.

16 F. Nixson, 'Import substitution industrialisation', in M. Fransman (ed.) *Industry and Accumulation in Africa*, Macmillan, London, 1982, p. 49.

17 T. Curtis, *Business and Marketing for Engineers and Scientists*, McGraw-Hill, Maidenhead, 1994, pp. 260–84.

18 A. Ventura, op. cit., p. 163.

19 Ibid., p. 164.

20 D. Conyers and P. Hills, op. cit., p. 25.

21 U. V. Reddi, op. cit., p. 30.

22 A. L. Mabogunje, op. cit., p. 30.

23 R. A. Onyango, 'Information, the nation-state and democracy', op. cit., p. 188.

24 C. Lagerstam, 'Business intelligence in Japan', in B. Cronin and N. Tudor-Silovic (eds) *The Knowledge Industries*, Aslib, London, 1990, pp. 69–77.

25 J. Sigurdson, 'Japan's pursuit of knowledge: reversing the flow of information', in J. Annerstedt and A. Jamison (eds), op. cit., p. 142.

26 C. Lagerstam, op. cit.

27 A. Ventura, op. cit., p. 169.

28 J. Sigurdson, op. cit.

29 J. L. Enos and N. H. Park, *The Adoption and Diffusion of Imported Technology: The Case of Korea*, Croom Helm, London, 1988.

30 R. A. Onyango, op. cit., p. 188.

31 P. J. A. Henriot, 'Development alternatives: problems, strategies and values', in M. P. Todaro (ed.) *The Struggle for Economic Development: Readings in Problems and Policies*, Longman, London, 1983, p. 35.

32 A. L. Mabogunje, op. cit., p. 41.

33 M. Smith, J. McLoughlin, P. Large and R. Chapman, *Asia's New Industrial World*, Methuen, London, 1985.

34 E. O. F. Reid, 'Internet developments and government diffusion: case of Singapore', in C. Chen (ed.), op. cit., pp. 219–30.

35 O. Obayiuwana, 'Nigerian authorities determined to block Internet access', *Owner-Kenya-net@AfricaOnline.com*, 20 December 1996.

3

SELF-RELIANCE
AND INFORMATION
MANAGEMENT

REDEFINING DEPENDENCY

Henriot[1] defined dependency as a situation in which major decisions that affect socio-economic progress within a country, such as those affecting commodity prices, investment patterns and monetary relations, are made by individuals and institutions outside the country; or a situation in which the economy of such a country is conditioned by developments in another country. The reality of dependence is thus in decision-making. But decisions are based on inputs of information about the environment. This puts information at the centre of the definition of dependency. Thus development as reduction in dependency can be seen as the capacity of a society or nation to enjoy autonomous participation in the productive activities of the international community and thus benefit from the international division of labour.

The dependency structure of LDCs begins with the disintegration of viable institutions in the society which follows contact with a powerful external social influence. The historical origins of this, initially coerced, arrangement are well-documented.[2] In sub-Saharan Africa, institutional disintegration began with the slave trade and colonization. This was followed by the establishment of plantations and the exploitation of minerals by foreign companies and investors. The institutions created to enforce and support these arrangements distorted market realities. This is the foundation of the post-colonial institutions that have proved unable to cope with open markets. They were designed to contain and subjugate, not to conceive and implement change.

The institutions of containment cultivated the tradition of uninformed decision-making, which has continued post-independence. These emphasize familiarity with and dexterity at manipulating routine procedures. This is because containment does not tolerate challenge and is inward-looking. Unlike in open markets with many uncontrollable variables, here the unfamiliar is ignored, denied or expurgated. Having to cope with the unfamiliar and the accompanying uncertainties of the situation creates the need for information in order to reduce the level of uncertainty.

23

Institutions that confront uncertainty take on a learning mode and constantly seek for and process information about the environment. In LDCs the institutions, unwilling to learn, have opted for imported, pre-packaged solutions in the form of blueprint plans and black-box technologies. This has both killed the urge to learn and transferred responsibility and accountability to remote parties.

This scenario is repeated on the technology front. For example, it was superior African mining technology and skills that first gave Europe the idea of acquiring skilled African miners as slaves to operate the gold and silver mines of South America. The acquisition or abduction of skilled manpower, to relocate a capability or reproduce a skill, was not new in history, but the scale of the exercise in Africa became destructive. Between 1451 and 1833, more than 160 million people were forcibly removed from the continent as part of the slave trade. As the most productive members of society were taken, the process accelerated the disintegration of communities and destroyed indigenous technologies and institutions. It also retarded primitive capital accumulation over centuries, annihilated productive capacity, and prevented the evolution and development of new technologies, skills and institutions.[3]

Colonialism intensified the inequality. The colonial system rested on a capitalist international division of labour and was based on a contrived framework of comparative advantages in which imperial countries specialized in manufacturing activities and the export of manufactures and capital to the colonies. The colonies were coerced into specializing in primary production of agricultural and mineral commodities for the colonialists' factories. Local manufacturing in the colonies was banned in order to preserve raw materials and markets for Europe. Indigenous craft skills and technology now atrophied through the disappearance of raw materials and local markets, prohibition of practice, and the non-absorption or reskilling of the displaced craftspeople into the new production facilities and industries.

Indigenous institutions, skills, knowledge and technological capacities have continued to be marginalized in post-colonial Africa. This process has been exacerbated by heavy foreign investment and involvement of MNCs in the definition of national development agendas and decision-making mechanisms. Craft skills have not evolved to artisan levels, nor has the deskilling caused by automated mass production been complemented by upskilling or reskilling in other sectors of the economy.[4] The potential for *polyvalence* – multiskilling that includes assuming supervisory and decision-making functions – promised by IT theorists remains remote in Africa.[5]

Recent studies confirm that modern training is not advancing national technical capabilities; it is now evident that the process of skills growth was seriously dislocated. Remedial measures are failing because the implementation of blueprint plans does not advance local decision-making and learning capacities.

Dependency becomes complete, according to Ventura,[6] at the point when a country is unable to define for itself where it is going or wishes to go. Mimicry and fawning then dominate the operations of national institutions, and the quality of performance is ignored. The institutions responsible for managing development mimic imported strategies, tactics and ideas without any consideration for the disparities in social structures, cultures and values. National thinking and learning stops.

Dependence is therefore defined in the realm of decision-making rather than the international division of labour, traditional forms of comparative advantages, or material conditions. To be able to take advantage of change, the ability, inclination and capacity for informed and autonomous decision-making are required. The dominance of MNCs in sectors such as consumer goods, machinery and equipment, electronics and chemicals has strengthened the cause of dependent cooperation in LDCs; it has become a pre-condition for keeping the industrialization process moving.

In the absence of a framework in which options are carefully identified, capabilities nurtured, and improved terms negotiated for, the arrangement degenerates into a dependency trap.

SELF-RELIANCE, INFORMATION MANAGEMENT AND INSTITUTIONAL CAPACITY

Interdependence between nations is a cornerstone of world trade. However, it becomes dependence pure and simple when dominant countries can expand and be self-sustaining, while dependent countries can grow only as a reflection of that expansion.[7] Thus, the production focus of a dependent country is geared primarily to the dictates of the dominant nation. The result is an unintegrated, dependent economy.

But the relationship depends on options, selection and decision-making mechanisms. As Henriot[8] asserts, dependence pertains not just to economic or social growth, but to the quality and nature of the decision-making process which defines control of the development process. The focus here is on a country's capacity and systems for setting out national priorities and for decision-making as an integral part of the development process. Autonomy in decision-making (not autarky) lies at the heart of self-reliance, where the choice and means for full mobilization of a society's resources are under its own initiative and direction.[9]

The essence of development is founded on institutional reforms which focus on advancing the process and quality of decision-making in the national environment enabling institutions. The optimality of the development path, identified by such institutions on the basis of reliable and up-to-date information, helps to decide the pace of the process. The underdevelopment cycle is therefore a product of national institutional arrangements and decision-making processes based on information management.

Mabogunje[10] identifies a failure on the part of African countries to 'correctly assess the nature of the situation facing them' as being responsible for many

25

development problems. Such assessment failures are a product of ill-informed or underinformed decision-making. The responsibility for this falls on national institutions. But 'institutions operating in Africa were established by colonial conquerors'.[11] They remain extensions and replications of institutions of the metropolis and continue to serve the wrong agenda. They were created to contain and preclude the unusual and unknown, and still operate accordingly. They obstruct change as a matter of course. Learning is prevented and no information input in decision-making is required because unknown scenarios are meant not to be coped with but to be removed. Having to cope with the uncertainties of the unknown would create a demand for more information and an improved knowledge of the terrain or landscape. This is what comes about when a nation's fate is considered from the international perspective, where realities have to be coped with rather than denied, wished away or administratively removed from sight.

Arturo[12] has argued that institutional development (with its focus on intangibles such as organization, rules and procedures, evaluation mechanisms and standards) has failed to receive appropriate attention in development policy studies because, unlike physical infrastructures, it is difficult to measure and fit into models. Roads, hospitals, schools and telephone lines are tangible indicators that economists, governments and donor agencies can show for their efforts. However, failure to give attention to the intangibles has led to under-utilization as well as misuse of the measurable physical inputs. In fact the failure to recognize and invest in and strengthen participative and accommodative intangibles of regulatory and institutional infrastructure in a land of great linguistic, religious and other differences now threatens the very existence of African nation-states as we have known them. The physical infrastructures failed to cement society together or to recruit widely to the national cause of shared values and unity in diversity in pursuit of competitive productivity in the global village.[13]

Institutional development provides a framework of analysis that would clarify the causes of performance that is poor despite the presence of costly physical infrastructure. Arturo also argues that it would focus attention on a clear set of operational principles that can be applied across a wide range of programmes and projects. It is also an appropriate path for studying capacity-building, particularly in the public-sector institutions of LDCs. Capacity-building is a learning process based on information and knowledge acquisition and use.

One way to study institutional and, by inference, national capacity-building is through paying attention to their information management processes. The foundation of organizations and institutions is the acquisition, storage, processing and dissemination of information. Arturo advances the view that more effective institutions operate on highly specific goals, methods and criteria for evaluation. The more specific these factors, 'the more intense the effects of good or bad performance'. Poor goal specificity and opaque evaluation criteria are characteristic features of underdevelopment that have been overcome in the Pacific Rim countries.

Underdevelopment can also be seen as a state of mind of a country and its institutions. It is not a simple consequence of environmental, social or technical impoverishment, as some studies have suggested. As Porter[14] asserts, national prosperity resulting from an effective development process is *created*; it is not a product of natural endowments as defined by previous perceptions of comparative advantages. To create its prosperity, a country needs to negotiate for the best terms in a competitive international arena that is continuously changing. However, equitable negotiation depends on equitable knowledge and information. A country's knowledge level depends on the knowledge stocks of its institutions and how they manage the process of learning. National information management and learning thus define the level of autonomy in decision-making or self-reliance.

The task of changing the institutions in which the 'thinking of individuals finds expression' is part of institutional capacity-building. The process needs to be deliberate and comprehensive. This requires political commitment if development is to be 'the movement of the whole social system upwards'.[15]

Within the conceptual framework of development as change, institutional, societal and cultural transformations are expected to occur. Dependency theorists have also observed that international transactions affecting LDCs become exploitative at the stage of acquisition and exchange and not at production. This points to poor bargaining by LDCs. This observation argues for an enhanced capacity for international negotiation as a vital component in development. Development should include the enhancement of negotiating capability. But this requires good knowledge of global events, which is predicated on good and objective information consumption by national institutions. The institutions require the orientation and capacity to draw up and implement intelligent decisions based on all available information and experiences.[16]

Ventura[17] reiterates that it is ignorance that undermines self-reliance. He identifies 'an astonishing lack of knowledge about themselves, their friends, their enemies and their technological, social, economic and ecological environment' among LDCs. This undermines meaningful negotiation in the international arena. But the ignorance is partly self-inflicted. Despite a costly information infrastructure of libraries, documentation centres, telecommunication networks and computers, and efforts at information acquisition, much information is dormant and unused. This is because the enabling institutions are not organized into dynamic systems that underpin informed decisions. The infrastructure of physical institutions only serves to 'adorn national prestige'. The resultant widespread practice of uninformed decision-making only serves to undermine self-reliance.

O'Brien and Helleiner[18] point to the 'quality of information input in national decision-making' as influenced by the 'institutional arrangements through which it is collected, communicated and processed'. Their view is echoed by Sagasti,[19] who identifies 'cognitive dependence' as underlying the dependency relationships of LDCs. This perpetually undermines the opportunity to arrive autonomously at optimum development decisions.

While proposing intelligence in national decision-making, Piganiol[20] argues for its diffusion. He states that 'intelligence must have a collective character', be 'widespread, and therefore communicated, disseminated and shared'. He advocates 'national mechanisms' to be used for creating and spreading such intelligence. These 'mechanisms' are the 'national institutions'.

Clearly, weak institutional and autonomous decision-making mechanisms, based on poor information and knowledge acquisition, have been recognized as factors in underdevelopment and dependency. Empirical studies of Japan and the Pacific Rim economies point to their lack of natural resources and their effective employment of internal and external information in autonomous decision-making. Their progress is characterized by limited use of the kind of blueprint packages that dominate African development planning.

What is lacking is the articulation of a holistic development statement which unequivocally places information in the development equation. This framework would make it possible to study the process of capacity-building in institutions and nations in a way that has so far eluded development studies. It is already accepted in mainstream thinking that capacity-building is a better way of appreciating the development process. What remains is the incorporation of the intangible aspects of capacity-building and learning into formal, measurable and testable models.

THE CASE FOR RECONCEPTUALIZING DEVELOPMENT STUDIES

Drucker[21] noted that fundamental changes in the world economy had left economic theories of development behind and that comparative advantages can no longer be based on labour costs or rare commodities or minerals; instead it is exchange rates that are critical. He suggests that LDCs can no longer realistically hope to finance their development by the exporting of raw materials or by low labour costs. LDCs therefore need to learn to negotiate the 'more complex and internationalist formula of production sharing and subcontracting' as the emerging, information-dominated 'symbol economy' takes hold. This symbol economy is founded on the electronic-based information and communication revolutions. A new development paradigm needs to incorporate this revolution, and requires flexibility to cope with the characteristic rapid changes that these revolutions entail.

By contrast, Mabogunje[22] proposes a new development strategy founded on the premise that every LDC 'has within its boundaries the two most important resources for development – productive land and the labour of its population'. He sees the development process as a country's 'application of rational thought to the mobilisation and utilisation of the two fundamental resources to improving the material conditions of its people as a whole'. He faults past paradigms for an undue focus on capital and a concern for what can be done for people 'rather than what the people can do together for themselves'.

Mabogunje implicitly advocates self-reliant decision-making and choice of development options.

Hyden[23] notes an emerging synthesis in the literature on development which is conceptually broader than development economics. The synthesis 'recognises traditional culture as intrinsic to development, as something development should enhance rather than as a nuisance to be ignored analytically or brushed aside politically'.

Nevertheless, Fransman[24] points to a 'new technological paradigm' that is reinterpreting the industrialization process. Based on technical change processes, it is in tune with the global information revolution. He traces its origins to four major events:

1 the rise of the newly industrialized countries (NICs) of the Pacific Rim;
2 the decline of the dependency theory;
3 the decline of neoclassical theory;
4 the emergence of a new paradigm labelled 'neo-Schumpeterianism'.[25]

Neo-Schumpeterianism accommodates the process of change, in a way that contrasts with neoclassical studies' analysis of equilibrium states. It considers instabilities as inherent in the change process accompanying industrialization and development.

Change and instability are accepted as an integral part of the competitive nature of industrial operations in developed countries. In those countries, industrial survival revolves around domestic manufacturers' increasing their competitive ability. Achieving rising competitiveness means instigating and coping with constant change. Organizations and institutions in developed economies accept this as the price of survival and advancement. But LDC institutions are configured to resist change. The neo-Schumpeterian approach helps illuminate these contradictions.

To cope with attendant instabilities of change requires an enhanced capacity to anticipate. This can be attained by 'investing in social innovations and change and accepting that creation is accompanied by some degree of destruction'.[26] Schumpeter identified 'gales of destruction' as innovations that challenge and undermine many existing branches of production, sets of skills, occupational structures, user–supplier relationships and social and economic institutions.[27]

The colonial legacy of inappropriate institutions created to contain and ensure stability rather than nurture change and development needs to be seen in this context. In the absence of a dynamic, adequate and experienced national private sector, the management of change and the accommodation of accompanying uncertainty and disequilibria fall disproportionately on the institutions and bureaucracies of the public sector. It is the public-sector bureaucracies that set the tone for change in the Pacific Rim countries. They managed this through a preparedness to accommodate accompanying social disruptions required for development and driving obstructive institutions, such as those supporting land speculations, out of existence.[28] This was managed through radical land distribution, a proactive posture and efficient information management to help cope with the attendant instability. Therefore the emphasis by colonial and post-colonial institutions of Africa on 'control rather than development'[29] is a major problem. Such institutions are prime candidates for creative destruction.[30]

The importance of the role of government in navigating development must be emphasized.[31] This situation remains, even with ongoing restructuring and privatization. After all, the economic miracle of the Pacific Rim has been credited mainly to intelligent government and capable institutions. But the centrality of government in LDCs is also a result of the following factors:

1 Domestic capital formation remains at a low level in most LDCs.
2 The private industrial sector is weak.
3 The economies are dualistic and unintegrated.
4 Economic and financial resources are concentrated in the public sector because of taxes levied on foreign trade and export commodities and bilateral and multilateral support funds. Despite the advent of non-governmental organizations (NGOs), governments remain major players. Only the state can mobilize financial resources, and has the mandate and responsibility to do so, to develop social and physical infrastructures necessary for national information management and carry out large industrial projects with long pay-off periods or requiring capital in foreign currency.
5 The need for foreign capital means that the governments will continue to be involved in negotiating terms and conditions with foreign banks and contractors and in regulating the pattern and volume of capital flow.
6 Government employs, and can requisition, the largest pool of the country's manpower resources and expertise.
7 Government still remains the only viable institution in LDCs that international banking practice recognizes as collateral.

The state also has a responsibility to gather and make available data and information required for long-term national management. It is responsible for ensuring that such information widens participation in development. Government is also a legitimate instrument of force, with the right to institute and regulate change. It can thus gather data and information on individuals, privacy rights notwithstanding. Thus, the government remains important to development management. But intangibles such as good and capable government, institutions, procedures, regulations and systems for participation in the development process will remain difficult to fit into models and/or study for some time to come.

The international scene and markets are particularly unstable from the position of most LDCs, which have little influence on events. The international division of labour and comparative advantages are no longer predicated on the endowments of nature. A country needs to define, shift and operate its niche beneficially under such arrangements. Faced with uncertainties, the information management capacity of national institutions becomes important. As Helleiner[32] has concluded, 'uncertainty is a product of incomplete information', a point also made by Tell.[33] National information management is central to a country's ability to cope with the inherent uncertainties of development.

National information management supports a country in its efforts to negotiate a suitable niche in the international arena. It is also crucial to the quality of decisions made in pursuit of change and in negotiating an internal consensus. Enos and Park[34] reiterate the centrality of negotiating, bargaining and, by inference, information management capability in LDCs. Their studies of technology transfer and industrialization point to negotiations, even more than good technology selection, as fundamental to success. Technologies, they say, are themselves neither profitable nor unprofitable; 'it is the terms on which they are obtained that determines profitability . . . where the deal is struck'. Therefore, national information management, as will be argued further in the following chapter, is also central to effective technology transfer.

Agrell[35] states that a modern society built on science and technology is heavily dependent on a continuous flow of detailed, accurate information. The intensity of information flow is thus a surrogate indicator of the intensity of the development process. The more complex and sophisticated a society becomes, the more intensified the information flow. National information management as a way of enhancing information flow is an important dimension of the development process.

Agrell adds that increased information flow makes 'each sector of society more transparent to observation'. He suggests that an advanced national knowledge industry serves to advance national transparency to observation. Transparency to observation, he argues, is a characteristic of developed economies. Effective national information management promotes transparency and, by this logic, advancement.

The development process needs to be reconceptualized to include the information element in the development equation. It is within this framework of information in development that the two studies (in Part II) of Kenya's technology transfer, industrialization and development efforts were carried out. The discipline of information science was used to look at the national framework of institutions that address technology identification, selection, acquisition and transfer. The focus was on the intangible attributes of informed decision-making, learning and memory within the social, organizational and institutional arrangements in Kenya.

NOTES

1 P. J. A. Henriot, 'Development alternatives: problems, strategies and values', in M. P. Todaro (ed.) *The Struggle for Economic Development: Readings in Problems and Policies*, Longman, London, 1983, p. 31.
2 W. Rodney, *How Europe Underdeveloped Africa*, Tanzania Publishing House, Dar es Salaam, 1972; K. Griffin, *Underdevelopment in Spanish America*, Allen and Unwin, London, 1969.

3 B. Onimode, *A Political Economy of the African Crisis*, Zed Books, London, 1988, p. 16.
4 P. Ainley, 'Three steps to the knack', *Times Higher Education Supplement*, 31 May 1991, p. 15.
5 M. Beirne and H. Ramsay, 'Manna or monstrous regiment: technology, control and democracy in the workplace', in M. Beirne and H. Ramsay (eds) *Information Technology and Workplace Democracy*, Routledge, London, 1992.
6 A. Ventura, 'Social intelligence: prerequisite for management of science and technology', in J. Annerstedt and A. Jamison (eds) *From Research Policy to Social Intelligence: Essays for Stefan Dedijer*, Macmillan, London, 1988, p. 164.
7 K. Griffin, op. cit., p. 68.
8 P. J. A. Henriot, op. cit., p. 31.
9 R. K. Hope, 'Self-reliance and participation of the poor: the Development Process in the Third World', *Futures*, vol. 15, no. 6, December 1983, p. 455.
10 A. L. Mabogunje, *The Development Process: A Spatial Perspective*, 2nd edn, Unwin and Hyman, 1989, p. 45.
11 G. Hyden, *No Shortcuts to Progress: African Development Management in Perspective*, Heinemann, Nairobi, 1983, p. 17.
12 I. Arturo, *Institutional Development: Incentives to Performance*, Johns Hopkins University Press, Baltimore, 1987.
13 R. A. Onyango, 'Information, the nation-state and democracy: an African perspective', in C. Chen (ed.) *NIT '96: Proceedings of 9th International Conference on New Information Technology*, MicroUse Information, West Newton, MA, 1996, p. 188.
14 M. E. Porter, 'The competitive advantage of nations', *Harvard Business Review*, March–April 1990, p. 73.
15 A. L. Mabogunje, op. cit., p. 46.
16 S. Dedijer and N. Jequier (eds) *Intelligence for Economic Development: An Inquiry into the Role of the Knowledge Industry*, Berg Publishers, Oxford, 1987, p. x.
17 A. K. Ventura, 'Jamaica's bauxite battle', in S. Dedijer and N. Jequier (eds), op. cit., p. 110.
18 R. C. O'Brien and G. K. Helleiner, 'The political economy of information in a changing international economic order', in R. C. O'Brien (ed.) *Information Economics and Power: The North–South Dimension*, Hodder and Stoughton, Sevenoaks, 1983, p. 3.
19 F. R. Sagasti, 'Techno-economic intelligence for development', in S. Dedijer and N. Jequier (eds), op. cit., p. 174.
20 P. Piganiol, 'Intelligence in science and technology', in S. Dedijer and N. Jequier (eds), op. cit., p. 184.
21 P. F. Drucker, 'The changed world economy', *Economic Impact*, vol. 4, no. 56, 1986, p. 12.
22 A. L. Mabogunje, op. cit., p. 50.
23 G. Hyden, op. cit., p. 193.
24 M. Fransman, *Technology and Economic Development*, Harvester, Brighton, 1986, p. 59.
25 J. A. Schumpeter, *The Theory of Economic Development: An Inquiry into Profits, Capital, Credit, Interest and Business Cycle*, Harvard University Press, Cambridge, MA, 1934.
26 M. Godet, 'From the technological mirage to the social breakthrough', *Futures*, vol. 18, no. 3, June 1986.
27 I. Miles and K. Robins, 'Making sense of information', in K. Robins (ed.) *Understanding Information*, Belhaven Press, London, 1992, pp. 1–26.
28 P. J. A. Henriot, op. cit., p. 21.
29 G. Hyden, op. cit., p. 19.

30 R. A. Onyango, op. cit., p. 195.
31 UNIDO, *Guidelines for Industrial Planning in Developing Countries: Basic Principles and Practices*, United Nations Industrial Development Organisation, Vienna, 1988, p. 12.
32 G. K. Helleiner, 'Uncertainty, information and the economic interests of developing countries', in R. C. O'Brien (ed.), op. cit., p. 30.
33 B. Tell, 'Libraries and social intelligence: experiences from the Third World', in J. Annerstedt and A. Jamison (eds), op. cit., p. 153.
34 J. L. Enos and N. H. Park, *The Adoption and Diffusion of Imported Technology: The Case of Korea*, Croom Helm, London, 1988, pp. 151–2.
35 W. Agrell, 'The changing role of national intelligence services', in S. Dedijer and N. Jequier (eds), op. cit., p. 38.

4

AN INFORMATION MANAGEMENT-BASED APPROACH TO TECHNOLOGY TRANSFER

INTRODUCTION

Technology is a product of the socio-economic and political environment. It represents the information and knowledge of a society as used to accomplish tasks, render service or manufacture products. It is all the elements of productive knowledge needed for the transformation of inputs into products, in the use of these in the development and rendering of services, as well as in the generation of further productive knowledge.[1] It is, therefore, a product of compromises among the competing interests in a particular society. These competing interests are projected and communicated as information flows. Technological artefacts represent a society's packaged compromises of such information flows. Technology, therefore, needs to be conceived as information and knowledge condensed into artefact, process or service in order to satisfy a need.[2] Technological artefacts as representations of a particular society's packaged compromises of information flows cannot be neutral.

Outsiders to Western technology evolution should not assume that it is universal in character. They need to analyse and unpackage the technology they import in order to introduce modifications to its various components and make them address the needs of the new terrain or landscape.

This chapter argues for a study of the technology transfer process within the interdisciplinary conceptual framework of information science. The approach emphasizes the need to recognize and adapt to change.

CHANGES IN THE INTERNATIONAL SCENE

There are changes in the international scene that call for a re-evaluation of past approaches to economic transactions. These changes, attributed to the information economy, are altering the fabric of world trade. For LDCs this means learning to cope with the unknown in circumstances that are already difficult.

Drucker[3] refers to 'uncoupling' changes in international economics. These changes have weakened the link between primary and industrial product

34

economies and have led to a situation in which the movement of capital rather than goods determines economic performance; the rules of international commerce have altered. But conceptual recognition of the reality is still lacking.[4] Drucker points to gaps in theories on international trade, technology transfers and development.

World commodity trade has been a victim of technological improvements. As a result of improved operations and reduced waste, raw material input per given unit of output is falling as outputs rise. High technology and biotechnology have also introduced cheap, better-quality substitutes and processes. This has marginalized commodity economies and weakened traditional development policies.

Manufacturing output is also not directly linked to levels of employment, especially of blue-collar labour. This has technology transfer implications for LDCs. Employment can no longer be guaranteed to rise with levels of manufacturing. Cheap labour is not, therefore, a crucial factor in the location of production facilities or the price of the final product. Recent spatial studies have identified a tendency towards localized and concentrated agglomerations of the industrial districts brought about by the new information and communication technologies in favour of the developed North.[5] These studies foresee a new global order marked by a new segmentation of on-line and off-line territories differentiating localities that can harness territorial endowments to the new network topology and those characterized by internal fragmentation and external disarticulation from the network. The trend is of production activities clustering together in a geographical space.

Options are limited. Drucker warns that resistance to change could lead to a total loss of production facilities in this increasingly competitive and open world.[6] Autarky is not an option.

The link between goods and services is disappearing and the symbols of money, credit and capital are also drifting apart in global trade. In the new symbol economy, exchange rates between major currencies have become an important factor of comparative advantage in international trade. This makes the inconvertible currencies of LDCs a bigger problem than before. But the reality of such changes has yet to appear in economic, development or trade theory. Traditional comparative advantages based on labour, raw materials, energy and transportation no longer suffice. It is increasingly clear, for example, that exchange rates influence comparative labour costs between countries, although the exact mechanisms have yet to be explained. It is also evident that within the global network topology across territories, capital is proving very sensitive to minute spatial differences in resources, labour supplies and infrastructures. This can only further weaken the negotiating capability of LDCs for investment or production facilities while strengthening the choice and position of MNCs. MNCs appear set to become key shapers of the world economy as the integration of their intensive and extensive activities becomes the primary dynamic of this period.

The absence of a conceptual grasp of the changes makes remedial action difficult amid already unfavourable arrangements. For example, in 1985 the USA manufactured 20 per cent of the world's manufactured exports, West Germany accounted for 18 per cent and Japan for 16 per cent. This totalled over 50 per cent of global production. The LDCs, with 70 per cent of the world's population and two-thirds of the world's nations, produced 11 per cent of the world's industrial products and accounted for 20 per cent of the world's trade.[7] The relative status of most LDCs continues to worsen. In the absence of a full conceptual understanding of technical change and technology transfer management, corrections to this imbalance will remain elusive. The intensity of the North–South divide at the World Trade Organisation (WTO) gatherings testifies to the problems.

INFORMATION AND ECONOMICS

Machlup[8] defined economics as 'the science which studies human behaviour as a relationship between ends and scarce means which have alternative uses'. Scarcity of means and resources and dealing with competing alternatives are thus the basis of economic conduct. Economics considers scarcity, choice and optimal resources allocation. But these are activities requiring information as input in the ultimate process of decision-making.

Studies on information in the economy are therefore founded on uncertainty, choice, decision-making and price mechanism in relation to optimal resources allocation or Pareto optimality. Information is also at the centre of the concept of competition and free markets. It is its effective signalling that underpins free-market concepts. In this framework, information is the 'intellectual product of human cognitive processing', intended to cope with uncertainty.

Uncertainty represents a lack of information, and the process of acquiring information is aimed at reducing uncertainty. The value of the acquisition of a specific piece of information then equals the utility gained from selecting a better choice among terminal actions or Pareto optimality.

Lamberton[9] described the 'economics of information and knowledge' as 'an emerging topic of interest for both economics and management science' as it analyses the processes by which information and knowledge are produced, diffused, stored and used. He felt that the attention given to information by mainstream economics was inadequate.

Economics has studied information as a dependent variable in models intended to explain price searching, purchasing when quality is uncertain, behaviour of insurance policy markets, financial markets and labour signalling markets.[10] However, the focus of the studies remained narrow. In the 1970s activity centred on economic uncertainty surrounding aspects of functioning markets. Production did not receive adequate attention, except as a spin-off of new information technologies such as computer-aided manufacturing or processing. Information in the creation and enabling of production has not been adequately addressed. Katz[11] feels that because of this, inadequate attention has been given to relations between information and economic growth. This is the approach that is required if a focus on information in development, and on the building of institutions that advance development, is to be cultivated.

This approach contrasts with the literature on the post-industrial society. The latter is specific to developed economies and over-emphasizes the electronic technology revolution and hardware and the convergence of microelectronics-based computer and communications technologies, as opposed to the organization, institutions and people that are required to integrate information in development. Studies of the information economy/post-industrial society that are founded on developed economies abound, but as yet such studies have failed adequately to locate Africa and LDCs in other parts of the world in the pre-industrial–post-industrial continuum.[12]

Before economists incorporated uncertainty into the model for competition, models bypassed the problem of uncertainty in decision-making. The firm or household was assumed to have available all information needed about the demand for its product(s), factor supply conditions and technology. The consumer was assumed to know about prices, the characteristics of the goods, and his/her preferences. An economics of information and knowledge model recognizes that an economic system is activated by decisions on many possibilities and is surrounded by doubts.

Introducing information into the traditional concept of the economy, however, disrupts old perceptions of competition, optimality and equilibrium. It raises epistemological problems. Incorporating information in international economics has raised doubts about the reality of perfect competition in a world in which asymmetry in the production and consumption of information and knowledge is widespread. Such information disparity permits oligopolists to coordinate their actions effectively. The resulting contrived stability undermines competition. The unequal information access to which LDCs are subjected makes international competition inconceivable unless this issue is addressed.

Addressing the problem is made difficult by the knowledge compartmentalization of structured disciplines. In 1983, for example, Martyn and Flowerdew[13] reported on the unfamiliarity of economists or accountants with the field of information – only surpassed by the ignorance of librarians and information officers of the fields of economics and accounting. In 1984, Lamberton saw 'information economics' as a response to deficiencies of economic theory built on unrealistic assumptions about such factors as the veracity of information available to decision-makers and the advent of intelligent electronics with enhanced capacities for communication, control and decision support. He saw in this the emergence of a new paradigm that would transform economics and other social sciences. He argued that intangible attributes such as information and organization demand recognition as fundamental economic resources with the capacity for initiating, responding to and controlling change.

The economist Kenneth Arrow put information in the framework of production, organization and industrial management. He perceived information-gathering specialization as forming the basis of economic organization. According to Arrow, the organization and division of labour aim at information-gathering specialization. Specialization allows individual workers to acquire skills for a particular task more effectively by restricting the range of the task. But the resultant efficiency gain, he argued, is actually due to the lower cost of information permitted by such specialization.[14] Arrow argued that individuals organize in order to permit effective acquisition and communication of information. He saw this as the basis of all organizations – private, public, charity, or profit-motivated. The degree to which an organization meets its set targets is, therefore, an indication of how effective are its information acquisition and communication efforts.

Hirshleifer and Riley[15] considered the economics of information as a study of the consequences of informational actions which allow individuals to overcome uncertainty. They see the management of organizations as information-generating activity (to induce disequilibrium, change and growth) and information-disseminating as activity to cope with the attendant disruptions. Management is, therefore, essentially the management of information.

In the real world, the decision-maker is either a group or an organization. The specialization in information-gathering by organizations is the means to attain objectives. For efficient decision-making, Lamberton advances the view of the organization as a variable and suggests that economics should draw on organizational and information sciences for appropriate concepts. He concludes that organizations are, in fact, information channels. Analysing organizational needs therefore requires a focus on their information-processing activities. He proposes a shift from the current focus on legal and managerial aspects of organizations and institutions; he sees them rather as incompletely connected networks of information flows.[16]

INFORMATION AND ORGANIZATIONS

Most major macrosociological theories associate information with organizations, society and the wider body politic.[17] Studies have shown, for instance, that media, domestic mail traffic and telecommunications can increase political participation, integration and nation-building. Such studies implicitly advocate mechanisms for improving information flows to weaken geographical isolation and advance national integration and economic activity. They have a development orientation. Early social theorists also conceived information as part of the cultural cement of political communities. Max Weber, for example, saw a common language and communications technology as determining features in nationalism.[18] Communications technology includes the press and media, which are means and tools for effecting information flows and permitting the sharing of information among members of a community. This framework recognizes that all society, as Sturges and Neill[19] emphasize, is underpinned by 'complex information systems at work'. Weber saw the development and degree of communications as determining the level of bureaucratic administration that could be imposed on a society.

The emphasis of study has changed with time. In the 1950s and 1960s the interest was on communications and information flows in nation-building, but later shifted to communications systems and socio-political change. In the 1970s it moved firmly towards the 'influence of information and communications on economic growth'.[20] This focus was, however, displaced by the 'cultural imperialism' arguments that underpinned the debate for the New World Information and Communications Order (NWICO). The cultural over-emphasis blunted and obscured the issue of information in development.[21]

The loss of the economic growth focus for information studies is also reflected in studies originating in LDCs. Studies of telecommunications, postal services and computer diffusion in LDCs focus exclusively on such economic variables as telephone provision and economic activity. The role of intangibles such as regulations, policies and the information-processing culture caused by, and affecting, change has yet to be studied.

Governments and their institutions regulate the expansion of telecommunications, computing and frequency spectrum allocations. This affects, and is influenced by, national information cultures which determine the intensity with which the physical infrastructures are used. Arturo[22] underlines this. He makes the point that it is easier to build highways, dams and telephone lines than it is to set up and improve institutions that use and manage them. However, the electronics-based information revolution of the 1980s shifted LDC attention away from institution-building and towards hardware acquisition. Most information policies in LDCs place undue emphasis on hardware acquisition, and little attention is paid to extant institutional operations that have led to underutilization of *in situ* infrastructures. The resultant post-industrial focus of current information studies has led to flawed perceptions of what the information sector actually consists of, particularly from the perspective of non-industrialized LDCs.

Studies of the information sector have been carried out in several economies. One of the biggest exercises was undertaken by the OECD in 1981. There have also been national studies covering the USA, France, Singapore, Australia, Papua New Guinea, Fiji and New Zealand. The studies were made difficult by the interwoven roles of information and organization, and the lack of an agreed terminology. The studies also failed to put information into the development perspective by not explicitly placing LDCs in the pre-industrial–post-industrial continuum that underpins the studies.

INFORMATION AND DEVELOPMENT

Katz[23] argues that the formation of a state as a political entity follows its acquisition of the attributes of an institution. Many of the attributes are symbolic. The success of the process depends on the capacity of the state to create and diffuse collective identities and loyalties among its citizens. The symbols support the material attributes through which the state controls, extracts and allocates resources. Without its institutional symbolism, the physical systems would be more difficult to enforce. But symbolism requires an adequate communications mechanism, therefore the technologies that support communications and information flows are central to the process of state-building. 'Technologies' here include all the mechanisms that enable information flows such as scripts, computers, telecommunications and radio.

Technologies help convey, and therefore advance, the process of developing the state's attributes. The technologies support the transmission, processing and storing of information needed by the state to achieve control over national territory and extract resources from society. But information technologies need to be diffused within what Katz refers to as 'communications ecosystems'. His studies show that information technologies diffuse in an ecosystem only where information flows are supported by previously available technologies already supporting societal information flows. New communications systems need to be devised in a manner that advances existing as well as newly created information flows. There are therefore problems with some information policies adopted by LDCs which over-emphasize the latest hardware at the expense of existing information flow mechanisms. Lack of an organic marriage between the systems could impede the cause of societal information flows. In Africa, this perceptual problem has led to investments in communications hardware but not enough in the content and procedures (or the software).

Weaknesses in the policy perceptions of information in development have led to the absence of information considerations in development planning and management. Sturges and Neill[24] refer to such circumstances in Africa. Here the information profession suffers low esteem: decision-makers, who do not use information anyway, remain unconvinced by the 'reasoned arguments' of the profession that information considerations are vital for development. Mchombu[25] reiterates the same observations.

The information credibility gap in LDCs permits the unrealistic pursuit of costly hardware acquisitions without preliminary internal information inventories that would clarify what Paez-Urdaneta[26] refers to as the level of 'societary informatisation'. This is the level at which a significant proportion of the population actively incorporates competitive amounts of information and knowledge into goods and services produced. It is what determines whether information technologies will be fully utilized.

Paez-Urdaneta attributes the conceptual gap in information in development to the philosophy that equated development with industrialization. This created the view that improved access to international scientific and technological information was all that was needed. The information systems that did focus on access, however, did not address the culture of incorporating and using information in official, public and industrial decision-making. But this 'societary informatisation' is what 'information for development' should be about. Raquel Salinas's[27] study of the Latin American debt crisis underlined the importance of the information culture in effective utilization of *in situ* infrastructure and in informed corporate decision-making.

What has evolved in LDCs is a culture of information as a social or academic service. This welfare perception has precluded its consideration as a competitive resource. The emphasis has been on supply of libraries and books rather than the stimulation of demand for development-related information. Arguments by the profession in support of real societary informatization remain unconvincing to an audience and system not structured for competitiveness and change. Without such a structure, the effective consideration of information in development remains remote.

O'Brien and Helleiner[28] have made the point that during colonial times information was irrelevant in LDCs because decision-making was externally located. Since independence, the need has arisen for LDCs to formulate and pursue policies that serve their own interests. This implies a search for new sources of information and expertise, new information systems, and new means for codification and use. But the results over the past three decades indicate a problem. O'Brien and Helleiner refer to LDCs' economic institutions as entering forms of bilateral and multilateral bargaining in which lack of information and expertise weaken their search for alternative markets and sources of supply. Despite the importance of improved access, the fundamental issue in LDCs remains societary informatization. The absence of information in decision-making and resource allocations, and the poor image of the information professions, are both aspects of the issue of information in development which undermine problem identification and the search for solutions.

Societary informatization or information socialization is a problem of attitudes. Attitude change needs to be founded on international realities, including the perception of LDCs as part of a wider competitive world. LDCs' problems thus need to be solved within a framework conditioned by factors not under an individual country's control. This means being as well informed as possible in order to optimize the opportunities that may arise.

The information sector of a country consists of existing technologies, information workers and the regulatory and policy infrastructure. Katz[29] suggests that there are 'as many profiles of the information sector as there are countries of the world'. This argues against LDC information sector policies that over-emphasize hardware acquisitions, as was the case with the information policies of India and Brazil in the 1980s. Kenya's projected informatics policy for the 1990s[30] also failed to give due emphasis to information in society. Policies that emphasize the glamour of hardware acquisition do not address the question of how existing or new technologies should be used to best advantage. Such a shift in focus is vital if national productivity is to be advanced and information is to be employed as an instrument of development.

To achieve this, national information management needs to be seen as the process of communicating and storing information in single and multi-dimensional ways supported by several technologies. Information transmission, processing and storage require individuals, organizations and societies to use multiple technologies deployed within communications ecosystems.

Many information policies in LDCs appear founded on the misconception that the 'information society' is a model based on a certain level of hardware infrastructure. What is required is a competitive use of information in decision-making within administration and production. Effective use of existing systems should ensure optimal use of additional systems.[31] This is the societary infor-matization upon which to build an LDC information sector. It is the basis for information in development. Only on this can one organically build the advantages of such developments as the multi-media/hypertext-, CD-ROM- and Internet-based systems.[32]

INFORMATION AND TECHNOLOGY

As stated at the beginning of the chapter, technology has been defined as knowledge and information that makes possible the accomplishing of tasks, provision of services or production of goods. It is a systematic application of a society's collective rationality to an identified need. Collective rationality implies compromise. Functional compromises are often packaged as rituals, tools, machinery, a process or a method of doing things. Thus the compromises take material forms as tools for productively coping with nature.

Fransman[33] refers to technology as activities involved in transforming inputs into outputs. This perception looks at production and technical change. By focusing on the transformation process itself, the approach looks at what goes on inside the 'black box' as opposed to what inputs enter it and what outputs emerge from it. Technical change focuses on the process of change, which is central to development. As Adongo[34] and Onyango[35] emphasize, technology is all elements of productive knowledge and information condensed into artefact, process or service in order to satisfy a need or want.

Productivity determines the maximum output that can be achieved with any given quantity of inputs. But productivity is determined by the state of existing technical knowledge. Knowledge, however, has to be created or acquired at some cost. In any case, the search for knowledge and information is fraught with uncertainty because it is difficult to predetermine the quality of what is being acquired. Transforming inputs into outputs involves knowledge of how to do things – although not necessarily why things work in the way they do.

Machlup and Mansfield[36] argue that information can be acquired by a stimulus, like being told, while knowledge can be a product of thinking. Thus information is a process and knowledge a state that gives capacity for creativity, invention and productivity. Therefore, the process of production is implicitly an information activity.

Fransman[37] sees buying, productivity and selecting as sources of information. He suggests that acquisition of improved components or better-skilled labour introduces new information into an organization, creating new possibilities. Production itself generates information flows which may form the basis of subsequent or improved actions. In addition, in a competitive environment, information on the activity of rivals provides an opportunity for 'learning by imitation'. But Fransman also refers to 'learning by doing' as a product of information flows generated by buying, producing and selling. However, the quality and quantity of information generated depend on the degree and effort allocated to facilitate the flows, such as improved response. This implies costs. The opportunity cost of acquiring new information and knowledge is complicated by the inherent uncertainties of the acquisition process.

The lack of a clear causal link between new information flows, learning and technical change draws attention to conditions necessary to optimize new information. These are determined by the existing information and knowledge arrangements of the society. This is the condition referred to as societary informatization or information socialization.

The complex nature of the technical change process is exacerbated by the difficulty of isolating and controlling the large number of determinants that simultaneously shape it. Fransman points to the importance of the state in the process. States encourage, shape and limit technical change and have an impact on generation and diffusion of technology. Katz[38] defines diffusion as the process by which new products, processes and ideas spread to members of a social system, and Reid[39] demonstrates how a state can manage the diffusion process. Sources for technical change and technology are identifiable from market- and non-market-mediated flows of information. But information-processing systems are country-specific in nature, and this makes generalizations difficult.

Most technology studies emphasize market-mediated information flows such as licences, patents and technology agreements. Not enough attention is given to non-market-mediated information transfer, learning and technical change. This has contributed to the failure to integrate information search as part of technology transfer management. From an LDC perspective, search constitutes the first step in the technology transfer process.

Despite the appearance of a terrain dominated by proprietary, and therefore market-mediated, information, over 90 per cent of technology information can be gleaned from public-domain sources. This is true of most types of information required by LDCs for technology transfer.

INFORMATION AND TECHNOLOGY TRANSFER

Fransman[40] defines international transfer of technology as a process where knowledge on production processes is acquired by entities within a country from sources outside the country. Enos and Park[41] see it as the acquisition of the entire body of knowledge necessary to fulfil a specific task – usually the production of a commodity. Such knowledge covers manufacturing techniques, the design, construction and operation of plants, training and improvements.

There is, however, no holistic theory or model of technology transfer. Enos and Park point to the scarcity of literature on technology adoption, which they define as the 'entire sequence of decisions made within a developing country determining how, when, where and with what consequences technology is employed'. They see technology adoption as a series of decisions and, therefore, information activities.

Existing technology transfer theories focus on inter-firm transfers, and fail to give attention to the whole macroterrain. In any case, LDCs tend to be dominated by MNCs, making such transfers intra-firm and creating a false picture. What is more, indigenous firms are too few in number to give adequate magnitude for such a study. In addition, indigenous firms in LDCs rarely participate in the technology scenario. The inadequate numbers of indigenous firms make them a weak mechanism for diffusing imported technology into the wider economy. This therefore leaves a gap in North–South technology transfer studies. The rising profile of small, medium and micro-enterprises (SMMEs) in the formal and informal sectors of LDCs, their improved access to support and resources, and their encouragement by NGOs to move into technology-based ventures could herald a new beginning.[42]

Technology transfer theories can also be faulted for assuming that knowledge and information are acquired instantaneously and without cost. As a result, they represent the local environment simply as different sets of relative prices, ignoring the challenges that the absorbing of new technologies in LDCs poses. What is more, the theories also assume a monolithic system of decision-making. However, the decision-making process in LDCs is characterized by bottlenecks, government regulations and controls, conflicts of objectives and interests, ignorance of risks, information asymmetry and uncoordinated decision-making.

Current theory attempts to capture societal learning through the framework of 'learning by doing'. Enos and Park describe this as a 'rogue theory',[43] because learning is not costless. But learning by doing offers a framework for analysing capability-building. Capability-building requires a system and mechanism for diffusion; but the limited number of firms in LDCs is a handicap for diffusing information and good practices throughout an industry or economy. Although the theory of technology transfer, which is based on the firm, suits developed economies, it is weak when applied to LDCs. This is likely to remain the case until adequate capacity is attained by new SMMEs.

The debate on the appropriateness of imported technologies has received much attention. It has led to arguments for the importing of intermediate or second-hand technologies by LDCs unable to cope with the latest sophisticated technologies. But this has been seen as an obsolete-technology trap that funds new technology in advanced countries. It saddles LDCs with uncompetitive and inefficient technologies that retard development.

The appropriate-technology debate remains unresolved. For instance, the Kenya Association of Manufacturers still argues for the withdrawal of government restrictions on second-hand machinery imports. This has gone on despite studies that have, for example, diagnosed Kenya's textile industry as suffering from off-loaded uncompetitive technology.[44]

One problem with the appropriate-technology debate is that it begins at importation stage and emphasizes final products and maintenance logistics rather than learning and competitiveness. It also focuses on complete technology packages and not the component parts important in technology adaptations. The debate also pursues a uniform blueprint culture for LDCs. Packaged solutions undermine development.

Ventura[45] states that for most LDCs all scientific and technological information has to be obtained from outside sources. Djeflat[46] expressed the same view. What is missing is a consensus on the means and ingredients to be considered.

Technology is a commodity not traded by the rules of the market, yet these rules are embodied in the models and debates of technology transfer. Market rules fail because of information and capability asymmetry in technology transactions. Technology is transacted by the following means:

1 incorporated in the form or 'package' of a product or material, such as machines, equipment or raw material;
2 as information on the constituent parts such as patents, licences, blueprints and conditions of use;
3 as a cost or price issue.

Djeflat refers to UNCTAD's division of technology into:

1 capital goods and direct material;
2 qualified and specialized manpower;
3 technical and commercial information.

Technology is marketed either as a complete package, or fragmented and unpackaged. The form it takes depends on negotiations, but the nature of the negotiations is decided by the buyer's knowledge and technical capabilities. Transactions are also determined by the structure of the technology market, which affects the negotiating strengths of the parties and the final contract.

Technology suppliers are often MNCs. These have the option of transferring technology through a subsidiary (internal arrangements) or to outsiders. But the buyer needs information and knowledge to unpackage the technologies, explore possible local inputs and alternative markets, and remove superfluous elements and costs from the contract. Superfluous additions to contracts, blueprints and even chemical compositions are just some of the defences against retro-engineering that Curtis[47] has described as non-functional additives to technologies. They act as smokescreens.

Djeflat[48] identifies three kinds of contract: packaged, unpackaged and 'turn-key' contracts. Although intended to guarantee deadlines, quality and quantity, packaged contracts commonly result in cost overruns, failed deadlines and very limited experience and capability transfer. The resultant supplier domination of decision-making precludes local economic considerations such as employment and sector integration. Unpackaged contracts could also lead to long completion times, high costs and 'self-delusion', particularly when the unpackaging is peripheral and does not cover the core technology.

Channels for importing technology also depend on buyer capability. Foreign direct investment, popular in Kenya and elsewhere in Africa and now considered a yardstick of investor confidence, does not require much knowledge in the importing country. But joint ventures have not worked any better, because often the management has been contracted to the foreign partner, which then also supplies or sells machines and expertise to the joint venture. Such organizations are joint ventures in name only.

Except in the Pacific Rim, technology transfer experiences in LDCs have not been encouraging. Djeflat[49] faults the mercantile instincts and lack of experience of LDCs' entrepreneurs. He also identifies a lack of time specificity for project completion and the exclusive control by foreigners of technology-related decision-making. As a result, technological information is withheld from LDCs, and local operators are restricted to handling peripheral administrative aspects of projects or contracts.

This arrangement allows foreign partners to steer purchases of capital goods towards their affiliated group, company or country. This does not lead to access to the most competitive technologies, suppliers or practitioners. This is evident in Kenya's sugar, textile and motor industries. Similar evidence can be observed in Botswana's textile sector.[50] Even where open tendering is required, inadequate information is made available and negotiations restricted to respondents to the tenders. However, not all technology players respond to tender requests from small countries. LDCs need to seek out as many participants as possible. But often, regulatory bodies, such as the Kenya Sugar Authority, restrict transactions to a static, centrally held list of suppliers. The practice is defended as cultivating supplier goodwill.

Djeflat[51] concludes that recent technology transfer contracts have resulted in supplier control and contravened free-market rules. But the problem was created by information and negotiating arrangements. Djeflat identified real and con-trived supplier oligopolies and monopolies in international technology trade, aided by buyer ignorance. Suppliers tend to have all the information, are aware of all choices and make decisions on behalf of buyers. Suppliers also have broader and longer experience in negotiating international contracts and come better prepared and informed. LDCs do not seek to be better informed and tend to surrender responsibility to suppliers.

Djeflat also refers to a UNCTAD report that identified LDC companies as lacking the information and commercial know-how required to assess the merits of what they needed. Many such companies showed limited aptitude for technology packaging, selection and preparatory work. They were also poorly informed on alternative sources, suppliers and markets. Many also turned to finance–technology packages because they lacked capital. This left suppliers with extensive decision-making powers. Kenya's sugar industry has been built on such finance–technology packages. The power alcohol programme, considered in Part II, was based on a similar structure created by middlemen with neither the technology nor the money, just an awareness of local weaknesses.

Technology–finance packages are made worse by bureaucracies and by uninformed decision-making practices. Ventura[52] considers technologies in enclaves as untransferred and contributing less than their potential. He argues for better information on technologies, the veracity of suppliers, their operation record, overall business profile, strengths and weaknesses, their competitors, and intimate knowledge about their negotiators. Only then, he argues, can an intelligent decision be made. Also relevant is Beirne and Ramsay's[53] assertion that the social specificity of technology's origins often limits the scope of 'infinite variations and recasting' possible at any given time. But exhaustive investigation of possibilities is feasible only among those with information and capability.

Learning and mastering core technology means developing the capability to 'manage' it. This means adapting and diversifying into similar or related industrial endeavours and moving towards independent product and systems development. It is conceptual confusion that has contributed to what Vo[54] refers to as industry transfer, instead of technology transfer. By industry transfer Vo means the transfer only of productive capacity and a little operational know-how, but not the technology itself. This is the case when MNCs export turnkey factories or firms undertake surveys or exploration, help build production or processing facilities, and provide equipment and technical devices. Some training of local personnel may take place, but not enough to ensure capability transfer. Diffusion does not take place because the countries do not have national domestication policies regarding the acquisition of basic engineering capability; or they have such policies but fail to enforce them.

Ventura[55] and Paez-Urdaneta[56] both point to the competitive nature of international negotiations, which requires adequate information management. By being uninformed and surrendering to suppliers, LDCs make themselves very transparent and vulnerable. It is the inequality in information between contracting parties in technology transfers that prevents efficient contracts from being made. Market failure from unequal information leads to adverse selection, which characterizes LDC terms of international trade, especially in their negotiations for technology transfer. This is worsened by the fact that the information encapsulated in a technology package is implicit, which gives the seller undue advantage in bargaining. An information-based approach to technology transfer study adds a new dimension to the activity.

NOTES

1 M. Adongo, *Science and Technology Policy*, Draft Proposal Document, 1996, pp. 1–13.
2 R. A. Onyango, 'Indigenous technological capacity: can social intelligence help?', *Social Intelligence*, vol. 1, no. 1, 1991, pp. 25–42.
3 P. Drucker, 'The changed world economy', *Economic Impact*, no. 56, 1986/4, pp. 6–13.
4 P. Drucker, op. cit., p. 7.
5 K. Robins and A. Gillespie, 'Communication, organisation and territory', in K. Robins (ed.) *Understanding Information*, Belhaven Press, London, 1992, pp. 147–64.
6 P. Drucker, op. cit., p. 10.
7 Ibid., p. 8.
8 F. Machlup, *Knowledge: Its Creation, Distribution and Economic Significance*, vol. 3: *The Economics of Information and Human Capital*, Princeton University Press, Princeton, NJ, 1984, p. 217.
9 D. M. Lamberton (ed.) *Economics of Information and Knowledge*, Penguin, Harmondsworth, 1971, p. 2.
10 R. L. Katz, *The Information Society: An International Perspective*, Praeger, New York, 1988, p. 53.
11 Ibid., p. 54.
12 R. A. Onyango, 'Information, the nation-state and democracy', in C. Chen (ed.) *NIT '96: Proceedings of the 9th International Conference on New Information Technology*, MicroUse Information, West Newton, MA, 1996, pp. 187–97.
13 J. Martyn and A. D. J. Flowerdew, 'The economics of information', *Library and Information Research Report 17*, British Library, London, 1983. See also R. A. Onyango, 'Strategic national information management and technology transfer: the case of Kenya', unpublished PhD thesis, University of Strathclyde, Glasgow, 1991, p. 58.
14 See D. M. Lamberton, 'The economics of information and organisation', *American Review of Information Science and Technology*, vol. 19, 1984, p. 3.
15 J. Hirshleifer and J. G. Riley, 'The analytics of uncertainty and information: an expositionary survey', *Journal of Economic Literature*, vol. 17, no. 4, 1979, p. 1393.
16 D. M. Lamberton, *Information Economics: 'Threatened Wreckage' or New Paradigm?*, Circuit Working Paper 1990/1, Centre for International Research on Communication and Information Technologies, Melbourne, 1990, p. 3.
17 A. L. Stinchcombe, *Information and Organisations*, University of California Press, Berkeley, 1990.
18 See A. L. Mabogunje, *The Development Process: A Spatial Perspective*, 2nd edn, Unwin and Hyman, London, 1989.
19 P. Sturges and R. Neill, *The Quiet Struggle: Libraries and Information for Africa*, Mansell, London, 1990, p. 7.
20 D. M. Lamberton, *Information Economics: 'Threatened Wreckage'*, op. cit., p. 3.
21 R. Salinas, 'Forget the NWICO . . . and start all over again', *Information Development*, vol. 2, no. 3, 1986, pp. 154–8.

22 I. Arturo, *Institutional Development: Incentives to Performance*, Johns Hopkins University Press, Baltimore, 1987, p. 18.
23 R. L. Katz, op. cit.
24 P. Sturges and R. Neill, op. cit.
25 K. J. Mchombu, 'The cultural and political dimensions of information resources management in Africa', in N. M. Adeyemi (ed.) *Reader on Information Management Strategies for Africa's Development*, UNECA/PADIS, Addis Ababa, 1995, pp. 103–24.
26 I. Paez-Urdaneta, 'Information in the Third World', *International Library Review*, vol. 21, 1989, p. 178.
27 R. Salinas, op. cit.
28 R. C. O'Brien and G. K. Helleiner, 'The political economy of information in a changing international order', in R. C. O'Brien (ed.) *Information Economics and Power: The North–South Dimension*, Hodder and Stoughton, Sevenoaks, 1983, p. 2.
29 R. L. Katz, op. cit., p. 139.
30 Republic of Kenya, *The Development Plan 1988–1993*, Government Printer, Nairobi, 1988.
31 R. L. Katz, op. cit., p. 139.
32 D. E. Riggs, 'Building a global information policy: issues, challenges and opportunities', in C. Chen (ed.), op. cit., pp. 231–5.
33 M. Fransman, *Technology and Economic Development*, Wheatsheaf, Brighton, 1986.
34 M. Adongo, op. cit.
35 R. A. Onyango, 'Information, the nation-state and democracy' in C. Chen (ed.), op. cit.
36 F. Machlup and U. Mansfield (eds) *The Study of Information: Interdisciplinary Messages*, John Wiley, New York, 1983, p. 644.
37 M. Fransman, op. cit., p. 40.
38 R. L. Katz, op. cit., p. 108.
39 E. O. F. Reid, 'Internet developments and government diffusion: case of Singapore', in C. Chen (ed.), op. cit., pp. 219–30.
40 M. Fransman, op. cit., p. 7.
41 J. L. Enos and W. H. Park, *The Adoption and Diffusion of Imported Technology: The Case of Korea*, Croom Helm, London, 1988, p. 26.
42 R. A. Onyango, 'New technology adaptions, SMMEs and reconstruction and development', paper read at the Science and Technology in Reconstruction and Development (STIRD) conference, University of Natal, Pietermaritzburg, South Africa, 23–26 September 1996, pp. 1–8.
43 J. L. Enos and W. H. Park, op. cit.
44 S. Langdon, 'Industrial dependence and export manufacturing in Kenya', in J. Ravenhill (ed.) *Africa in Economic Crisis*, Macmillan, London, 1986, pp. 181–212.
45 A. Ventura, 'Social intelligence: prerequisite for the management of science and technology', in J. Annerstedt and A. Jamison (eds) *From Research Policy to Social Intelligence: Essays for Stefan Dedijer*, Macmillan, London, 1988, p. 167.
46 A. Djeflat, 'The management of technology transfer: views and experiences of developing countries', *International Journal of Technology Management*, vol. 3, nos. 1 and 2, 1988, p. 152.
47 T. Curtis, *Business and Marketing for Engineers and Scientists*, McGraw-Hill, Maidenhead, 1994, pp. 260–84.
48 A. Djeflat, op. cit., p. 155.
49 Ibid., p. 159.
50 J. Senabye, 'Atlas textile firm collapses in Selebi-Phikwe', *Daily News*, 7 May 1996, p. 1.

51 A. Djeflat, op. cit., p. 164.
52 A. Ventura, op. cit., p. 470.
53 M. Beirne and H. Ramsay, 'Manna or monstrous regiment', in M. Beirne and H. Ramsay (eds) *Information Technology and Workplace Democracy*, Routledge, London, 1992.
54 X. H. Vo, 'The role of transnationals in technology transfer', *Economic Impact*, no. 60, 1987/4, p. 47.
55 A. Ventura, op. cit., p. 172.
56 I. Paez-Urdaneta, op. cit., p. 187.

USING THE CONCEPTUAL FRAMEWORK OF INFORMATION SCIENCE

THE INFORMATION SCIENCE FRAMEWORK

Machlup's[1] study of information in economic activity identified a tendency among decision-makers to accommodate themselves to information deficiency, whenever the cost of additional information proved prohibitive, by adapting to the uncertainty. He thus argued for an alternative conceptual framework for pursuing Pareto optimality under a new science. Defining science as knowledge acquired by sustained effort, Machlup[2] saw the new science as advancing the frontiers of information and knowledge, combating ignorance, error, risk and uncertainty, and, therefore, advancing autonomous decision-making. Information science is one such discipline. It offers an appropriate framework because it is interdisciplinary and multidisciplinary. Its lack of a homogeneous set of tacit and shared paradigms[3] permits the importation of ideas from other disciplines.

Information features in nearly forty fields. Most social sciences have sub-sectors addressing information and knowledge in society. For example, anthropology and politics enquire into knowledge and information, while social psychology has its own literature on information and knowledge. Amid these are many direct specialities that consider information a major constituent, including computer and information science, library and information science, information theory, general systems theory, linguistics, semiotics and several others.

Information science is a framework covering the role of information and knowledge in economies and in international relationships. Its adaptability to new concepts and paradigms is made possible by the pervasive nature of information and its integral part in all human endeavours as a resource, commodity and 'constitutive force in society'.[4] As Miles and Robins[5] point out, all tasks to which human labour is applied inherently involve some measure of information-processing.

Machlup[6] traces a trend in which the rules of science are shifting in favour of flexibility. The trend is marked by a reduced emphasis on methodological perfectionism in favour of pragmatism, sensitivity to reality and applicability. This research trend makes the flexibility of information science a bonus in the study of development and technology transfers. The trend towards flexibility and generalizations is, in any case, blurring traditional distinctions between disciplines. Whereas this 'leakage' unsettles professional convictions, it is also a source of innovation.[7]

Stonier[8] ascribes the failure of many disciplines to cope with the full implications of the information and electronics revolution to a lack of an 'interdisciplinary and future-oriented' framework of education and training. As we saw in Chapter 2, the Pacific Rim countries are trying to address this matter.

The term 'information management' was first used in the USA in the 1980s.[9] It covers subjects ranging from library services to database management, and can be defined as the economic, efficient and effective coordination of the production, control, storage, retrieval and dissemination of information from external and internal sources, in order to improve the performance of an organization. As Hills[10] points out, information management is critical because it constitutes the fundamental processes of government, business, industry and education. What is more, organizations are organisms held together by the means of acquiring, using, storing and transmitting information. The essence of effective management revolves around acquisition and protection of sound, vital information and knowledge. This is what makes it possible to staff, direct, coordinate, report and budget, or, in other words, to manage.[11]

Information resource management is a concept that links managerial effectiveness, information acquisition and use. It represents a synthesis of a range of ideas based on the premise that effective decision-making and strategic thinking cannot be divorced from information considerations. It covers the organizational/institutional capability to translate diagnostic results into specific information needs based on adequate knowledge of the requirements of the situation.

However, technological convergence has sometimes led to confusion in the literature between information and information technologies (ITs).[12] Information is the intellectual product of human cognitive processing and IT the technical ability to process and transfer the information product. It is erroneous to equate technology in the hardware sense with information and the use of information. As referred to earlier, this error permits the adoption of IT equipment as a representation and measure of how well an economy is handling information even though the reality may be different.[13]

Information technologies are a broad set of technologies ranging from cabinets, shelves, telephones, telexes, computers and the added-value derivatives. The current electronic-based ITs are thus at the end of a long chain of structural and organizational changes in developed economies going back to the industrial revolution. IT-led productivity is a result of many attendant and contributory factors that have created an appropriate organizational or institutional environment on to which the new technologies have been beneficially grafted. Good information management first requires the creation of an appropriate and transparent institutional environment for such organic grafting. This institutional attitude is societary informatization.

Information can also be referred to as 'intelligence'. Dedijer and Jequier[14] define intelligence as 'the ability of institutions to acquire new information and knowledge, make judgements, adapt to environment, develop new concepts and new strategies, and act in a rational and effective way'. Ventura[15] identifies social intelligence as the information that fuels action by providing confidence for the use of otherwise static information. He suggests that this is the information that directs and shifts society out of acquiescence and complacency with existing levels of knowledge, and thus causes change.

When information is used to plan and advance the future and to cope with the attendant uncertainties, it is referred to as strategic information. The following case studies focus on national and institutional management of the kind of information that stirs activity and moulds future response to future events. Informed strategic decisions are, however, founded on good-quality information about prevailing circumstances. This accords with the perception of social intelligence as the 'organisational capacity of a nation, a government, a corporation or any social organism, to acquire and use information in order to probe its environment, identify new threats and challenges, and respond in a creative way to new circumstances'.[16] This intelligence at national level is referred to here as strategic national information management. The responsibility for this rests with national institutions.

In technology transfer, strategic national information management involves monitoring technological developments in developed countries, evaluating their probable impact, making optimal decisions on the basis of information which is often incomplete, and dealing with future events.[17] Such strategic decisions require an 'independent world technology reconnaissance capability' to support autonomous decision-making and also technology transfer negotiations.

NATIONAL INFORMATION MANAGEMENT AND CAPACITY DEVELOPMENT

Efficiency in information infrastructures encompasses aspects such as organization, attitude, confidence, motivation, and rules, regulations, procedures and institutions. The hardware infrastructure is not, in itself, sufficient.

As stated previously, governments play an important role in information management in less developed countries (LDCs). Central government is an ideal locus where information, documentation and mass communication policy is formulated and implemented.[18] But government bureaucracies manage information on the basis of history and routine procedures rather than logic. Transparent procedures for institutional flows of information within a national information policy framework could improve fluidity of information transmission. However, the ways in which decision-makers receive information from subordinates and colleagues depend on patterns of authority and networks of mutual trust within the institution or society. These may need reviewing and attitudes may need to be changed. The policy emphasis needs to be on enhancing transparency and addressing information attitudes.

From an informational perspective, secrecy is artificially created uncertainty. It is, however, a form of government operation, and states need a degree of secrecy. But accommodating transparency is important.

Katz[19] has argued that future LDC development will have to be information-driven. The reason he gives is that the public information sector in LDCs is overmanned but underused. What is lacking is innovative ways to mobilize it. It is important to view political structures as information-processing entities which generate demand for both information workers and technologies, and to conceive development plans with this view in mind.

Therefore, a policy challenge for LDCs is not so much to increase physical infrastructure or size of the knowledge industry, as to create a favourable information environment and attitudes for effective operations.[20] Although the efficiency and speed with which information is transferred are conditioned by quality and density of the infrastructures, related actions or decisions are influenced by intangibles such as attitudes to secrecy, social values, personal relationships, cultural traditions and structures of authority. The value of information depends not only on 'its intrinsic importance, its relevance or its veracity, but also on its timeliness'.[21] The policy framework needs to address the trade-off between timeliness, reliability and secrecy and the means for effecting societal, institutional and attitudinal changes.

Most LDCs accept the modern scientific enterprise as central to enhancing national capabilities. But new science continues to be initiated in the West. However, knowledge creation dependency need not be an obstacle to technology transfers, as the Pacific region testifies. The lesson here is that 'careful planning and correct policies lead to real and beneficial technology transfers'.[22] Real technology transfer is, however, a multi-stage, multi-level process of 'domestication, indigenisation, and diffusion'. This combines well with Reid's five innovation attributes of relative advantage, compatibility, complexity, triability and observability.[23] She refers to Rogers' model of diffusion as the process by which an innovation is communicated through channels over time among members of a social system. Djeflat[24] sees the technology transfer stages as covering costs, adaptation by local operatives, internal capacity inventory, technology choice, importation, channel selection, and negotiations. Enos and Park[25] add monitoring of implementation and enforcing of contracts and deadlines. During this process, core technology needs to be mastered and the capability to adapt the foreign technology to suit local demand and manufacturing conditions developed.

However, imported technological components transfer only if they fit into the local design framework.[26] Freeman[27] explains the Japanese success as being founded on a great use of indigenous scientific and technical resources to assimilate and improve on the imported techniques. Effective inventory of local capability is therefore important to technology transfer. In most LDCs, indigenous technologies are left to peasants and ignored, despite their forming the backbone of the country's economy. The technologies are thus not improved on, and most resources go to importations of foreign technologies. The result is the importing of obsolete, irrelevant technologies that cannot be absorbed, maintained or improved on to suit local conditions.

The failure to take stock of, and use, indigenous resources and traditional strengths has been costly. National capability inventory and management need to be at the core of capacity development.

INDIGENOUS TECHNOLOGICAL CAPABILITY AND INFORMATION MANAGEMENT

Vo[28] considers the most important element of transfer in industrial technology to be the accumulation of experience concerning project implementation and manufacturing operation at the middle and top management levels, and down to the maintenance level. Training, the participation of local personnel and the institutional mechanisms for storing, processing, using and diffusing experience and learning are all crucial to the indigenization of appropriate human resources.

The technical know-how and operational experience acquired in any one field should spread to other industrial endeavours if the recipient country is to build indigenous capability. A first step towards generating indigenous technology is the ability to diversify into related fields using experience learned from the area in which foreign technology was imported. However, transplantation requires a favourable environment characterized by a transparent institutionalized 'techno-logical culture', in which communication of specific as well as general industrial knowledge plays an important role. *Real* technology transfer assumes that each enterprise for which foreign technology is sought contributes to the diffusion process. Only countries like those in the Pacific Rim appear to have made this significant progress in real technology transfer. Many LDCs have achieved the ability to transplant some industrial technology. In such circumstances, Vo considers the transfers as 'apparent', not real. He also considers technologies transferred through MNCs as unable to accommodate and address local peculiarities and applications. Information management helps address collective accumulations of learning and experience. Through information management one can evaluate transfers across sectors and projects in terms of completion times, local content rise, adaptations, and innovative applications of skills acquired to new areas.

Technology transfer failures have been blamed on the modality of the transfer, the environment in the recipient countries and a lack of government leadership. Despite being a channel for firm-specific technological transfers, foreign direct investment, for instance, does not contribute to indigenous capacity. The lack of an adequate infrastructure of indigenous firms able to use the technologies in the forms transferred prevents diffusion into the wider economy. This vacuum requires alternative government-instituted mechanisms to unpackage and diffuse the technologies, and must be the responsibility of specific institutions.

Vo considers licensing arrangements a better channel for product technology transfers. However, the experiences of the Pacific region indicate that licensing arrangements alone are inadequate; correct public policies are vital. Korea's transfer success is, for example, attributed to an excellent physical and financial infrastructure, an adequate supply of skilled labour, and a pool of high-powered technical and scientific knowledge founded on one of the oldest systems of mass education in the world.

Market imperfections mean that much technology transfer is intra-firm and internalized within MNCs. MNCs bypass external markets in order to maximize net benefits through mechanisms that include transfer pricing. MNC systems have thus led to controversies about the way transfers take place, the nature of technologies transmitted and the impact of such transfers on the technological capabilities of LDCs. But the debate on the appropriateness of the technology drew attention away from the contribution of information asymmetry to the perpetual vulnerability of LDCs in technology imports.

LDCs have to negotiate with MNCs in technology matters. Ventura[29] describes the MNCs as 'brimming with a solid stock of specific technological knowledge woven into high level social intelligence fabrics'. The corporations often know more about the needs and weaknesses of their LDC customers than the customers know about themselves. LDC teams are often characterized by superficial understanding of technological market alternatives and a lack of preparation that forces them to depend on whatever information the technology suppliers are willing to divulge.

Technology transfer does not take place if the recipient country is not ready. The readiness is conditioned on its ability to build economic and physical infrastructure, improve and consolidate human resources, and establish sound institutions. The role of public policy is important in bringing that about as well as in conceiving imaginative solutions. Technology transfer will depend on enhanced national social intelligence. The required strategic national information management is, however, the responsibility of national institutions. How they generate and assimilate new information and knowledge is important.

KNOWLEDGE DEPENDENCY AND TECHNOLOGY MANAGEMENT

Technology is a product of a society's knowledge creation endeavours, where knowledge is the pool of its tested and structured information, consisting of rules, procedures, rituals and skills concerned with doing things or carrying out duties and tasks. Every human grouping constructs its map of physical reality, tests it against reality, and adapts it accordingly.[30] After a map is legitimized it becomes absorbed into the rituals of society. Annerstedt[31] concluded that organized knowledge is the key factor of a society. He sees society as resting upon a continuous flow of diversified information. This facilitates production and change by creating new knowledge. A society therefore needs new knowledge to understand and control changes in its natural and social environments.

Change, creativity, growth and development are products of new knowledge caused by breakthroughs in attempts to formulate new views of reality.[32] This process of growth and evolution of knowledge should be endogenous, self-perpetuating and self-sustaining. However, the source for new stimuli or insights to changes in reality need not be endogenous. International reality demands that stimuli be sourced from global scanning and research – research being 'any creative systematic activity undertaken to increase the stock of knowledge, and the use of the knowledge to devise new applications'.[33]

Science, as knowledge actively acquired by society, is influenced by political and economic considerations. This is especially true of industrial science and science-based technologies. Economic imperatives dictate funding of particular scientific and technological developments by both state and private-sector organizations. Therefore, the social structure of modern science is dependent upon the social, economic and political organization of society and is sensitive to changes in this environment.

As a result, knowledge creation in LDCs faces a problem from dependent infrastructures. Social dynamics influence what is produced and the areas of knowledge investigated. Because research is founded on previous findings, relativism is strong. New knowledge is established by reference to an audience and what it accepts. It defines acceptable areas of concern, sets standards, and decides legitimate uses for the new knowledge. The audience is therefore central to scientific claims.

Under this framework, sub-Saharan Africa is disadvantaged in knowledge creation endeavours. In 1980, for example, at the start of the 'lost decade', Africa's share of global research and development reached 0.3 per cent.[34] This means that the region must look outside for mainstay knowledge out of necessity. But this has inherent risks.

It is the specialized research community that filters research output and decides what are to be recognized as 'facts' within a body of scientific knowledge. 'Scientific truth' is, therefore, arrived at partially by social processes such as the defining of acceptable credentials, keeping the right peer set, selecting acceptable problems and methodology, and communicating results through accepted media. Theories can be formulated, accepted and abandoned as a result of social fashion. Influencing this fashion is important., but to do so depends on where the influential parties reside.

Normally, knowledge develops in relatively autonomous ways while remaining porous to external influences and selecting from external, cultural realms the ideas which, in a broad sense, fit its internal social criteria. Cross-cultural borrowings are made both across contemporary cultural boundaries and across time boundaries. Knowledge and information are thus a process of constant interaction within the socio-economic environments, moving in response to changes in those environments. The addition of new knowledge that accrues to an existing body of social knowledge should consist of those elements that respond adequately to the internal and external social environments. Therefore when a particular community or sub-culture is beset by uncertainty, it should tend towards greater receptivity to new ideas.[35]

However, the knowledge creation and technological frontier facing LDCs is not a normal one. Contact with European science has led to much of what now constitutes universal legitimate scientific problems and methodologies being defined by the prevailing intellectual climate in Europe and North America.

As a result, most formal knowledge creation activity in LDCs is removed from the immediate needs of society. With research mainly supported by the public sector, the situation is self-perpetuating.

Much of what is traditional and indigenous and affecting the majority of the people receives no resources to update and develop it. This has contributed to ignorance of the traditional knowledge creation processes and technologies. Ventura[36] points to this divorce of information and knowledge generation from national priorities as contributing to the weaknesses in national technological infrastructures. At the point of technology negotiations, the subsequent ignorance of local realities leaves negotiators without relevant information on how to commercialize technology in a manner that relates to their special interests. This also contributes to the credibility problem encountered by information professionals attempting to place information in mainstream development knowledge management.[37] Mchombu,[38] for example, points to library systems and services that are not open to use by over 90 per cent of the population. The information and knowledge they collect and manage remains alien to immediate national needs; and the formal sector to which the profession addresses its arguments is accustomed to purchasing, rather than searching for and formulating, solutions. The sector does not need competitive information to run such an arrangement.

Goonatilake[39] has concluded that European-created knowledge has stultified non-European countries that have absorbed it. It has had the effect of delegitimizing large amounts of valid, relevant knowledge from these countries. In Africa, European knowledge discouraged the evolution of a culture built on a search for consensus in new knowledge creation. The culture of importing blueprint solutions has stunted thinking in national institutions and spawned imitations and mimicry.

The system of legitimizing new knowledge by reference to external practices marginalized all forms of indigenous scientific, cultural and knowledge-creating endeavours and skills. It is now difficult to distinguish between creativity and mimicry in mainstream national culture; in national institutions this is supported by opaque regulations that penalize creativity. These institutions cannot be held to account because their performance standards are externally conceived and cannot be evaluated locally. Resource limitations also contribute to the production, in universities and research institutes, of knowledge with little relevance to the immediate environment. The funders, located externally, determine the research agenda.

Scientific and technological 'xenophilia' dominates LDC markets, making direct intra-LDC trade difficult. Entry into another LDC market needs to be arbitrated through Western legitimizing systems, thus undermining any advantages resulting from propinquity. Success in Western markets is required in order to establish credibility within LDCs. This was the case with the Malaysian national car, the Proton. Its successful entry into the UK market was instrumental in its acceptance by, for example, African markets. This pattern of knowledge creation, adoption and acceptance has serious implications for technology importation, the process of creativity and intra-LDC trade policies and concepts. The practices pursued by knowledge-creating institutions in LDCs undermine objectivity and creativity. Ventura[40] suggests 'goal specificity' in review procedures as a remedy. Knowledge creation needs clear plans and set goals. He refers to a 'plethora of private and public concerns' from LDCs searching for technologies with no clear perspective on wider national direction, responsibilities, or the other parties involved. The tendency to import packaged knowledge and solutions has led to low search culture among institutions and a preference for proprietary information despite high costs and alternative public sources. What is more, such costly information is not even diffused once acquired.

REDEFINING TECHNOLOGY AND THE TRANSFER PROCESS

Technology can be considered the intermediary in humans' interaction with the environment and a tool in coping with nature.[41] This underlines the absence of 'universal technologies' as such. What do exist are specific solutions for specific socio-economic pressures, requiring adaptation whenever transplanted.

Particular technologies are outcomes of configurations of particular socio-economic forces at particular times. Beirne and Ramsay[42] have argued that technology is not produced in a vacuum and that it develops from past location-specific technological and scientific understanding. Technology reflects class relations of a society, the nature of its economic system, its patterns of conflicts, conflict management and conflict resolution. This limits the scope for its variation. What is more, social constraints or determinism conspire to further squeeze out abstract technical options opened by new technology.[43] To be transferred effectively, these components of a technological package need to be unpackaged, identified and understood before they can be grafted organically on to a different economic system, history and terrain.

It is the successful evolution of Western technology into mass production and its ability to provide an unending supply of high-quality goods and services that makes it attractive to countries outside its immediate socio-economic context. Western technology should not, however, be perceived as universal. What should be possible is the adoption of dynamic and long-term structural policies that prepare the new terrain for an organic rather than illusory transplantation of technology.[44]

Western technologies are capital-intensive, create divisions between mental and manual skills, and de-emphasize manual and craft skills that, incidentally, predominate in LDCs. European society favours mental skills. This is confirmed by, for instance, project management methods that play down labour costs. This tends to make human resource utilization a residual issue for top management. What is more, it has been observed that European styles of management show little inclination towards worker involvement in change management. Beirne and Ramsay[45] ascribe this to the European history of class conflicts in which the worker tends to lose anyway. But this trend spells problems for countries where cultural ideals and indigenous forms of production are differently inclined, but which are nonetheless interested in Western technology. The solution lies in seeking locally conceived and devised compromises as part of technology transfer management.

The Pacific Rim's success in incorporating and reproducing Western technology involved important changes and compromises in social relations. But most important was the identification and recognition of the social and organizational problems. This recognition continues to elude Africa's planners generally, as is glaringly illustrated by the cases studied in Part II of the book.

Fransman and King[46] advocate the need to immerse knowledge creation in local traditions. This would make it possible to immerse the imported technology into people's creative talents and establish the management of change firmly within the society. Without such well-considered measures, the result of technology transfer efforts will remain technology enclaves. In LDCs, effecting such measures requires institutional changes.

This is illustrated, for example, by a report[47] on a Kenyan scientist who was forced to sell a coffee invention based on ultraviolet light to a European manufacturer. The manufacturer, after developing it, then sold the equipment to Kenya's coffee industry. The inventor found no supportive local institutions. Until December 1989,[48] Kenya's Patents Registration Act[49] allotted the responsibility for managing Kenya's inventions to the United Kingdom. Only patents registered at the British Patent Office, under UK patent law, were recognized in Kenya. Many African countries still lack the institutional framework for managing local creativity. The Director of the Kenya Industrial Research Development Institute (KIRDI) has complained of inventors suffering from lack of incentives, motivation and funding, and of a national lack of confidence in indigenously produced technology.

It is therefore important that means be devised to engineer an association with imported technology, whether on a technical or an organizational basis. What is important is that the society is able to identify with the goals generated by the technology. Formulating this compromise requires sound knowledge of the social and productive goals of the technology, and of the production mores of the importing society. This is the lesson to be learned from the Pacific Rim experiences. The alternative is to marginalize the pool of a nation's unique indigenous skills, dynamism and other innate abilities that have evolved through centuries of interacting with the local environment. This is the dilemma confronting much of sub-Saharan Africa.

INFORMATION, INSTITUTIONS, AND TECHNOLOGY TRANSFER

Djeflat's[50] technology transfer studies have concluded that LDCs need to pay more attention to:

1 the kind of technology they intend to import;
2 the type of contract to be used;
3 the channel for importation;
4 the nature of the negotiations involved.

All these steps depend on information and knowledge concerning alternative sources, markets, competitors and substitutes. Only then can equitable and meaningful negotiations take place.

Negotiators and market participants in LDCs are disadvantaged by their information poverty. The specialized use of information, and the deployment of new technological capacity to convey it, is the determinant of future economic competition between nations. It is therefore important for a country to be able to integrate or synthesize pieces of information into coherent units for pursuing its development goals. But this requires an effective infrastructure consisting of organizations able to use the information gathered and to define correct policies.

Djeflat's remedy is the introduction of mechanisms to strengthen the bargaining power of LDCs. For this he recommends that LDCs:

1 are properly informed about suppliers and products;
2 unpackage the technologies as much as possible;
3 avoid supplier financing;
4 use group buying.

He argues that LDCs need to allocate more time and effort to preparations for technology transfer negotiations. Djeflat advocates intensive and wide use of search capacity in order for the team to be better informed.

From their study of South Korea, Enos and Park[51] report on active and intense government participation in all technology negotiations before 1979. The government's objective was to ensure that Korean parties were as informed as possible, which it achieved by making its import regulations clear. The Korean technology transfer landscape was therefore well documented and transparent. Industrial targets were precise and the government adhered to its targets.

Korea therefore bears testimony to the benefits of transparency, goal specificity and documentation in planning and implementation. The Korean government also insisted on exhaustive surveys of alternative techniques, technologies, suppliers, markets and the possible combinations.

In the Korean technology transfer landscape, supplier profiles are emphasized and updated. Also important was that all potential suppliers were sought and negotiated with, whether they responded to tenders or not. This requires good international reconnaissance. Korea emphasized implementation time schedules and full capacity utilization, and held technology suppliers accountable for undertakings made during negotiations, including support in entry to export markets. Technology diffusion was ensured through conferences and trade exhibitions. What Enos and Park describe is a proactive government, institutions with a sense of purpose and organizations that learn between projects, as shown by improved time schedules, higher utility of installed capacity, and lower implementation costs between related projects over time. Improvements in institutional learning curves and memory were evident, starting in and inspired by the public sector and then infusing into private-sector operations.

There are advantages in a purposive informational approach to industry management through an appropriate information policy approach. For example, the Japanese motor industry frequently operates cooperative ventures between various firms from different sectors as temporary industrial groups called *keiretsu*. These are loose, temporary confederations of independent or semi-independent companies, maintained through effective flows of information. The *keiretsu* depend more on mutual cooperation, and information flows among members of the group, than on levels of financial and legal integration that underpin Western corporations. This gives *keiretsu* the advantages of large organizations but without the accompanying disadvantages of size, having to maintain buffer stocks, vertical integration and multiple sourcing of components. A country like Kenya, with its dearth of dedicated finance, supplier, distributor and franchise-holder organizations in any defined industry, could learn from such innovative arrangements. But innovation depends on the inclination of national institutions.

Clark and Juma[52] see technological innovations as involving constant improvements on the adaptive parameters of national systems. These are achieved by matching previously unmatched environmental features or adapting to new changes. They recognize that innovations can disrupt market niches and make existing equipment, skills, materials, components, management culture and organizational capabilities obsolete. They can bring about the attendant disruptions that accompany change and development. The analysis of patterns of information flow makes it possible to predict the dimensions of shift.

Patterns of information flow are seen as having value as predictors of possible trends. Thus a study of an economy's information flow and infrastructure patterns contributes to predicting the direction the economy may take. With the environment in constant flux, technological entrepreneurship becomes complex and full of uncertainty. However, the levels of uncertainty for young industries can be reduced if national environment enabling institutions work towards enhancing operational terrain transparency. In a transparent terrain patterns of information flow are more discernible and comprehensible.

Institutional organizations, inherent in a policy framework, are intended to ensure that information and knowledge are generated and disseminated in a less random way. Institutions thus help to channel and manage change. New technologies require new institutional arrangements and, by inference, new information configurations. Reorganizations are needed because old institutions are repositories of old codes, regulations, channels and practices. Not only are their capacities to handle information requirements for new technologies limited, but they could inhibit development of new technologies because they have inappropriate channels, continue to follow inappropriate or outdated practices, or are sustained by vested interests.

Vested interests can become powerful obstacles to change and the learning process. But keeping abreast of rapid technological change requires a preparedness for rapid reorganization. This has implications for public policy and for how vested interests should be coped with. A science-based approach to managing vested interest lies in wider exposure to the reality that without change, little self-sustaining technological capability can develop, which ultimately leads to economic decline.

Japan and Korea have demonstrated that research leadership and total mastery of knowledge generation are not crucial to international competitiveness. What is important is the ability to utilize available technical information in the process of economic evolution and niche-making. This ability depends on the capacity of countries to establish institutions which can facilitate the process. An important goal for such institutions includes ability to smoothen the flow of information and resources pertaining to planned tasks. This requires flexibility, extensive diversity, experimentation and relative autonomy in decision-making.

CONCLUSIONS

Most of the information and knowledge acquired by an institution at project level will probably not contribute to overall policy learning unless deliberate action is taken to create and regularly activate documentation and institutional memory processes. The capacity to accumulate and to mobilize knowledge and experience depends on how well existing institutions can retain and reproduce experiences. This is what constitutes policy learning. Political will is needed because it is in the political arena that broad evolutionary paths are defined.

In most LDCs, policy learning is hampered by vested interests and limited flows of newly generated information. Terrain opacity does not serve the learning process. This opacity is also due to the operational nature of bureaucracies. Under conventional government practice, activities of the bureaucratic machinery are distributed in a fixed manner in the form of official duties or functions. Tasks which fall outside the jurisdictional domain are ignored, explained away, or passed to other officials. But, as situations tend towards complexity, new requirements for technological development cannot be met without destabilizing the bureaucratic system. Since the bureaucratic machinery is meant to create and maintain a stable state, contradictions follow.

The bureaucratic rationality accorded government departments is based on the view that all information and knowledge required to implement projects are available and all resources can be mobilized by government fiat. But projects, especially of a technological nature in LDCs, encounter problems related to the fact that every step in the implementation process is unpredictable and non-routine, and requires new pieces of information that are sometimes unavailable locally. Thus most bureaucracies are bound to, and do, fail in project implementations even with the best of intentions. Such a failure featured at the early stages of Malaysia's national car project – the Proton. The manner in which government officials handle information limits or obstructs wider capacity to learn from emerging situations and stultifies the contribution of the learning process to adaptive change.

This style of managing information is based on office documents or files made inaccessible by government secrecy regulations. The information is seldom synthesized or analysed for useful lessons. Secrecy prevents the information from being subjected to recombination or selection for purposes of institutional or technological learning and innovation.

Transparency is vital in the make-up of a technology learning model for an LDC. It enables recombination, synthesis, selection and objective reviews of activities for learning and accumulation of experience. But it conflicts with secretive bureaucratic procedures. The tendency towards secrecy, or lack of transparency, is a major contributory obstacle towards efficient use of experience and available information in LDCs. It also obstructs accumulation of learning and improvement of societal knowledge and undermines negotiating capabilities.

Evidence from recent technology transfer studies indicates the need for flexible, adaptive, accountable and semi-autonomous institutions that assume uncertainty and therefore emphasize learning and the flow of information through dynamic networks. But such policies for long-run economic change are possible only where institutional and political contexts permit adaptive change.

In a world of increasing complexity, integration and competition, political institutions and human resources need to take on a corresponding character or else the nation will be overtaken by nations that do adapt in this way. The growing disparities between LDCs bear testimony to this. A high-profile civil service able to direct technology transfers, flexible and sensitive to international changes, underlines the Pacific Rim success. The economic cost of accommodating institutions that act otherwise is demonstrated in the case studies that follow. In any event, the already overmanned bureaucracies can be made productive only by such mobilization. The option of redundancies carries a big political price for countries with small and diminishing formal employment sectors. Poor negotiating capability and an unwillingness or inability to mobilize the service into a productive posture has driven many African countries into implementing the World Bank/IMF-initiated retrenchments. The social cost of doing so is bound to be felt soon.

The following case studies set out to evaluate the information-handling capability of the environment enabling institutions which support the operations of economic agents in Kenya. This combination of existing information, technologies and workers is considered the national development capital upon which effective technology transfer can be constructed. The evaluation of this capital requires the multidisciplinary framework of information science. The Kenyan case studies illustrate an LDC's attempts at managing a technology transfer process with institutions and methods that have as yet to recognize information as central to development management.

NOTES

1 F. Machlup, *Knowledge: Its Creation, Distribution and Economic Significance*, vol. 3: *The Economics of Information and Human Capital*, Princeton University Press, Princeton, NJ, 1984.

2 Ibid., p. 217.

3 B. Cronin and L. Davenport, 'Profiling the professors', *Journal of Information Science*, vol. 15, 1989, p. 13.

4 D. M. Lamberton, *Information Economics: 'Threatened Wreckage' or New Paradigm?*, Circuit Working Paper 1990/1, Centre for International Research on Communication and Information Technologies, Melbourne, 1990, p. 8.

5 I. Miles and K. Robins, 'Making sense of information', in K. Robins (ed.) *Understanding Information*, Belhaven Press, London, 1992, pp. 1–26.

6 F. Machlup, op. cit., p. 231.

7 F. Machlup and U. Mansfield (eds) *The Study of Information: Interdisciplinary Messages*, John Wiley, New York, 1983, p. 363.

8 T. Stonier, *The Wealth of Information: A Profile of the Post-industrial Society*, Thames Methuen, London, 1983, p. 42.

9 D. P. Best, 'The future of information management', *International Journal of Information Management*, vol. 8, no. 1, 1988, p. 13.

10 P. Hills (ed.) *International Journal of Information Management*, vol. 8, no. 1, 1988, p. 3.

11 A. Ventura, 'Social intelligence: prerequisite for the management of science and technology', in J. Annerstedt and A. Jamison (eds) *From Research Policy to Social Intelligence: Essays for Stefan Dedijer*, Macmillan, London, 1988.

12 N. Roberts and T. D. Wilson, 'Information resources management: a question of attitudes', *International Journal of Information Management*, vol. 7, no. 2, June 1987, p. 68.

13 D. M. Lamberton, op. cit., p. 5.

14 S. Dedijer and N. Jequier (eds), *Intelligence for Economic Development*, Berg Publishers, Oxford, 1987, p. xi.

15 A. Ventura, op. cit.

16 S. Dedijer and N. Jequier, op. cit., p. 227.

17 Ibid., p. 4.

18 Ibid., p. 85.

19 R. L. Katz, *The Information Society: An International Perspective*, Praeger, New York, 1988, p. 137.
20 S. Dedijer and N. Jequier, op. cit., p. 227.
21 Ibid., p. 231.
22 X. H. Vo, 'The role of transnationals in technology transfer', *Economic Impact*, no. 60, 1987/4.
23 E. O. F. Reid, 'Internet developments and government diffusion: case of Singapore', in C. Chen (ed.) *NIT '96 Proceedings of the 9th International Conference on New Information Technology*, West Newton, MA, 1996, pp. 219–30. Reid refers to E. Rogers' book *Diffusion of Innovations*, 4th edn, Prentice-Hall, Hemel Hempstead, 1995.
24 A. Djeflat, 'The management of technology transfer – views and experiences of developing countries', *International Journal of Technology Management*, vol. 3, no. 1/2, 1988, p. 15.
25 J. L. Enos and W. H. Park, *The Adoption and Diffusion of Imported Technology: The Case of Korea*, Croom Helm, London, 1988.
26 A. Rahman, 'Science, technology and modernisation', in J. Annerstedt and A. Jamison (eds), op. cit., p. 14.
27 C. Freeman, 'Quantitative and qualitative factors in national policies for science and technology', in J. Annerstedt and A. Jamison (eds), op. cit., pp. 114–28.
28 X. H. Vo, op. cit., p. 47.
29 A. Ventura, op. cit.
30 S. Goonatilake, *Aborted Discovery: Science and Technology in the Third World*, Zed Books, London, 1984, p. 1.
31 J. Annerstedt, 'The global R & D system: where is the Third World?', in J. Annerstedt and A. Jamison (eds), op. cit., p. 129.
32 S. Goonatilake, op. cit., p. 2.
33 J. Annerstedt, op. cit., p. 139.
34 Ibid., p. 138.
35 S. Goonatilake, op. cit., p. 81.
36 A. Ventura, op. cit., p. 167.
37 P. Sturges and R. Neill, *The Quiet Struggle: Libraries and Information for Africa*, Mansell, London, 1990.
38 K. J. Mchombu, 'The cultural and political dimensions of information resources management in Africa', in N. M. Adeyemi (ed.) *Reader on Information Management Strategies for Africa's Development*, UNECA/PADIS, Addis Ababa, 1995.
39 S. Goonatilake, op. cit., p. 87.
40 A. Ventura, op. cit., p. 169.
41 S. Goonatilake, op. cit., p. 120.
42 M. Beirne and H. Ramsay, 'Manna or monstrous regiment – technology, control and democracy in the workplace', in M. Beirne and H. Ramsay (eds) *Information Technology and Workplace Democracy*, Routledge, London, 1992.
43 S. Lubbe, R. Eggert and N. Hawkes, 'Determining the significance of decision criteria in the selection of IT investment in South Africa', *Information Technology for Development*, vol. 6, 1995, pp. 125–38.
44 X. H. Vo, op. cit., p. 50.
45 M. Beirne and H. Ramsay, op. cit.
46 M. Fransman and K. King (eds), *Technological Capability in the Third World*, Macmillan, London, 1984, p. 60.
47 'The patents debate', *The Weekly Review*, 24 February 1989, p. 21.
48 Republic of Kenya, Industrial Property Act 1989, Government Printer, Nairobi, 1989.

49 Republic of Kenya, The Patents Registration Act Chapter 508, Revised 1982, Government Printer, Nairobi, 1982.
50 A. Djeflat, op. cit., p. 165.
51 J. L. Enos and W. H. Park, op. cit., p. 231.
52 N. Clarke and C. Juma, *Long-Run Economics*, Pinter, London, 1987, p. 168.

Part II

STRATEGIC NATIONAL INFORMATION MANAGEMENT

6

RESEARCH METHODOLOGY CONSIDERATIONS

INTRODUCTION

The 1980s was a period of descriptive studies of the information sector, when studies from both developed and developing countries identified growth in the sector. The reasons for this growth were, however, different.[1] In developed countries the growth was driven by the private sector. It marked advanced reorganization in production methods. In LDCs, this growth was largely in the public sector, and took place despite deteriorating productivity. It was caused by political intervention intended to absorb the output of training systems out of step with national productivity needs. It represented an overmanned and unproductive bureaucracy.

These were studies in the tradition of the post-industrial economy of Daniel Bell.[2] Most of them invariably failed to locate LDCs in the pre-industrial–post-industrial continuum.[3]

The studies of the 1990s have focused on analysis of the information sector. For LDCs, this has been informed by the realization that the prospects of 'leapfrogging'[4] are far more complex and remote than previously assumed. There have followed specific studies of events and projects in an attempt to understand the role of information management and its potential benefits to operational, tactical, project and strategic management.[5] These have gone hand in hand with studies that have attempted to cost the consequences of poor information management.[6]

Such studies have implications for the design of information sector study for developing countries. Information sector studies can focus on:

1 information technologies;
2 information workforce;
3 information industries; or
4 social information flows[7] or societal informatization, to use Paez-Urdaneta's term.[8]

Information technology studies in LDCs often end up as censuses of equipment and vendors.[9] Some LDCs, such as India and Brazil, have adopted information policies intended to boost information technology industries. The second kind of study, of the information workforce in LDCs, as indicated, usually reveals the workforce to be an unproductive bureaucracy.

Most LDCs have no information technology industry; they import these products. But little has been done to understand the societary informatization of these countries. A study that did seek to do so for Latin America, by Salinas,[10] identified structural and cultural constraints that undermined improved information management despite additional technologies or improved international information access. Salinas's study emphasized societary informatization above acquisitions of high technology. This study adopts the same approach and focuses on Kenya as an example of a developing country.

FOCUS OF RESEARCH

The data collection for this research took place in two stages. The first took the form of a survey of Kenya's information infrastructure between December 1987 and June 1988.[11] It covered thirty educational and research bodies, the national postal and telecommunications authority, and professional, industrial and commercial associations. The survey found differing levels of information facility availability and use, reflected in resources dedicated to information support. It also confirmed that there was little use of competitive information in decision-making in Kenya, as is also the case in other LDCs according to Paez-Urdaneta[12] and Sturges and Neill.[13]

In order to study Kenya's societary informatization effectively, a case study approach focused on project implementation was chosen. This was intended to identify institutional coordination in common tasks. It was considered important to look at how the relevant institutions galvanize resources and synchronize their operations over time.

The industrial sector was identified as the best location for the case project because, as in other LDCs, industrialization is an area of national development priority, but one which, according to Matthews[14] and Bennel,[15] has had a poor performance record. This problem has been traced to technology transfer. This national problem was to be subjected to a new information-based diagnosis.

As I have argued before,[16] there is no accepted holistic technology transfer model. However, Enos and Park[17] refer to the 'rogue theory' of 'learning by doing' as offering a framework for analysing capability-building. This study is based on the premise that capability-building at institutional and national level requires information-diffusing mechanisms, and it therefore looks at corporate or institutional skills, learning, memory and experience accumulation and transfer mechanisms among Kenya's technology management institutions.

The study acknowledges government secrecy in project management and assesses whether the Official Secrets Act advances or obstructs efficient project implementation.

THE ASSUMPTIONS

This study assumes that understanding the information economy is important in defining the national development path in the context of global trends. The trends need to be taken account of in development and technology studies.

The study also assumes that Kenya, like other LDCs, will, for the foreseeable future, need to import most of its technology requirements because of its dependent knowledge creation position. Improving capability for negotiations is therefore important.

Recent studies, such as those of the Pacific Rim, have emphasized the importance of government and public-sector enabling institutions in managing technology transfer. Katz[18] also underlines improved use of public-sector bureaucracies (the information workforce in LDCs) as crucial to future development. This study focuses on the navigational role of government institutions, how they improve terrain transparency and how they facilitate national learning.

The study acknowledges that declared policies are not always in step with practice. Therefore, documentation procedures are looked at as aids to transparency in policy and practice. It is also assumed that documentation aids reviews and supports goal specification and accountability.

In what follows, the term 'environment enabling institutions' covers public-sector institutions as well as professional and business associations. These institutions constitute fora in which ideas are conceived and formulated into policies and agendas for project definition and implementation. The focus is therefore on the institutions as economic navigators, and less as economic agents.

In order to evaluate institutional goal specificity, experience transfer and learning, an adequate time period needed to be covered by the study. Enos and Park[19] refer to performance improvements in Korean institutions between projects over time, as reflected in improved completion times, higher utilization of installed capacity, and falling costs relative to similar and related projects over time. These occurrences testify to institutional learning, experience transfer, goal specificity and objective review procedures. In order to take on board the element of time, this study adopts two cases and looks at events between 1973 and 1990. The repercussions, manifesting themselves between 1990 and 1996, are also taken on board for policy implications and to test the veracity of conclusions drawn.

The cases were also selected on the basis of their importance and ability to galvanize and marshal wide national political and institutional attention and resources. The cases are looked at against the reality of other countries, organizations and forces in the international arena involved in similar projects. The result is an inventory of Kenya's information-processing capital.

OBJECTIVES OF THE STUDY

The objective of the study is to test the hypothesis that efficient national identification, selection and management of strategic competitive information aids effective technology transfer and development. The study assesses the use of strategic national information management in unpackaging imported technology and aligning its components to indigenous technological and cultural capabilities, talents and traits.

This is an information policy study. It looks at how information policy supports the mechanisms for keeping the long-term national development agenda in focus despite pressures of short-term considerations. This supports policy learning through institutional memory and learning, and objective, transparent and documented evaluation procedures. Such institutional ability is considered vital to identification of, selection of, negotiation for and transfer of suitable technologies.

It is the intention of this study to look at measures that define inter- and intra-institutional and sectoral synchronization in project implementation. Also of interest are extant procedures and guidelines for accessing local and external expertise, evaluating alternative technologies and suppliers, environmental appraisal, and accessing strategic and competitive information on technologies, suppliers, financiers and donor markets. Attention is also paid to guidelines for purchasing and paying for identified technologies, and procedures and practices in monitoring technology transfer processes and enforcing contracts and commitments.

The mechanisms for institutional acquisition, retention and generation of expertise and enhanced learning and memory capacities receive special attention as means of seeking to evaluate the role and capability of enabling institutions in advancing the national learning curve in the handling and absorption of alien technologies.

RESEARCH METHODOLOGY

This was a novel research theme significant in its holistic and multidisciplinary approach to the information-based concepts of development, technology acquisition and organic transfer. It breaks new ground on information management systems in development management and is broad-based because no previous groundwork has been carried out.

After the preliminary survey,[20] the research on societary informatization took place between December 1989 and April 1990. Thirty-two organizations were visited and fifty-six people interviewed.

The questions were intended to identify operational search culture. Questions were asked about alternatives and options for suppliers, techniques and markets and the related operational requirements for using the alternatives. It was also intended to identify whether informed decision-making, institutional capability inventory, proceduralizing and documenting of experience, monitoring project implementation and enforcing schedules, contracts and reviews were considered as operational requirements among the institutions in particular, and in the wider Kenyan terrain in general.

The study used open-ended questions administered in personal interviews. A guideline of the interview structure was forwarded in advance to the interviewees. The questions were intended to capture and address operational practice for comparison with the official role of the institutions, as checked against official documents. The emphasis on practice in relation to the cases was intended to reduce restatements of the official position. As many institutions as possible with an interest in the cases were included.

The aim was to visit as many institutions and interview as many individuals as possible within the time frame, so as to obtain adequate data, enable all actions to be understood, as far as possible, and reduce, as much as possible, gaps in the description of events surrounding the cases. The evidence would then be used to confront and test the hypothesis. Therefore the diversity of information sources was deliberate and meant to capture the actual reality.

Published reports and studies of the events were looked at, including newspapers, journals, government reports and studies (internal and published) and seminar papers referring to the projects. As many as possible past and present participants in the events under study were interviewed, as well as those considered to have related or relevant expertise in the fields. In some instances, opinion was sought outside the usual informed circles in order to comprehend the perceptions of the wider public affected by the cases.

The strategy was to capture and assess the posture of Kenya's institutions in coping with internal and global changes while navigating these specific local developments. Attention was paid to procedures and requirements for documenting, disseminating and institutionalizing information, knowledge and experiences acquired and used in project planning, appraisal and implementation of national programmes. The flexibility and ability of institutions to anticipate, accommodate and cope with the unexpected were looked at.

CRITERIA FOR CASE SELECTION

With the aim of being as comprehensive as possible within the time frame of the study, the institutions and organizations selected were those with an influence on technology selection and adoption in Kenya, either as environment enablers or as technology participants. The need to understand the capabilities and role of these institutions determined case selection.

The cases were required to:

• need the dedication of several enabling institutions for their success. Participation of the institutions would thus expose their operational guidelines and practices;

- be within the core area of identified national interest, although government equity participation was not necessary (both the cases selected, however, had government equity);
- be of a scale and importance to require inter- and intradepartmental, sectoral and ministerial coordination and synchronization. This permitted the assessment of information flow patterns. Scale also indicated level of importance to the country;
- be of the kind to need foreign partnership. This permitted a review of search procedures and negotiation preparations and capabilities;
- be of a sophistication as to need use of the best national research, skill and entrepreneurial capabilities. This made it possible to evaluate national capability inventory procedures;
- be able to call upon use of institutional memory-building and benefit from transfer of experiences from other projects or sectors. This was in recognition that participants in projects move on, and the information management issue is whether capabilities remained in institutions as foci for social macro learning or departed with individuals. The cases were thus intended to exercise the memory of institutions that had participated in previous high-profile projects and evaluate institutional learning across projects.

The study recognized the inadequacies of the theory of the firm in development. The focus was therefore on the national landscape or terrain, a focus that was intended to identify the process of change on the continuous national technology landscape and thus capture evidence of learning.

Capability-building in Kenya's technology transfer terrain was to be evaluated on the basis of procedures and practices founded on:

- credible and documented planning and evaluation;
- search and survey of alternatives;
- preparations and transacting of negotiations;
- scheduling and implementation; and
- diffusing of capability between industries, sectors and projects over time.

The cases chosen were the National Power Alcohol Programme and the National Car Project.

THE NATIONAL POWER ALCOHOL PROGRAMME

The power alcohol programme first featured in 1973 and partially came on stream in 1985. Possibilities for its expansion are kept alive by Kenya's continued vulnerable dependence on the volatile Middle East for its commercial energy supply. In addition, the sugar industry on which the programme was founded is in serious need of vertical integration to improve operational margins. At the political level, this agenda continues to raise much heat. Political heat needs to be managed as an integral part of resolving conflicts.

This programme presents an opportunity to test institutional memory, learning and project management practices. Because power alcohol remains on the national research agenda as the local alternative source of liquid fuel, it is an ideal case for studying policy learning in national institutions between 1973 and 1990. It also provides a lesson on problems of managing the demobilization of a failed project in circumstances of poor information management.

THE NATIONAL CAR PROJECT

The National Car Project was new and ongoing at the time of study, and thus presented logistical problems. Officially launched in 1984, the project was in official documentation until 1986/87, when it was classified. The project, however, offered a surrogate means for assessing national machinery capability. For tactical reasons, it was often necessary to refer to 'machinery capability' in written research correspondence. The project would then be referred to only in the course of the interview.

In the course of the fieldwork, however, the prototypes were unveiled and, for a period, the project was openly discussed. But even while it was still classified, many interviewees remained willing to discuss it. The reservations in other quarters, however, underlined the different interpretations of secrecy requirements of government in Kenya.

As an ongoing exercise, this project raised some conceptual questions of research legitimacy. However, this was an information management study looking at the management of information in pursuit of laid-down objectives. It was treated accordingly.

A comparative international framework was included as an evaluative benchmark of Kenya's ability to tap into global stocks of information, knowledge and experience. This made it possible to put the learning dimension in the context of global realities of the motor industry. But most important, the case was an opportunity to evaluate synchronization efforts, consensus-seeking among institutions, clarity of objectives, and experience transfer between projects. It offered an opportunity to assess policy learning in Kenya. The fact that, despite its failure to take off commercially, it remains alive so long afterwards is a further indication of decision-making difficulties in circumstances of poor information management.

LIMITATIONS OF THE RESEARCH

A limiting factor was time. Despite two visits to Kenya in the course of three years, putting fieldwork logistics in motion took a lot of time. As a result, not all identified institutions could be visited, with the danger that the picture may not be a complete one.

Another limitation was related to funds. The mechanics for obtaining funding approval created unexpected demands and led to a reduction in the amount of time spent at some institutions and the number of interviews conducted.

Although terrain opacity was among the research parameters, it sometimes made it difficult to assess institutional learning processes conclusively. Aided by the Official Secrets Act, terrain opacity sometimes made it hard to distinguish between secrecy, lack of capability, lack of information and ignorance.

Finally, this is an empirical study of societary informatization in Kenyan institutions. It reflects an information culture moulded by the players in Kenya's technology sector, a sector dominated by multinational and state corporations, marketing boards and political institutions that nurture certain traits. The culture might not be similar in an environment with a different combination of factors. It is important to be aware that some information cultures are country-specific.

NOTES

1 R. L. Katz, *The Information Society: An International Perspective*, Praeger, New York, 1988.
2 D. Bell, *The Coming of Post-industrial Society: A Venture in Social Forecasting*, Basic Books, New York, 1973.
3 R. A. Onyango, 'Information, the nation-state and democracy: an African perspective', in C. Chen (ed.) *NIT '96: Proceedings of the 9th International Conference on New Information Technology*, MicroUse Information, West Newton, MA, 1996, pp. 187–97.
4 U. V. Reddi, 'Leapfrogging the Industrial Revolution', in M. Traber (ed.) *The Myth of the Information Revolution*, Sage, London, 1986, pp. 84–98.
5 N. Moore and J. Steele, *Information-Intensive Britain: An Analysis of Policy Issues*, Policy Studies Institute, 1991.
6 C. Burns, 'Three Mile Island: the information meltdown', in F. W. Horton, Jr and D. Lewis (eds) *Great Information Disasters*, Aslib, London, 1991, pp. 45–54; B. Norton and S. Gotts, 'The events of October, 1987', in F. W. Horton, Jr and D. Lewis (eds), op. cit., pp. 107–23; J. R. Wertzel and D. A. Marchand, 'The US stock market crash of 1987: the role of information system malfunction', in F. W. Horton, Jr and D. Lewis (eds), op. cit., pp. 185–201.
7 R. L. Katz, op. cit.
8 I. Paez-Urdaneta, 'Information in the Third World', *International Library Review* vol. 21, 1989, pp. 177–91.
9 Price Waterhouse Associates, *Kenya Computer Buyer's Guide 1986*, Price Waterhouse Associates, Nairobi, 1986.
10 R. Salinas, 'Forget the NWICO . . . and start all over again', *Information Development*, vol. 2, no. 3, July 1986, pp. 155–9.
11 R. A. Onyango, 'Report on in-country fieldwork carried out in Kenya between January and May 1988', mimeograph.
12 I. Paez-Urdaneta, op. cit.
13 P. Sturges and R. Neill, *The Quiet Struggle: Libraries and Information for Africa*, Mansell, London, 1990.
14 R. Matthews, 'Appraising efficiency in Kenya's machinery manufacturing sector', *African Affairs*, vol. 90, no. 358, January 1991, pp. 65–88.
15 P. Bennel, 'Engineering skills and development: the manufacturing sector in Kenya', *Development and Change*, vol. 17, 1986, pp. 303–24.
16 R. A. Onyango, 'Information, the nation-state and democracy', in C. Chen (ed.), op. cit.

17 J. L. Enos, and W. H. Park, *The Adoption and Diffusion of Imported Technology: The Case of Korea*, Croom Helm, London, 1988.
18 R. L. Katz, op. cit.
19 J. L. Enos and W. H. Park, op. cit.
20 R. A. Onyango, 'Report on in-country fieldwork', op. cit.

7

THE KENYAN NATIONAL POWER ALCOHOL PROGRAMME

PREAMBLE

This is a study of Kenya's programme for the production of alcohol, or ethanol, as a fuel. It mainly covers the activities between 1975 and 1990, but also includes recent events that add light to the study.

The origins of the programme can be found in the global petroleum crisis that followed the 1973 Yom Kippur War over the Sinai. Oil prices rocketed and reached US$58 a barrel at some stages. The pursuit of an alternative dependable and cheaper source of motive fuel became global in nature. The price benchmark, of course, remained petroleum. Its price fluctuations needed close monitoring even as efforts in other directions gathered momentum. Much effort was dedicated to research into possible alternatives such as solar, biomass and recyclable sources. Because of the magnitude and global nature of this event, the Kenyan programme is a useful means of evaluating the information management capability of Kenya's environment enabling institutions. A comparison is made with parallel events and the international issues at play at the time. Matters are put in an information context as much as possible.

Different countries reacted differently to the crisis, as determined by their various capabilities. The USA and its European allies, for instance, threatened to invade and occupy the oilfields – a threat kept alive by military patrols in the region to this day. Japan worked on reducing its petroleum consumption and integrated these efforts in national energy management measures. It also dedicated itself to a more active posture in the search for tranquillity in the Middle East, largely through backing US and Western European efforts. Such measures demonstrate options based on capability.

A small developing country needed to consider its options in a careful and informed manner. This study is about how one such country sought to do so. It examines how informed the processes were, the information available, identified and accessed, and the process of decision-making within the context of local peculiarities. The focus is mainly on information available in the open domain: free/public and proprietary; this study did not focus on information that may involve espionage. This is not a serious limitation, because studies have shown that over 90 per cent of the critical information required for decisions in commercial and international relations is in public sources. Intelligence focused on ability to synthesize data into information and the use of this in decisions, in actions and in the accumulation of knowledge and the building of institutional memory.

INTRODUCTION

Kenya's National Power Alcohol Programme was built on the sugar industry. Power alcohol was intended to reduce the extent of dependence on imported petroleum, which accounted for over 85 per cent of Kenya's commercial energy needs. Events in 1973 pointed to the need for a local and reliable alternative source of liquid motive fuel. Ethanol or power alcohol (also known as ethyl alcohol) seemed to fit the bill.

The post-1973 crisis that disrupted the OPEC (Organization of Petroleum Exporting Countries) price consensus gave ethanol a price competitiveness previously missing. It became part of the 1970s movement for renewal energy sources.

Ethanol has a lower energy content than both petrol and diesel but burns at a higher thermal efficiency and has a higher octane rating. It can be used neat as a motive liquid, as in Brazil, where over 2.2 million cars run on neat hydrous ethanol. Cars using neat hydrous ethanol are fitted with small petrol tanks and the engine exhaust is placed in contact with the intake manifold so as to pre-heat intake air without additional fuel cost.

Ethanol can also be blended with petrol to boost octane ratings and to replace lead, which is toxic. Thus the current lead-free movement promises to keep ethanol on the motive liquid fuel agenda. For blending purposes anhydrous ethanol is used. The mixture of ethanol and petrol, referred to here as *gasohol*, reduces the carbon monoxide emissions of motor vehicles by as much as 20 per cent[1] while also reducing the amount of petrol consumed.

Although based on renewable biological materials, ethanol production requires some sophisticated technological intervention. The extent to which such capabilities resided in Kenya was then unknown. Kenya's power alcohol programme, therefore, constituted an exercise in technology transfer management. This chapter looks at how Kenya's national institutions managed the technology selection and implementation of the power alcohol programme. The institutional arrangements underpinning the sugar industry are addressed to see how they affected the programme, and to see whether there were lessons transferred from it to the programme. The system of institutional documentation and transfer of learning and experience between projects, and how this informed debate, discussions and decisions concerning the new programme, is addressed.

THE ETHANOL TECHNOLOGY PROCESS

Ethanol processing technology developed in the beverage, rather than the energy, sector. It involves fermenting simple sugars. The *batch fermentation system* takes 36–48 hours, has an efficiency of between 90 and 95 per cent, and requires little skilled labour. The *cascade process* uses tanks connected in series, which saves down-time and reduces chances of infection. In the more advanced *continuous fermentation process*, both substrate and yeast are recycled, reducing down-time and increasing volumetric efficiency, but the system employs more capital equipment and needs skilled labour. Later developments in this area include *computer-aided fermentation* (CAF).[2]

Simple sugars can be obtained directly or indirectly from a wide range of biological materials available in Kenya (Table 7.1). Starch can also be converted to simple sugars and fermented to produce ethanol. As a result, some developed countries, such as Finland, use grains as 'feedstock', or input, in ethanol production. Such countries find the use of starch-based plants attractive as a way of absorbing their surplus grain. But starch-based plants do not generate adequate independent energy, and sophisticated technology is required to address this problem. This could have a bearing on production costs.

Feedstock options also include cellulosic material such as agricultural residue or municipal solid waste.[3] Wastes, however, require complex and costly modifications to existing technological systems to achieve economic conversion to fermentable sugars. This too has a bearing on final costs.

Feedstock access and pricing are critical, and should be based on national availability and relative cost, especially as the oil industry's competitive capacity

Table 7.1 Kenya's alternative sources of ethanol feedstock

Crop	Yield (tonne/ha/yr)	Ethanol	
		Litres/tonne	Litres/ha/per year
Sugar cane	50–90	70–90	3,500–8,000
Sweet sorghum	45–80	60–80	1,750–5,300
Wheat	1.5–2.1	340	510–714
Barley	1.2–2.1	250	300–625
Rice	2.5	430	1,075–2,150
Maize	1.7–5.4	360	600–1,944
Sorghum	1.0–3.7	350	350–1,295
Potatoes	10–25	110	1,110–2,750
Cassava	10–65	170	1,700–11,050
Sweet potatoes	8–50	167	1,336–8,350
Grapes	10–25	130	1,300–8,000
Molasses	—	245	—

Source: Adapted from National Academy of Sciences, Washington, DC; quoted in N. Clark and C. Juma, *Long-Run Economics: An Evolutionary Approach to Economic Growth*, Pinter, London, 1987, p. 120

is formidable and entrenched. Kenya adopted molasses, a by-product of the sugar industry, as feedstock. But direct cane juice, tubers, grains or cassava (Table 7.1) could also have been used.[4] Molasses has a wide range of other end-uses, including use as animal feed or for human consumption, and in technical applications. In Kenya, molasses constitutes about 3 per cent of cane tonnage milled.[5] When subjected to fermentation, molasses yields a range of potentially marketable products. But to find the right niche requires careful consideration of market and technological potential.

Molasses also creates pollution problems, either on its own or as slop or stillage in ethanol processing. Early surveys of molasses use in Kenya thus focused on managing the pollution threats. Every litre of ethanol produced discharges about 20 litres of stillage. This makes pollution an important consideration in the choice of technology to be adopted for ethanol programmes.

Some technologies emphasized this. For example, the Swedish engineering company Alfa-Laval had designed a process that utilized concentrated feedstock. Instead of leaving 15–20 litres of stillage, this Biostil process released between 0.8 and 4 litres. The Biostil process is marketed by AC Biotechnics, a subsidiary of both Alfa-Laval and another Swedish company, Cardo.

Kenya's choice of molasses as feedstock prevented examination of existing alternatives. This was occasioned by project proposals which came from organizations with an interest in the sugar industry. It was not, therefore, the result of a considered decision by government institutions. Information on options was not brought to bear at this stage.

KENYA'S POWER ALCOHOL SCENE

Juma[6] estimated that between 1973 and 1976, Kenya's sugar mills (Table 7.2) produced about 60,000 tonnes of molasses a year. About 70 per cent of this was exported, 7 per cent used in local industry, 10–19 per cent used as cattle feed, and 2 per cent dumped in the cane fields – which was a cause of pollution. Unsteady export prices, rising transport costs and weak environment inspection regimes continually made dumping an easy alternative for the factories.

The proposers of ethanol production saw it as a means to enhance value added, regularize the profit flow of sugar mills, meet some of the country's liquid energy needs, and reduce environmental risks. A government-initiated study by Tate and Lyle of the UK (now operating as Booker Tate) in 1975 was followed in 1977 by three proposals for ethanol projects. Two of these, submitted by the Mehta Group and the Madhvani Group respectively, were approved.

Mehta and Madhvani were companies owned by two Asian families originally based in Uganda and with a long-standing presence in the East African sugar industry (owning the Lugazi and Kakira factories respectively). They moved to Kenya from Uganda following the expulsion and appropriation of Asian businesses in the latter country by the Idi Amin government. For the companies, this was an opportunity to build expertise in downstream operations of the sugar

Table 7.2 Sugar mills in January 1988

Factory	Year established	Ownership	Management	Capacity (tonnes/year)
Miwani	1922	Hindocha family (Kenyan/Indian)	Hindocha family	60,000 (1,200 tcd)
Ramisi	1927	Madhvani Group International (Indian)	Madhvani Group	30,000 (1,530 tcd)
EASI-Muhoroni	1966	Kenyan government	Mehta Group* International (India)	60,000 (1,800 tcd)
Chemelil	1967	Kenyan government	Booker McConnell† (British)	55,000 (2,235tcd)
Mumias	1973	Kenyan government	Booker McConnell (British)	180,000 (7,000 tcd)
Nzoia	1978	Kenyan government	Kenya Government‡	60,000 (2,000 tcd)
Sony	1979	Kenyan government	Kenya Government§	60,000 (2,000 tcd)
WKS¶		Bhiku Patel	Patel Family	4,000

Notes:

tcd – tonnes of cane crushed per day

*   Under Kenyan government management since June 1990, when the Mehta Group contract expired and unexpectedly was not renewed.

†   Under local management since 1985.

‡   Currently under local management although facing intractable problems.

§   Sony was under Mehta management until 1985. It was temporarily under local management and then under Booker Tate.

¶   West Kenya Sugar Company – privately owned and currently the only operational OPS (open-pan sulphitation; see p. 87) facility in Kenya.

The Ramisi factory closed for good in 1989. The Miwani factory closed in 1989 and reopened as a joint venture between the government and the Dolphin-Dubai Group in 1990. Booker Tate now runs Sony, Mumias and Muhoroni. It is reportedly set up to take over the management of the ailing Nzoia and the planned Busia factory.

industry. The third proposal, which was shelved, was by a Kenyan entrepreneur, Dr Oluoch Okeyo,[7] a pharmacist by training. None of the three applicants had any experience in ethanol production.

At the time of submitting the proposals, the Mehta Group had equity interest in, and managed, East African Sugar Industry (EASI) in Muhoroni and the South Nyanza Sugar Company (Sony) (Table 7.2). The Madhvani Group owned and managed the Ramisi sugar factory on the coast. In the end, only the Mehta project, the Agro-Chemical and Food Corporation (ACFC), came on stream. ACFC is annexed to EASI although it maintains a separate management hierarchy. At the time, EASI was managed by Mehta Group International while ACFC was managed by International Investments Corporation (IIC), a subsidiary of Mehta International.[8] The corporation was created in 1979;

construction work began in February 1981 and commercial production in June 1982.

ACFC has an installed capacity of 60,000 litres per day of power alcohol and 4.0 tons per day of baker's yeast. The government had a 56 per cent equity in ACFC through two parastatals, the Agricultural Development Corporation (ADC) and the Industrial and Commercial Development Corporation (ICDC), each holding 28 per cent. The Bermuda-registered IIC held 34 per cent and was also given the management contract. The balance, 10 per cent, was held by Vereinigte Edelstahlwerke GmbH (VEW), an Austrian state-controlled engineering firm.

Over 80 per cent of the foreign exchange funding for ACFC came from Girozentrale und Bank der Österreichischen Sparkassen AG of Vienna, Austria. The technology was supplied by another Austrian organization, Vogelbusch, controlled by VEW. Vogelbusch remained a technical consultant for ACFC.[9]

According to government records in 1989, four other ethanol plants were approved, in Busia, Mumias, Sony and Riana. Both Busia and Riana were approved for 60,000 litres a day. But up to the end of 1996, no work had begun on either. Neither had Sony or Mumias begun work on ethanol annexes. In any case, the ethanol agenda as an alternative or supplementary motive energy was dead, to all intents and purposes.

The groundwork for ethanol introduction was conducted under the shadow of the Kenya Chemical and Food Corporation (KCFC), the Madhvani Group's proposed company. KCFC was a joint venture between the government (with 51 per cent equity), Advait International SA of Luxembourg (15 per cent) and Chemfood Investment Corporation SA (CIC) of Switzerland (34 per cent). This still-born project, which remains controversial today, was initially financed by Union Bank SA of Zurich, Switzerland, and Process Engineering Company AG (PEC), also of Switzerland, which supplied the technology. Eximcorp SA of Panama was the project manager.

Work on KCFC stopped in August 1982 amid controversy and cost overruns. By this time construction was 80 per cent complete. There has been no work done on the other four approved projects. The lack of clarity and information has politicized the manner of handling these projects; discussion of them has moved into the arena of politics with no substantive plans or direction and little documentation to go by. This state of limbo can misdirect national efforts, resources and energies away from capability enhancement.

Kenya's national power alcohol programme was eventually confined to ACFC. Up to 1985, capacity utilization at ACFC was below 30 per cent. This created liquidity problems and debt arrears for the company from which it has yet to recover.

ACFC first marketed power alcohol for 10 per cent blending with premium petrol in May 1983. This followed problems with the oil companies that control the acquisition, processing and distribution networks for liquid fuel. Sales improved after 1985 and capacity utilization rose to 75 per cent, but only through a government directive which extended blending to all petrol sold around Nairobi from November 1985 onwards.

Although gasohol in Nairobi was intended as a pilot programme preceding nationwide coverage, the rest of the country never came on stream. However, the Nairobi area accounts for 70 per cent of Kenya's liquid fuel consumption.

ACFC is designed to use molasses, exclusively, as feedstock. It consumes 70,000 tonnes of molasses and produces around 16.5 million litres of alcohol per annum. Although designed for 18 million litres, a design fault limits output.[10] This is the output that determined Kenya's national ethanol requirements.

Political statements continue to hint at possibilities of extending gasohol use in the country and plans to annex more ethanol units to existing sugar mills, and even to change the product mix of such facilities. What is more, KCFC, as a corporation, has yet to be formally wound up, and attempts to wind it up are steeped in political intrigue and litigation. However, active government attention to power alcohol as an alternative strategic energy ceased in 1985 when references to it disappeared from official government planning documents. The steadying of oil prices since 1983 has also altered official calculations concerning national liquid fuel needs. Ongoing privatization too is expected to reduce government participation in this sector.

There had, however, been ongoing national research interest. KIRDI (Kenya Industrial Research Development Institute) records from the period after 1987 referred to a 'power alcohol project' in collaboration with IPT Brazil.[11] A local plant prototype was designed and modelled in 1986 but never fabricated or put up. The prototype was intended to be small and within the means of Kenyan enterprises and resources. Final fabrication was expected to involve UNDP, UNIDO and an export agency in the UK. Although this indicates bilateral and multilateral international agency interest, nothing came of it.

THE CHOICE OF MOLASSES AS FEEDSTOCK

As indicated, feedstock options available to Kenya other than molasses were not explored. Private-sector initiatives from firms with links to the sugar industry foreclosed this step. They presented proposal packages complete with feasibility studies which, at the time, appeared to save the government the cost of carrying out its own studies. The proposals assumed, and the government approved, that the sugar industry was the most suitable foundation for the national power alcohol programme despite the unstable track record of the industry. No government documentation on the approval process refers to the instability of the sugar industry.

The instability in the sugar industry was caused by global over-production. Before the collapse of the Soviet Union, over 80 per cent of sugar was traded through 'special arrangements' unrelated to production costs or demand.[12] This made the industry particularly vulnerable to political events. For instance, the Soviet Union's withdrawal from the market disrupted the industry immensely.

A major player, Cuba, faced an immediate and unprecedented economic crisis as a result.

Basing ethanol production on sugar cane processing mills did, however, have technical advantages in Kenya. Sugar cane furnishes its own processing energy from its fibrous residue, bagasse, used as fuel in steam boilers. One tonne of wet bagasse is equivalent in energy output to a barrel of crude oil. Under normal conditions, therefore, modern cane factories employing vacuum boiling methods are self-sufficient in energy and produce a surplus. Steam and electricity produced from excess bagasse can be fed to attached refineries and distilleries. Some cane mills around the world even deliver power to irrigation systems and national grids.[13] The surplus energy makes it economic to annex ethanol units to sugar mills. Therefore, the choice of cane processing technology is important when ethanol production is under consideration.

The boiling process is the primary source of scale economies in sugar processing. Because the boiling point of water is lower under vacuum conditions, it was realized, in the mid-nineteenth century, that granular sugar yields could be increased if the boiling process could take place in a semi-vacuum spherical pan – referred to as the vacuum pan (VP). This reduces energy costs in the boiling process and offers an additional advantage over the older method in which juice is boiled off in a series of open pans – the open-pan sulphitation (OPS) process.

A major difference between OPS and VP is in heat demand for juice boiling. The VP process is more energy-efficient. It draws heat and power from a central steam-raising plant, and the centralization results in an efficient utilization of the energy in the bagasse. The relatively small size of the OPS furnaces, their simple construction and lack of a heat recovery system lower efficiencies.[14] The energy efficiency makes VP plants suitable for annexation of ethanol units.

But a case could still be made for OPS systems in Kenya within the context of an ethanol programme given the capital and foreign exchange intensity of VP mills. The flexibility of OPS mills allows them to produce economically a mix of either cane juice, sugar and liquid molasses, or sugar and solid molasses. Large-scale VPs may be fairly efficient in processing cane to sugar, but managerial and distributional diseconomies associated with ensuring sufficient cane deliveries continue to offset such economies. What is more, the capital intensity of VP plants makes the cost of sub-optimal capacity utilization particularly high. This cost has foreign exchange implications. With the intended government withdrawal from direct participation in this sector, the future of Kenya's VP mills, with their inflexibility, will be seriously threatened.

The introduction of OPS along with VPs, and use of their partially processed products within a framework of independent ethanol units and units annexed to VP mills, could improve the overall performance of the sugar industry. In addition, the cost of OPS is within reach of local entrepreneurs and could open up the industry to wider private-sector participation and competition. The large government presence concealed inefficiencies and other costs in the sugar industry. These costs were carried into the ethanol programme and effectively barred private-sector entry. Privatization moves, belatedly forced on government by external events, could still alter or tilt the playing-field in the sugar industry.

GOVERNMENT PRESENCE AND THE TRANSFER OF LESSONS AND CAPABILITY

Commercial sugar production started in Kenya in 1922 following the establishment of Miwani and Ramisi Mills (Table 7.2). Two privately owned OPS plants were established in 1974 and 1977 in Kabras and Yala but did not survive for long. The other OPS proposal, the Opapo Project, faced approval delays because of government fears of encroachment on Sony cane supplies. Farmers contracted to Sony have, however, always preferred an alternative outlet.[15] This remains the case with all sugar nucleus estates, as we shall see. Only government presence and enforcement have prevented the mushrooming of small-scale OPS and jaggery plants (jaggery is a part-refined brown sugar in paste form used as input in informal-sector activities, including illicit brewing).

Kenya's sugar industry is dogged by factories operating below capacity and farmers facing liquidity problems. The result has been an increase in sugar imports.[16] Government presence has, however, prevented objective diagnosis of the problem. The government has majority shares in the mills (Tables 7.2 and 7.3), although it contracts out the management of most plants.

State entry into the industry was funded by finance–technology packages as turnkey projects from several countries. Thus, Mumias was funded and supplied by British technology, Chemelil is German, Nzoia French, Sony Indian (with German turbines) and Muhoroni Dutch (Table 7.2). This has made it difficult to pursue a defined industrial technology acquisition policy or seek economies of scale on parts and components purchases. But most important, it has undermined technological learning and transfer of related 'core' technological experience between projects. The fact that technology–financing agreements have also involved management contracts has led to the unintended exposure to different work cultures. Without institutionalized measures to synthesize the

Table 7.3 Sugar milling ownership structure: transition to 1990

Factory	Government equity (%)	Management agents
Miwani	0	Hindocha Group
	45	Dolphin-Dubai Group(1990)
Sony	92	Mehta International/Booker Tate (1985)
EASI-Muhoroni	74	Mehta International/Local (1990)/Booker Tate
Mumias	71	Booker McConnell (Tate)
Chemelil	100	Booker McConnell/Local (1985)/Booker Tate
Nzoia	97	Technisucre/Local (1985)/Booker Tate

systems, the results have been seen in confusing and conflicting management practices, particularly when management agents are changed, as happened at Sony in 1985 and later at Muhoroni.

The government also determines the price of cane by direct and indirect controls, intervenes in sugar marketing, determines prices, and authorizes sugar imports. Sugar schemes are established by government fiat and government makes the finance–technology selection decisions.[17] It appoints the boards of directors of the mills, who determine the industrial policy, and awards the management contracts for running the mills. This has led departmental conflicts in central government to have ripple effects in the industry, over, for example, appointment of management agencies. Such conflicts have undermined efforts at a common policy that may advance national capability in the sugar industry, one of the longest-established industries in Kenya, and in the world. These weaknesses were reflected and carried over into the implementation of the ethanol programme.

Government presence in milling and distribution of sugar shifted the burden and costs of bureaucratic inefficiencies in the industry onto the farmers. Proposals that mills sell directly to wholesalers have been opposed by interests in distribution businesses. As a result, despite being the third-highest revenue-generating industry in the country after tea and coffee, cane farmers face perpetual liquidity problems to a degree unknown in other cash crop enterprises in Kenya. In addition, discussions of the industry attract the participation and interest of middlemen such as transporters and wholesalers to an extent that has not helped inform the industry. This confusion was transferred to discussions on power alcohol.

The mills make losses, but government association allows them to conceal this by depreciating capital at levels below replacement and to accumulate excise tax backlogs. Even older mills operate below capacity, indicating little 'learning by doing' in the industry. What is more, despite the time lapse, Kenya has yet to independently plan, design, build and commission a mill without a large foreign presence and direction. As late as 1979, Sony was designed and implemented by the Mehta Group together with Lonker, an Indian firm.[18] Current plans for the new sugar mill to be located in Busia are on a similar turnkey and management contract. National capability in this industry is yet to be tested. This tendency to preclude local expertise was transferred to the implementation of ethanol projects.

The strong government presence means that the establishment of this industry in western Kenya was not entirely determined by ecological, economic or market suitability needs. Cane farming is not the most profitable enterprise for the region (Table 7.4), but government policies do not permit alternatives. Cash crop participation in Kenya is based on regions. It was this that led to the ethanol programme being located in western Kenya even though it was to supply Nairobi, 400 kilometres away in central Kenya. This has cost and efficiency implications.

Table 7.4 Average annual gross margins per hectare of sunflower, tea, sugar cane and maize interplanted with beans by region (Kenyan shillings @ 1986 prices)

Crop	Nzoia	Mumias	Chemelil	Muhoroni	Miwani	Sony
Sunflower	947	947	947	947	947	947
Tea	55,089	55,089	55,089	55,089	55,089	55,089
Maize and beans	3,910	3,910	3,910	3,910	3,910	3,910
Cane*	4,769	4,376	4,462	4,386	1,807	981

Source: Adopted from J. E. O. Odada *et al*, *Incentives for Increased Agricultural Production: A Case Study of Kenya's Industry*, Friedrich Ebert Foundation, 1986, p. 60
Note:
* In relation to the mill, the supply areas are designated as Zones A, B, C and D depending on their distance from the mill. Margins fall with distance from the mill. The figures given here are for Zone C

THE COST OF REGIONALISM

Cane competes for land, labour and financial resources with alternative crops, including tea and coffee, that suit the ecology of the sugar belt (Table 7.4). Some of these are considered 'high-earning crops' in official government categorization.[19] But the option is foreclosed.

Kenya's regionally based agricultural divisions are rooted in colonial history.[20] The foreign-exchange-earning cash crops were intended for the privileged settler community. National communication patterns, urban centres and industries were designed to serve them. Settler agriculture received monopoly advantages in national marketing boards, regulatory institutions and planning committees. These institutionalized advantages remained intact after independence and have spanned new, influential pressure groups that work against regional redistribution measures and any attempts to alter the *status quo* – irrespective of the global realities. Such interests are, of course, alarmed by the prospect of privatization and government withdrawal.

Consequently, government policy underpins returns on most agricultural commodities and their geographical distribution within the country. Possible changes are circumscribed by international commodity trade arrangements, therefore export cash crops cannot be introduced in former 'native reserves' because national quotas are already met.[21] Only a redistribution of this quota would address the problem, but this is resisted by groups that have inherited privilege. Western Kenya thus cannot participate in 'high-earning' export agriculture because the national quota was distributed to other regions.

In Kenya, like everywhere else, powerful groups influence the distribution of resources in an arrangement in which economic power is unequally and regionally distributed[22] on the basis of cash crops grown. The situation is worsened by patron–client frameworks based on tribal loyalties, which are an ingredient of African politics.[23] This reality underpins distribution and location of industries, despite its being the responsibility of national institutions to formulate and present objective and consistent project evaluation methods that can be used to effect and support positive change.

Even a commodity industry with insufficient returns could be justified if it forms part of a national industry chain creating opportunities and adding value. The sugar industry provides substantial employment in a region deprived by history.[24] To evaluate the contribution of this industry requires a broader approach than the standard financial yardsticks applied by government departments and international finance agencies. Such evaluation is particularly important when considering extensions to the industry, as was the case with power alcohol. The pre-packaged models for project evaluation used did not reflect the peculiar national realities. But leaving such interpretations to the discretion of officials only served to politicize and subjectivize the process. This did not inform and improve decision-making processes.

It is important that evaluation methods and standards and models explicitly and transparently include the social and political dimensions. When, for example, the power alcohol debate became public, no reference was made to regional compromises that underpin Kenya's foreign exchange earnings. All opportunity cost calculations, therefore, identified the programme as unnecessary and costly. But the calculations did not consider imperfect domestic markets and other national peculiarities, or the continuing uncertainties of the Middle East, from where Kenya continues to get its oil. The Kuwait–Iraq war substantiates the point. Isolated models and calculations cannot, therefore, inform such debates and decisions.

Kaplinsky[25] argues that 'social appropriateness' calculations are required when evaluating a crop such as cane and its spin-off sectors. For example, cane production is more labour-intensive than many other Kenyan crops. It requires 1,764 person-hours per hectare (hours/ha) as compared to, for example, 325 for maize. Thus a sugar policy that, in addition, emphasizes OPS technology would contribute significantly to employment generation. This would be important in a region, like western Kenya, that has suffered long-term structural unemployment and has the country's highest rural poverty levels. But this needs to be specified, documented, made consistent and transparent if it is to inform decision-making at the time and in the future. It is inconsistency that, for instance, makes debate on OPS technology controversial even within a specialist unit such as the Kenya Sugar Authority (KSA),[26] with some for and some against. This points to serious institutional weaknesses in informing national debate and decision-making via transparent parameters, especially when objectivity could be clouded by partisan regional interests.

Inconsistency is also evident in procedures for calculating the price structures for sugar.[27] This formula leaves much to the discretion of individual officers allocated the responsibility at the time. The routines for calculations are thus sustained, with varying degrees of strictness, depending on the officers responsible and the political alliances at play.[28] Such discretion has, however, had the effect of politicizing the exercise and making it unpredictable.

The absence of specific guidelines also fuels inter- and intradepartmental conflicts caused by decisions and data that do not tally. This undermines the development of institutional expertise. Without informed, objective and consistent expert guidance, politics has gained a high profile in industrial decisions and sidelined the need for expert input. The practice of not seeking objective expert advice in decision-making processes, common in the sugar industry, was transferred to the ethanol programme.

For example, sugar mills fall under different ministries. But whereas KSA is intended to advise the whole industry, operating regulations do not require that it be consulted. Nor is the advice it gives binding. This practice undermines the seriousness and accountability of the technical expertise at KSA. The power alcohol projects were, for example, approved and implemented with minimum identifiable local expert input. It was not sought.

The government's ownership of mills and the poor documentation of its decision processes prevented a rigorous and consistent discussion of the pricing formula for the sugar/ethanol industry. The price structures that followed were thus unrealistic and based on subjective compromises. The mills have, for example, obstructed a pricing system that shares the benefits of bagasse and molasses with farmers. In other countries, farmers are paid on the basis of sugar yields, molasses and bagasse. In Kenya, payment is confined to tonnage. The mills have argued that these are 'by-products' and that paying for them would make milling unprofitable.[29] The mills, however, sell molasses and use bagasse to generate energy. What is more, during discussion on molasses pricing for the ethanol programme, the mills argued that 'a product with effective demand could not be considered simply as a by-product'.[30] Contradictions like this were permitted by procedures that are not consistent, documented and transparent and by weaknesses in national institutional memory.

Poor national institutional memory can lead to serious problems. Integration of regions in the development process is a prerequisite for the general equalization of incomes. It is a means to attaining wider economic participation, which can hasten the pace of development, as has been illustrated by the Pacific Rim nations. Retardation of some regions puts the rest of the economy behind by excluding their contributions from the synergistic process of national wealth creation. Balanced regional development also mitigates against possible large and disruptive migrations and can stave off inter-regional frictions. In Africa, regional frictions are tribally based and can interfere with and disrupt 'nation-building' and other development efforts. Institutional memory backed by adequate documentation of processes leading to decisions can reduce the possibility of such occurrences.

Poorly integrated economies generate forces that defend regional imbalances and obstruct positive, flexible and participative development. Such forces influence development plans and objectives, and will colour debates on new projects unless weakened by documented institutional memory. The power alcohol programme had to contend with such forces.

Extension of the sugar industry to ethanol production needed to be supported by clear and specific statements on goals to be attained and structural weaknesses to be remedied or addressed by the new activities. These statements needed to include documented acknowledgement of the sugar industry as a part of the country's effort at internally balancing its global role as a commodity supplier. It needed to be specified, as part of the documentation, that western Kenya's option of engaging in coffee or tea production is precluded by international quota restrictions and, in exchange, the country needed ethanol as a value-added activity in the industry and, only secondly, as a strategic motive power source. The responsibility for such definition of the framework rested with national environment enabling institutions. Their failure coloured subsequent discussions, especially as the impact of the devastation caused by the petroleum price hikes faded.

DOCUMENTATION, INSTITUTIONAL LEARNING AND MEMORY

Kenya's development plan documents do not recognize and address the realities of regionalism. The country has sought to maintain traditional export markets and find new ones with the same institutions and products for over three decades, despite global changes. Juma[31] points to 'expectations of normalcy and upturns' as shaping Kenya's political outlook and ruling ideology. He sees Kenya's institutions as, therefore, able to manage only minor reforms.

Government documents and attitudes to documentation reflect this. One document, considered its most thoughtful to date, was *Sessional Paper No. 1* of 1986.[32] It reiterated strategies for the next decade based on 'the prime commodities' of coffee and tea. It saw the end of the coffee agreement in 1989 as an opportunity to expand quotas and increase sales to non-quota markets. As a result, Kenya planned to expand national output of coffee and tea to meet this anticipated expanded global consumption and, implicitly, tied the introduction of coffee in western Kenya to this expected upturn.[33]

The document did not acknowledge rifts within the International Coffee Organisation (ICO) or anticipate competition from old and new producers. It pointed to Kenya's 'stable political system, sound growing economy, central position in Eastern Africa, and its record of fiscal and monetary responsibility' as inevitable attractions to foreign investors. It did not note divestment trends from the continent to other parts of the world, protectionist and competitive activities in neighbouring countries, the evolution of regional trade blocs such as SADC (the Southern Africa Development Community) or the changing attitudes of international monetary and donor agencies towards 'fiscal responsibility'. It did not acknowledge the strong indications of donor fatigue or speculate on its possible fall-out. This document was drawn up under the shadow of the shocking debts of LDCs but was deludedly upbeat. Instead, in 1989, the coffee agreement collapsed, donors cut aid levels and international lenders applied the squeeze.

The country has yet to recover from this unpreparedness. This paper confirmed the government's awareness of western Kenya's ecological suitability for coffee but it tied this to expected upturns in the international markets. These assertions were never reviewed or referred to in subsequent related government documentation. National institutions do not seem to consider documentation of learning processes important. The absence of relevant follow-up documents fuels suspicions that documents such as these are intended to impress potential donors and lenders as a short-term strategy rather than as a serious statement of intent.

Institutional changes assume normalcy and continuing growth rates, despite glaring shifts in reality. For example, informed calculation is required to address the choice between VP and OPS technology in the country. The OPS technology avoids the social and environmental risks and costs associated with VP mills such as mandatory large nucleus estates and the subsequent economic devastations that follow mill closures.

For instance, the Mumias plant serves a radius of 21 square kilometres, over 20,000 small farmers, an acreage of over 36,000 hectares and a nucleus estate of 3,500 hectares. The closure of Mumias affects a whole region. It is probably such overwhelming responsibility that has left its management in the trusted and tested hands of Booker Tate since its inception. But this undermines local learning. The moderate cost of OPS would open up the industry to wider indigenous participation, increase the number of mills per target crushing capacity and reduce impact of such accidental closures. But VP technology remains preferred on the basis of efficiency and output calculations, and of models that do not consider realistic scenario studies.

Recent rehabilitation programmes in the sugar industry indicate no change in direction or attitude. Rehabilitation started in 1982 and was intended to expand national sugar output. But at Sony, for instance, the exercise, scheduled to cost KShs 512 million (KShs = Kenyan shillings), was designed to achieve the 1979 capacity of 2,000 tonnes of cane crushed per day. The technical opinion of staff at Sony was that this target crushing capacity had been over-costed. However, the parameters and finance for this exercise were worked out without local technical input.

The rehabilitation arrangements at Sony were concluded between Booker Tate management agents and the government-appointed bureaucratic directors of Sony, based in Nairobi. Booker Tate negotiated and packaged the financing and contract with the Commonwealth Development Corporation, the African Development Bank and Agriculture International. These are, however, agencies with which Booker-Tate enjoys frequent dealings as part of its global sugar operations. In Africa, for instance, Booker's operations stretch from Sudan to Swaziland. Any trade-off spill-overs negotiated are, therefore, likely to benefit Booker Tate's other worldwide operations rather than accrue to Kenya. In any case, Booker Tate was at the time involved in negotiating the financing of the larger Finchaa Valley sugar project, which it had packaged for Ethiopia, with the same organizations. Such packages preclude local experts, stunt local learning, and leave expertise and capability firmly resident with the agencies. Kenya's sugar rehabilitation programme was designed with minimal local technical input despite decades of national experience in the industry. The ten-year activity has not contributed to advancing local expertise in sugar milling project management.

Rehabilitation should have afforded Kenya the opportunity to review and examine alternatives with the intention of deploying resources more efficiently per target crushing capacity. It should have been an opportunity to take stock of capability gained from over seventy years' association with the industry. An option should have included, for instance, introducing more private OPS plants in the national equation. India, with over 8,000 OPS mills alongside VPs, has shown that recent technological developments make OPS profitable and that the effect of having varied technologies in competition in the industry is to enhance national performance.[34]

Kaplinsky[35] saw increased OPS participation as opening up an innovative power alcohol programme arrangement in which juice extraction is carried out at several OPS mills and then shipped to VP mills in tankers. This would create technological diversity in the industry, maximize benefits from the higher energy and technical efficiency of the VP process, stimulate the economic and social benefits of small-scale production, and remove the need for OPS to buy-in energy. It would allow for optional installation of independent or annexed ethanol plants that can take direct cane juice or molasses, or a combination of both, as feedstock from various OPS and VP mills. This would reduce the impact and cost of mill closures and improve capacity utilization in the capital-intensive VPs. It would give the sugar industry the 'flexible specialization'[36] required to respond to international trends in ethanol/molasses/sugar and petroleum prices.

But such considerations require fine-tuned planning, which is difficult to accomplish when decisions are discretionary and based on personalities, politics or finance–technology turnkey packages without deliberate measures to improve institutional learning and memory.

DECISIONS ON IMPLEMENTATION OF THE POWER ALCOHOL PROGRAMME

In May 1973 the Madhvani Group, in conjunction with some foreign organizations, submitted a molasses utilization proposal to the government. It was accompanied by a feasibility study and details of how the project would be managed.[37]

The first government-initiated study was carried out by Tate and Lyle Technical Services in 1975. It surveyed alternative uses for molasses, which, because of export problems, was becoming a potential environmental hazard. It reported a high sugar content in Kenyan molasses, and a survey in 1981–5 confirmed the sugar level at over 50 per cent. The mills have reported improvements that have brought the level to 42 per cent.[38]

The early studies and proposals did not address national energy requirements. They were a search for domestic use of a by-product whose export prices were no longer feasible and whose dumping created pollution. The Tate study was intended to inform government decision-making. It linked molasses disposal with energy, but only as part of and basis for a bigger organic chemical industry. Power alcohol was to be a first step in the development of a broader industry. Despite the global energy crisis at this time, the boom in coffee prices still shielded Kenya's institutions from the reality.

In 1976, the Industrial Survey and Promotion Centre (ISPC),[39] a unit in the then Ministry of Commerce and Industry, submitted another report, but adopted the technical data from Tate and Lyle. It did not undertake separate studies or attempt to verify the technical assumptions of the Madhvani and Tate and Lyle studies. The ISPC report weakened government competence in handling related technical negotiations because of the ISPC's lack of an independent institutional capacity to evaluate proposals. Matters were worsened by failure to prioritize aspects and phases of the intended 'organic chemical industry' and the absence of a government master-plan against which to evaluate and/or influence proposals on the basis of compatibility.[40] It was assumed, incorrectly, that it would be economically viable to recover all technically recoverable by-products of molasses.

Without independent data or a plan of the industrial arrangement the country required, ISPC reported government intention to 'promote any viable proposal for industrial utilisation of molasses'. It also reported intentions to encourage a working relationship between sugar mills and oil companies which might be interested in participating in the manufacture of power alcohol.[41] This task was, however, not allocated to any specific government department, so no action was taken to bring the oil companies on board until after ACFC started production in 1983. Such loose-ended, unspecific and uninformed but documented commitment exposed government departments to pressures and manipulation.

In June 1977, the government announced the approval, and committal of public funds, to a resubmitted Madhvani proposal. This resubmission had few modifications as compared with the original, but no attempt was made to verify and, if necessary, make updates to the data. The description of the project in the joint-venture agreement signed with the government refers to government undertaking 'to arrange the supply to the company of adequate molasses at reasonable prices and all other local supplies necessary for the company's business'.[42] The government guaranteed supplies of molasses (and 'other local supplies') without ascertaining how much was to be required and what national output levels were. The Madhvani proposal also estimated molasses prices at KShs 160 per tonne at a time when exports were fetching KShs 246 per tonne. It is clear that Madhvani expected subsidy, but this was not formally recognized in government records.

The government depended wholly on data submitted as integral parts of project proposals. It adopted the data as its own for the purpose of evaluating subsequent proposals. However, the expertise input accompanying the proposals was from interested foreign parties and required verification. The Madhvani study was undertaken in collaboration with Process Engineering Company (PEC) of Switzerland. But PEC hoped to co-finance and become technology supplier to KCFC. The Mehta Group's study was undertaken by Vogelbusch, which became technology supplier to ACFC.[43] These studies required impartial alternative verification mechanisms or data. At the minimum, national institutions needed a master-plan against which to evaluate proposals submitted. None existed.

Government negotiators did not attempt to establish the identity and reputation of the parties they were dealing with and assess whether they could deliver their part of the bargain. No corporate profile of the parties was compiled, which contravened Ministry of Industry guidelines.[44] It also permitted Advait Holdings and IIC to pass for foreign experts in ethanol technology, which they were not.

In fact, these were corporations owned by Kenyan residents with no experience in ethanol. Advait was, for instance, concurrently involved in a similar joint textile venture with the government, Kenya Fibre Corporation (KFC), in Nanyuki.[45] Both KFC and KCFC later faced similar problems, were abandoned incomplete in 1982, and left the government to shoulder the liabilities.

IIC and Advait were incorporated in offshore tax havens: Bermuda and Luxembourg respectively. This improved their foreign exchange access facility status. The companies were thus able to sell joint-venture proposals, guaranteed and funded by government, generate revenue from sale of equipment and management fees, while shielding themselves against liability and possible litigation as government partners. Approval of KCFC even breached existing government finance guidelines concerning participation in ventures that involve foreign parties. These ventures were required to be subjected to various scenario studies before approval.[46] This was not done.

Gachuki and Coughlin[47] point to several instances in which national institutions have similarly disregarded guidelines. This indicates that guidelines are no guarantee of an informed and documented government decision-making process. But guidelines can help identify sources of failure and can aid remedial measures if used properly. This is why, for example, Odidi's[48] diagnosis of the inconsistencies exposed by KCFC traces faults to the recommendation procedures of the New Projects Committee (NPC), which approved it.

The NPC was an *ad hoc* interministerial committee set up to evaluate proposals and negotiate with potential investors. The 1974–8 Development Plan refers to the NPC as the main 'technical organ through which the government will administer legislation to regulate the establishment of industrial capacity'. But though intended to receive legal status, the NPC legislation, which would have required firms to obtain government approval to increase manufacturing capacity, was never enacted. The NPC remained an *ad hoc* committee with neither a clear mandate nor legislated responsibilities to enforce or implement. But the 1978–83 Development Plan still insisted that 'projects not approved by NPC will not receive the Approved Enterprises Status under the Foreign Investment Protection Act and will not be entitled to any concessions or investment allowance'.[49]

Until it was abolished in 1985, the NPC had no legal status and had fulfilled none of the roles indicated. Its *ad hoc* nature undermined continuity and accountability, and left critical gaps in the documentation of its decision process. These events underline differences between policy and practice in institutional management. They also point to documentation as an inadequate barometer of intended government action in some LDCs such as Kenya. However, existence of guidelines can support the process of diagnosis, which in turn can aid remedial action. Coupled with review and evaluation procedures, it can make a difference.

The government sent representatives to a UNIDO workshop in Vienna in March 1979 to improve its institutional appreciation of the ethanol sector. But not all government institutions were actually ignorant of the sector at this time. The problem had more to do with poor coordination. For example, Ministry of Commerce and Industry records indicate awareness of India's attempts to produce fertilizer from molasses and the problems India encountered.[50] This was important to government policy because fertilizer was an option in its 'organic chemical industry' scheme. Such knowledge compartmentalization was exacerbated by government equity participation in the projects. Participation pre-empted a rigorous interministerial evaluation process because implementation automatically became the responsibility of a particular department. Implementing departments are not required to seek expertise input from other units, nor, if they do, are they bound to accept it. That is how the regulations stand.

Therefore, consultations between promoters of KCFC and the Ministry of Commerce and Industry culminated in government approval, and subsequent inclusion of the project in expenditure estimates, without exhaustion of the laid-down formalities. For example, the required detailed specific examination of the project by NPC prior to government approval and commitment did not occur. This would have required an expert report on the viability of the project, a report on national availability and utilization of molasses, and a scenario study of possible impact of project collapse. Instead the process and decisions on KCFC were unusually hurried, and by 16 July 1977 ministerial signature to the project had been finalized[51] (Table 7.5). Doubts and questions raised by other quarters or departments were ignored, including amendments to the joint-venture agreement recommended by the Attorney-General's Office.

Juma[52] has contrasted this with Rhodesia/Zimbabwe's approach to a similar programme. Here good communication between local business and government prevailed, sharpened by international trade sanctions following unilateral

Table 7.5 Kenya Chemical and Food Corporation (KCFC)
proposal for a power alcohol programme

Expected date for commissioning:		October, 1980
Quantity of molasses required:		110,000 tonnes per annum
Products:	power alcohol	20 million litres per annum
	dry baker's yeast	1,800 tonnes per annum
	citric acid	3,000 tonnes per annum
	vinegar	2 million litres per annum
Total project cost:		KShs 502.5 million (US$67.0 million)
Managing Agents:		Advait (Madhvani) International

Source: O. Odidi, 'Financing of recurrent expenditure in Kenya's industrial sector', paper given at the Kenya Economic Association's Workshop on Recurrent Costs of Public Investment and Budget Rationalisation in Kenya, Nairobi, 27–29 April 1988, p. 46

declaration of independence (UDI) in 1965. Project managers emphasized international technological reconnaissance, knowledge of alternatives and well-informed choices. Scenario studies included the possible impact of sanctions on the project, and informed technology choice decisions. Zimbabwe emphasized national institutional learning and capability-building, and selected technology that could be implemented locally and independently.

In Kenya, the need for review and appraisal of the project, required by established regulations, was ignored. For instance, the designs of the proposed projects were not studied by independent experts. The now admitted design faults of both KCFC and ACFC were therefore never identified and discussed in time. The External Aid Division of the Treasury was not asked, as is required, to give its views on the possible impact of project failure,[53] in foreign exchange terms, on government finances.

Kenya's bureaucracy depends on a civil service trained in containment procedures[54] and ministerial positions that do not require particular expertise. The civil service is relied on to implement technical projects despite acknowledged doubts about its capacity to handle non-routine programmes. Some ministries, such as Agriculture, often suffer project overloads (over 200 in 1990) but are not required to engage external expertise. Instead, the option of discretionary use of expert facilities has led to its abuse through, for example, point-scoring during interdepartmental conflicts.

For instance, the Ministry of Agriculture has been known to engage foreign consultants to legitimize its decisions on the sugar industry if they conflict with KSA recommendations. One such consultant even recommended the dissolution of KSA, although this was not part of the terms of engagement. KSA did not, therefore, find it unusual that KCFC and ACFC were approved before a request was sent to KSA for data on national molasses levels,[55] data which in any case would already have been too late to inform the required decisions.[56] Table 7.6 shows molasses availability and projected consumption over the years 1979–85.

Table 7.6 Molasses availability, 1979–85, and projected consumption
('000 metric tonnes)

	1979	1980	1981	1982	1983	1984	1985
Availability							
Miwani	12.0	14.0	18.0	20.0	22.0	23.0	25.0
Chemelil	17.0	17.0	17.0	17.0	17.0	18.0	21.0
Muhoroni	15.0	19.0	20.2	24.0	24.0	26.0	26.0
Mumias	38.7	53.0	53.0	53.0	53.0	53.0	53.0
Nzoia	16.7	19.5	20.0	24.0	24.0	24.0	24.0
Ramisi	8.5	10.5	12.1	12.1	13.0	15.0	17.0
Sony	—	16.0	20.0	24.0	24.0	24.0	24.0
Other factories	2.0	2.0	2.0	2.5	3.0	3.0	3.0
TOTAL	109.0	151.0	162.3	176.6	180.0	186.0	193.0
Consumption							
Miwani distillery	5.7	6.0	6.0	6.0	6.0	6.0	6.0
Exports	74.6	78.6	15.1	—	—	—	—
Animal feeds	29.6	30.4	31.2	32.1	32.8	33.7	34.6
KCFC	—	35.0	110.0	110.0	110.0	110.0	110.0
ACFC	—	—	—	50.4	63.0	63.0	63.0
TOTAL	109.9	150.0	162.3	198.5	211.8	212.7	213.6
BALANCE	—	—	—	(21.9)	(31.8)	(26.7)	(20.6)

Source: Kenya Sugar Authority and Ministry of Livestock

It is not that Kenya's civil service is ignorant of business practices. Civil service regulations permit engagement in business by incumbent officers, and many indigenous entrepreneurs are former public-sector employees. This has only served to fuel suspicions of conspiracy when their actions and decisions contravene guidelines or appear inexplicably negligent.

Such conspiracy theories receive sustenance from conflicting interdepartmental information and decisions. For example, a survey by ISPC[57] reported that about 12,000 tonnes of molasses in the mid-1970s was used as animal feed but the Ministry of Livestock Development put the figure at about 30,000 tonnes.[58] The Ministry projected a demand rise of 7.0 per cent per year while KSA put it at 3.0 per cent. The estimates by the Ministry were difficult to justify on existing or projected livestock nutrition patterns in the country. But without incontrovertible data and information, informed debate was hampered.

DECISIONS ON THE GASOHOL NICHE

Kenya's oil refinery, a parastatal, was built in the 1960s under the ISI framework to meet domestic needs and those of neighbouring countries. Initially built to handle 1.8 million tonnes of crude oil a year, it was expanded in 1969 to take 4.8 million tonnes. Its introduction consolidated petroleum as Kenya's commercial energy base. It meant that attempts to introduce alternative liquid fuels would have to contend with this established interest in which government impartiality could not be assumed, as it held equity in it.

The government has an arrangement with representatives of international oil companies giving them the right to purchase crude oil, plan for its processing at the refinery, and organize a national distribution network. In exchange, the companies make their technology available to, and support, the refinery. This arrangement between the refinery and the international oil companies means that efforts at alternative liquid fuel sources must reckon with an arsenal of international experience in dealing with potential competition. In Kenya's dependent scientific terrain, the participation of such a degree of sophistication tilted the playing-field against any agenda intended to address domestic specific needs.

In 1973 Kenya lacked independent operational mechanisms or institutions for dealing with disruptions in normal channels of oil supply. The country could not, for instance, take advantage of concessionary offers from some OPEC members to LDCs because it did not have an independent means of importing and distributing the fuel, and in any case, this would have infringed existing commitments to the oil companies.

Kenya's GDP growth rate fell from 6.5 per cent between 1963 and 1972 to less than 1 per cent between 1973 and 1975. Acute balance of payments problems followed. In November 1979 the Ministry of Energy was set up. The new ministry identified with the ethanol programme. But without independent data, it could not advance the cause of informed debate.

Many of the sugar and ethanol technology requirements are within the design and construction capability of most large international engineering firms. There is no distinct ethanol technology market as such, although some firms are highly reputed suppliers of distilleries to the beverage sector. Some of these are subsidiaries of large corporations. But these beverage-focused firms do not always have a high profile in ethanol. In 1977, the period under study, Brazil was the main ethanol technology market following the launch of the Programa Nacional do Álcool (Proalcool) and had an institutional interest in ethanol going back to the formation of the Institute for Sugar and Alcohol (whose name in Portuguese is abbreviated to IAA) in 1933. This led to the fuel ethanol technology trade being dominated by Brazilian firms such as Codistil, Zanini and Conger. The firms also supplied sugar technology because much of the equipment used consists of fabricated vessels rather than intricately constructed machinery.[59]

Firms from industrialized countries located in Brazil while Brazilian firms established links with them in order to access emerging technologies and also in order to supply their own. For example, Zanini entered into technical cooperation agreements with Zahnräderfabrik Renk AG of Germany and Foster-Wheeler of the USA, while Conger, whose technology PEC sold to KCFC, took up a 5 per cent equity in Vogelbusch of Austria, the technology suppliers to ACFC. Conger intended to access the stillage-reducing technology from Vogelbusch.

Some large firms supported university research. Oil companies also funded research in this area. For example, the Atlantic Richfield Company supported enzymatic fermentation research at the University of Arkansas during this period. The oil companies wanted to keep abreast of advances in this field of potential competition.[60]

The ethanol technology market that Kenya faced therefore consisted of a number of organizations whose design control was distributed over several sectors, including the food, engineering, pharmaceutical, chemical, beverage and oil sectors. Many of the firms with the engineering capability did not, however, anticipate or seek markets outside Brazil.[61] This therefore made Brazil an important location from which to learn about this technology. But it also underlined the need for international technology reconnaissance, because much initiative was required from the interested country if optimum terms for technology acquisition were to be obtained.

NATIONAL INSTITUTIONS AND ETHANOL PROJECT MANAGEMENT

The Oluoch Okeyo proposal was submitted ahead of the Madhvani second version of May 1977. This Madhvani submission is reported to have had more technical data than Okeyo's. But after the joint-venture agreement was signed in July 1977, Madhvani resubmitted new technical data for the official portfolio. This event has raised questions about the validity and motive for earlier data.[62]

It has been suggested that the first set of data was merely intended to undermine the Okeyo proposal – which would imply that Madhvani was privy to government records. It has also been suggested that the new technical data may have been sought from Madhvani to be used to justify retrospectively the rejection of the Okeyo proposal.[63] What is certain is that the Madhvani proposal constituted the standard against which the Okeyo proposal was evaluated and rejected, confirming that the government did not have a separate independent plan, standard or benchmark.

ACFC and KCFC emphasized different products (Tables 7.5 and 7.7), which made comparisons difficult. The ACFC proposal concentrated on potential financial returns while KCFC emphasized foreign-exchange savings, employment, local sub-contracts, technology diffusion, employment for local specialists, improvements in food and nutrition, and superior products for local production. Comparison was impossible without an independent national plan. In any case, a plan was required if the submissions were to conform to comparable standards. In the event, information from the proposals could not inform and improve decision-making. What is more, no measures were put in place to ensure that the commitments in the submitted proposals would be delivered. The approval process was characterized by the kind of institutional weaknesses that Djeflat[64] identified as undermining technology transfer efforts in LDCs.

Table 7.7 Agro-Chemical and Food Corporation (ACFC) proposal for a
power alcohol programme – Muhoroni

Expected commissioning date:	January 1982
Quantity of molasses required:	63,000 tonnes per annum
Products: power alcohol	18 million litres per annum
active baker's yeast	1,104 tonnes per annum
dry fodder yeast	550 tonnes per annum
Total cost of the project:	KShs 212,000,000 (US$18.4 million)
Government 56% equity, IIC 34%, VEW 10%	
Managing agent:	IIC (Mehta Group International)

Source: Adapted from E. O. Awilly, 'Introduction to chemical processing technology',
unpublished manuscript, Kenya Sugar Authority, Nairobi, 1989, p. 13

Madhvani and Mehta indicated plant costs of US$60.4 million and US$18.3
million respectively. These capital costs were not independently evaluated before
approval. The Centre for Industrial Development (CID) of the EEC and the
Africa, Caribbean and Pacific (ACP) countries reported to the Ministry of
Industry in July 1977 that a plant with the capacity of KCFC should cost
between US$18 million and US$24 million. But this information did not influence the signing of the joint-venture agreement. In 1978, an ISPC report also
indicated that KCFC was over-priced. But this information was a year too late.
A government team that visited Brazil in 1980 made similar observations on
its return. Institutional learning processes were either initiated late or excluded
from discussions.

There was no independent assessment of national ethanol needs prior to
decisions on the proposals. National needs later had to be tailored to decisions
made by PEC and Vogelbusch. The proposals were considered in isolation, without local technical input or contributions from local industrialists. For example,
engineering firms in Kenya have proven capability in metal fabrication and have
been involved in large and complex projects in the region. As was indicated,
fabrication capability underpins both sugar and ethanol processing technologies.
Local expertise in fabrication of stainless steel had been demonstrated at a new
brewery facility in Kisumu and in the components of a geothermal plant in
Olkaria, near Naivasha, during this period. Fabricating brewing distillation
columns demands more skill than that for fermentation plants used in ethanol
production. Geothermal columns must withstand high-pressure steam and have
to undergo X-ray testing. This is a higher quality requirement than that expected
in ethanol fermentation or sugar processing.

But this established local capability was neither sought nor utilized for the
ethanol programme. The finance–technology–supplier conditions negotiated by
Madhvani and Mehta, and the absence of a national institutional framework
requiring use of local technological capabilities, precluded this step. Excluding
local technical input gave the projects an unnecessarily high foreign-exchange
content which required government guarantees. This exposure was used to justify

government equity participation. But equity prevented rigorous evaluation and a search for alternatives.

It has been pointed out that any experienced chemical engineer or sugar technologist would have identified the design problems with both KCFC and ACFC.[65] However, no such local expert was included in the government team. Decisions were influenced more by financial sourcing than socio-economic or technical considerations. This practice has contributed to the bureaucratization of technological decisions. The result is that technology choices are consistently left to contractors and financiers. This may have a bearing on what Lubbe *et al.*[66] have referred to as the predominance of financial objectives and cost control in European project management styles and culture. It may work for Europe, where transparent technology and other resources choices exist, but it has consistently failed in LDCs. The Pacific Rim's alternative emphasis on investment in human resources and transparent initiatives and efforts needs to be explored and pursued.

In any case, the Kenyan government did not search for and compare alternative financing sources or terms. The efforts of PEC and Vogelbusch, as repackaged by Mehta and Madhvani, were accepted as adequate. PEC and Vogelbusch arranged for loans with their respective national banks but made it conditional on their supplying the technology. Vogelbusch supplied its new, and as yet untested, cascade process. Madhvani accepted the batch process fabricated by Conger despite indications in the proposal that PEC would deliver a continuous process. Lax institutional management of the implementation phase allowed early breaches of the contract to take place without penalty. These infringements, therefore, increased with time.

Kenya's institutions also failed to identify the Vogelbusch–Conger connection. The batch process delivered by PEC from Conger was an adaptation of an Austrian technology transferred to Brazil in the 1930s. Through its equity in Vogelbusch, Conger also had access to Vogelbusch technology (and vice versa). The country could have negotiated a more favourable disposition for two orders from either Conger or Vogelbusch. But there were no institutional procedures for exploring such possibilities.

Little institutional learning has taken place in the ethanol sector. ACFC continues to maintain stocks of Vogelbusch-supplied spare parts and retains it as consultant. ACFC argues that the equity of VEW assures it of a favoured status with Vogelbusch.[67] ACFC has therefore not seen the need to be familiar with the plant designs and blueprints. These are still kept by Vogelbusch in Austria. ACFC believes that this arrangement speeds up trouble-shooting communications and parts orders. However, such institutionalized complacency perpetuates the dependency cycle.

The arrangements have the institutional backing of units such as KSA, which itself keeps a list of approved spare-parts suppliers to the sugar industry. Orders with foreign-currency implications have been checked against this list before the Central Bank could approve expenditure. The list is rarely updated, as KSA argues that this technology sector is stable and that it is loyalty to suppliers that ensures sympathetic terms. The reality is, however, different. In any case, such an arrangement does not nurture learning and independent capability-building.

Bureaucracy and compartmentalization of government departments undermined and delayed implementation of the projects. Thus, the release of land for siting KCFC was delayed because some departments considered the amount of land and approved lease term excessive. Even though KCFC was a government-controlled corporation and the local council in Kisumu gave the land, the Ministry of Lands and Settlement in Nairobi withheld its approval (it later compensated KCFC for the delays). The issue of excessive land continues to haunt what is left of KCFC. The government now seeks to off-load the facilities but without the land. This has been an issue of recent litigation between government and the leading bidder, East African Spectre, which insisted that the facilities were worthless scrap metal without the land. Government determination to hold on to the land is leading to delays in burying the project that are every bit as bewildering as the KCFC saga itself was.

The delays proved costly in foreign exchange terms at a time when the value of the Kenyan shilling was in decline *vis-à-vis* convertible currencies because of the recession induced by rocketing petroleum prices. For example, the Swiss loan for KCFC equipment was signed in November 1977, but the papers were not presented to Parliament until June 1978. KCFC missed the tender price deadline and had to start fresh negotiations at higher prices. This delay added US$2.5 million to the cost of KCFC, a sum equivalent to the payment made to Conger for the equipment.

Delays in approving the marketing of ethanol also caused problems for ACFC. The rapid devaluation of the Kenyan shilling – by 15 per cent in September 1982 and 14 per cent in December 1982 – under IMF pressure[68] increased interest and loan repayment liabilities to Girozentrale und Bank. Although commercial production started in June 1982, marketing was delayed until May 1983 and full operations until 1985.

The total cost to ACFC of the prolonged plant closures was estimated at KShs 3.0 million per month. The cost of the project escalated from KShs 259,582,000 in October 1980 to KShs 300,208,000 in January 1983 – much of the increase being due to exchange rate fluctuations.[69] The plant and machinery were, unlike KCFC, however, supplied under a fixed-price contract and did not face similar cost escalations. ACFC failed to pay its first loan instalment to Girozentrale und Bank, due in December 1982, and an application had to be made to reschedule the loan.

KCFC engaged Epcil (Kenya) to undertake civil engineering work from June 1979. But Epcil withdrew from the project in January 1980 claiming turnover problems, and went bankrupt. The contractual breach was settled out of court, in case litigation delayed construction, and the circumstances remain unclear. The work was then retendered to Solel Boneh, an Israeli firm. The erection phase was managed by an Indian company, Deweto International, under a PEC sub-contract. Therefore, local participation was also precluded from civil works, even though studies of Kenyan engineering by Bennel[70] and Matthews[71] point to civil engineering as being highly developed. Instead, all civil work decisions were made, and work undertaken, with little local technical input.

Without local participation, the open-ended contracts allowed contractors to inflate foreign-exchange costs. Whether by default or design, higher capital costs positively influenced management fees. Raising pre-start-up capital costs raised earnings. This made delays in construction beneficial to management agents because they could capitalize such expenses. In any case, they continued to generate revenue as long as there was some work on site. There was no time specificity or clauses in the project agreements that penalized delays.

THE MANAGEMENT CONTRACTS

Both ACFC and KCFC were proposed as turnkey projects to be managed under technical management contracts by IIC of Bermuda and Eximcorp of Panama respectively. In practice, they were managed by locally resident members of the Mehta and Madhvani families, who were paid in foreign currency at a time of foreign exchange squeeze. The management contracts were open-ended, had low attainment targets and were difficult to enforce.

Clark and Juma's[72] study of these contracts is revealing. The Project implementation management agreement between KCFC and Eximcorp, for example, gave Eximcorp an annual management fee of US$150,000, payable to a London bank. Eximcorp was also to receive 5 per cent of all capital expenditure (except the cost of land) on the project upon its completion, in US dollars. Eximcorp would receive 2 per cent of KCFC sales monthly, in US dollars, and 3 per cent of KCFC's annual profits before interest and tax deductions. The terms had no productivity targets. Eximcorp carried no risks but would continue to receive income whatever befell the project. The government accepted the terms without making alternative proposals and without negotiations.

Higher capital costs had implications for ethanol prices and could reduce the fuel's competitiveness. But the government carried all the responsibility for marketing ethanol. In any case, the market niche was protected. Eximcorp had little incentive to keep costs low and ensure that ethanol was competitively priced. There were also no clauses requiring PEC to search for the cheapest source of equipment. The extent to which the activities of Eximcorp and PEC inflated costs has fuelled doubts about whether Madhvani intended to bring KCFC on stream at all.

The unequal sharing of responsibilities and liabilities between the government and the other parties was entrenched by the interlocking partnership of the investors, particularly elaborate in the case of KCFC. For instance, the joint-venture agreement made the participation of Chemfood Investment Corporation (CIC), with 34 per cent equity in KCFC, conditional on the *technical engineering agreement* appointing PEC as machinery and equipment supplier. Similarly,

Advait International's 15 per cent equity was conditional on the appointment of Eximcorp (Panama) as project manager.

But in the joint-venture agreement, PEC and CIC are represented by the same signatory and give the same office, telephone number and address in Mannedorf, Switzerland. Advait and KCFC also have the same signatory, Nittin Madhvani, and Madhvani admitted to owning Eximcorp.[73] Therefore, KCFC consisted of the government and two interlocked investment groups selling equipment and finance and managing construction. Nobody in this group had prior experience in ethanol technology projects.

These complicated arrangements are not recognized in government documents prior to signing of the joint-venture agreement. Rescinding parts of the joint-venture agreement, the project implementation management agreement or the technical engineering agreement was precluded by other sections of the contracts. Cancelling the whole project would, however, leave the government shouldering all liabilities plus a *force majeure* compensation of US$500,000 in foreign currency to Eximcorp. In any case, records confirm that the Attorney-General's recommended amendments to the joint-venture agreement were not considered by the NPC and did not therefore inform its decision process.

The Mehta Group opted for a fixed annual management fee of KShs 600,000 payable in Swiss francs and a five-year management contract, although IIC continues to manage the now faltering ACFC. The partnership of VEW led to Vogelbusch being appointed technology supplier and consultant. But it also gave ACFC a powerful ally in the form of the Austrian embassy in Nairobi, which was able to pressurize Kenya's bureaucracy in a manner that only a government with leverage over another could.

INFORMATION, DECISIONS AND CONTROVERSIES OVER FEEDSTOCK

As indicated earlier, molasses supply was an early issue of contention. In 1978, Madhvani unilaterally reviewed the KCFC proposal (Tables 7.8 and 7.9). This pointed to the open nature of the contract and lax institutional supervision of implementation. This was identified by Djeflat[74] as an attendant danger in 'open-ended product-in-hand turnkey contract' packages. Djeflat pointed to the tendency among contractors, in such circumstances, to inflate prices and include superfluous infrastructures and security measures.

KCFC activities were characterized by this trait (Table 7.10) starting only months after approval. Notable in the KCFC revisions was the tilt of the project away from ethanol, the initial centre-piece of the project approval process (Table 7.9).

It is possible that the KCFC revisions were intended to pre-empt moves to approve ACFC through cornering of molasses supply. The Mehta proposal was

Table 7.8 Original and revised proposals for the Kenya Chemical and Food
Corporation (KCFC)

Product	Original (May 1977)	Revised (March 1978)
Fuel ethanol	9.2 million litres	16 million litres
Citric acid	2,200 tonnes	3,000 tonnes
Dry baker's yeast	1,200 tonnes	1,000 tonnes
Fresh baker's yeast	1,700 tonnes	3,000 tonnes
Vinegar	1.7 million litres	2.2 million litres
Sulphuric acid	—	7,500 tonnes
Ammonium sulphate	—	2,000 tonnes
Oxygen	—	6,800 tonnes
Methane	—	60 billion Btu (63 billion kJ)

Source: C. Juma, 'Evolutionary technical change: the case of ethanol in developing countries',
unpublished PhD thesis, University of Sussex, Brighton, 1986

Table 7.9 Kenya Chemical and Food Corporation (KCFC) capital allocations,
1982, by product

Unit	US$ million	Percentage
Citric acid	49.7	39.8
Yeast	36.9	29.5
Ethanol	23.0	18.4
Anamet water treatment	7.6	6.1
Vinegar	4.1	3.3
Oxygen	2.6	2.1
Sulphuric acid	1.2	1.0
TOTAL	125.0	100.0

Source: Kenya Chemical and Food Corporation, Nairobi, 1981

submitted in February 1978 and Madhvani submitted the revision in March
1978 (Table 7.8). The original KCFC proposal was designed to use 55,000
tonnes of molasses annually. The revised version required 110,000 tonnes per
year (Table 7.5). With the ACFC proposal of 63,000 tonnes (Table 7.7),
Miwani requirements (Table 7.6) and the Ministry of Livestock Development
projections, adequacy of molasses availability became doubtful. However, in July
1978 the government approved and took 56 per cent equity in ACFC.
Government decision-making did not seem concerned with such details. But
KSA was asked to supply data on national molasses availability, although this
could not have influenced the direction of events.[75]

Both ACFC and KCFC were designed exclusively for molasses. This was
unnecessary, because only minor adjustments were required to the technology
to enable use of molasses, cane juice or a combination of both. This design
failure, however, gave molasses undue importance at a time when the country

Table 7.10 Kenya Chemical and Food Corporation (KCFC) capital allocations (KShs '000), by type of activity

Item	Original	Revised
Land and preparation	2,125	10,702
Buildings	14,450	17,849
Machinery and equipment	385,900	564,619
Oxygen plant	—	13,478
Sulphuric acid plant	—	6,584
Fire-fighting equipment	—	3,750
Factory equipment	—	6,640
Incoming water system	—	5,082
Foreign exchange adjustment level	3,859	4,755
Sales tax	38,590	59,649
Clearance/freight/insurance	3,400	21,747
Erection and commissioning	17,000	40,126
Training	2,125	2,142
Furniture and fixture	—	2,677
Water treatment	1,700	—
Vehicles	12,750	10,711
Pre-start expenses	17,000	114,897

Source: Kenya Chemical and Food Corporation, quoted in C. Juma, 'Evolutionary technical change: the case of ethanol in developing countries', unpublished PhD thesis, University of Sussex, Brighton, 1986

was faced with excessive cane supplies, inadequate factory outlets and cane rotting in the fields. The choice of technology for Kenya's ethanol programme had completely failed to address local peculiarities.

Juma[76] points out that Zimbabwe's concurrent programme addressed this issue. Triangle, the Zimbabwe company, chose to design and install two plants able to use molasses, cane juice or a combination of both. Zimbabwe was concerned with sugar market fluctuations, and in this design flexibility integrated the alcohol programme with the rest of the sugar industry. In Kenya, technology choice was left to Vogelbusch and PEC without adequate briefing from their local partners. Flexibility was needed by both the sugar industry and the planned ethanol programme.

KCFC wanted long-term molasses supply commitments from the sugar mills. It argued that molasses had a zero opportunity cost. But sugar industry representatives countered that a resource with an effective demand could not have a zero opportunity cost. The mills had reversed their stand but the low institutional memory of the arbitrating organs of government undermined their role as effective brokers in the government-arranged series of negotiations that followed.

KCFC wanted a ban on export of molasses, a practice applied, for example, in cases of identified strategic input in other industries. It is the case with scrap metal, considered a strategic input for the informal sector.[77] KCFC also wanted the price of molasses sold to it to be fixed. Prices of all inputs and outputs in the sugar industry were regulated anyway.

But the mills preferred to sell on the most competitive markets available, because world prices were showing an upturn at the time of negotiations. The mills also successfully resisted the imposition of export duty on molasses which would have encouraged local utilization. During the negotiations, no reference was made to previous studies by Tate and Lyle and ISPC that had identified ethanol production as a way of stabilizing export price fluctuations and the attendant pollution dangers. This failure to use previous studies to inform negotiations illustrated weak institutional memory, a disregard for learning processes and lack of preparation on the part of government.

The government asked the parties to negotiate procurement procedures and fix prices but did not specify direction, time or framework of policy to guide negotiations. As a result, the parties concentrated on short-term returns, and past studies, reports and information in government possession were not used to inform the process.

Without the benefit of government direction, Miwani saw KCFC as threatening its own future plans and announced its intention to expand its spirit operations. Mumias, Sony and Nzoia indicated their own ambitions to annex ethanol plants. These mills could not, therefore, give long-term guarantees on molasses.

Almost two decades later, nothing has come of the Sony, Mumias and Nzoia plans, and when Hindocha's Miwani finally shut down in 1988, there was no evidence of such expansion work. What is more, Miwani did not replace the production manager of its spirit operation when he moved to ACFC in 1983.[78] Miwani's expansion proposals may have been intended to bar the entry of a potential competitor, but the actions of other mills were undirected, and reflected an uninformed and uncharted negotiation process.

Without reliable independent data, guidelines and yardsticks, government arbitration lost objectivity. Frequent changes in departmental representation at negotiations further weakened institutional knowledge and competence to arbitrate. Without departmental guidelines, representatives articulated personal views, which confused matters. The initial broad goals of the ethanol programme were soon lost and not referred to. Nor were matters of plant design, technology choice and selection, and feedstock flexibility adequately addressed.

In 1981, the Ministry of Energy suggested a switch in feedstock from molasses to cane juice, pointing to national oversupply of cane and mill closures. But the decision was left to ACFC and KCFC, which remained unwilling, without pressure, to make concessions and effect the technological adjustments. By the beginning of 1981, KCFC construction was 75 per cent complete and work on ACFC had begun, but this issue was still unresolved. This remained the situation when KCFC construction was abandoned in 1982.

INFORMATION, DECISIONS AND THE GASOHOL BLENDING CONTROVERSY

It was not until construction of KCFC was in progress that the oil companies indicated their disapproval of any blend that would require them to modify equipment and stations. The refinery also indicated its disapproval of any blend or blends that would require modifications to the refinery process.

The oil companies wanted to conduct road tests to ascertain the suitability of fuel ethanol, the tests to be paid for by KCFC. They also wanted KCFC to indemnify them from any legal liabilities arising from use, blending, handling, storage, sales, supply and distribution of ethanol. They wanted blending done at their depots while KCFC remained responsible for ensuring quality standards, delivery schedules and any costs of modifications, consumer education and legal costs.

Government arbitration was uninformed here too, weakened by the 'musical chairs' syndrome and the absence of a policy framework for conducting negotiations. Departmental representatives took sides, and in the end no agreement was signed between the companies and KCFC. Matters were only later resolved by government fiat. This indicated institutional weaknesses in managing negotiations and arbitrations caused by uninformed and undocumented intervention procedures.

There were also problems with the pricing formula for the blend. The oil industry proposed that KCFC sell it ethanol at a price less than half the indicated production cost of KCFC.[79] At this price, the oil companies would have retained revenue from the differences in price between regular and premium petrol and earned fortuitous extra revenue. The companies would also use ethanol as a substitute for tetraethyl lead but would not include the savings in the price they paid. This was a strange proposal coming from international commercial operators. Again no agreement came out of the negotiations.

Price affects the competitiveness of a product, but in neither the KCFC nor the ACFC feasibility studies was the pricing of ethanol addressed. Only production costs were indicated. Whereas Madhvani expected the government to fix the price of ethanol, Mehta intended to free-ride on an arrangement carved out by Madhvani. Since ethanol costs normally tend to be higher than those of petrol, government intervention should have been anticipated and neutral arbitration abandoned in favour of directed negotiations. Failure to gain the early cooperation and commitment of the oil companies, as desired by the ISPC report of 1976,[80] proved an expensive oversight. Government guarantee of foreign loans made it an interested party in ensuring that the projects met their foreign loan obligations, and they were granted a price that would ensure this. But this reality was lost on government departments and their negotiating teams.

THE CONSEQUENCES OF INSTITUTIONAL
WEAKNESSES

Lack of informed debate gave the ethanol programme a political twist. Government departments vied to defend their patch and adopted positions based on information supplied by the interested parties, who took advantage of poor institutional knowledge of the sector. For example, when the debate became public, KCFC management issued statements arguing that KCFC could not be compared to any plant in Kenya and, by virtue of its product mix, to any in the world.[81] Nittin Madhvani rejected both World Bank and UN Industrial Development Organization (UNIDO) criticisms of KCFC as uninformed. It became difficult, in these circumstances, to gain an objective picture of events, and politics moved to centre stage.

Because KCFC had the potential to become a big employer in this economically poor region, local politicians argued for strong government support and advanced a 'conspiracy theory' to explain the unexpected difficulties facing the largest government-led project in the region.[82] Nittin Madhvani accused the press of being 'divisive and malicious',[83] and propagating the sentiments of foreign firms (presumably the oil companies) who supplied the press with the information used to question the viability of fuel ethanol programmes. The questions raised by the press were, nonetheless, credible because by 1981 oil prices were steadying. Selective presentation of facts that excluded past reports and studies of the sugar industry and molasses disposal problems as well as the post-1973 energy crisis could appear quite convincing. Such presentations needed to be countered with comprehensive and holistic fact-based arguments. These were not forthcoming from any quarter.

Instead, Madhvani appealed to patriotism. He argued that, in line with presidential calls for exports, KCFC intended to export citric acid and baker's yeast products[84] (Table 7.9). He used this to justify the cost overruns but without specifying the export markets. In February 1982,[85] another press statement argued that KCFC was a pioneering venture comparable in complexity to nuclear and space technology development programmes in the USA. KCFC was described as a 'high-technology investment'.

There were no informed responses to KCFC assertions. It was not pointed out, for instance, that KCFC had been approved for completion in 1980 (Table 7.5) and that similar projects had been brought on stream, on time, in Zimbabwe, Malawi and Swaziland. Nor was it indicated that the unilateral shift of emphasis away from ethanol contravened the letter and spirit of the joint-venture agreement.

Inter- and intraministerial conflicts later became public. For example, on 16 May 1979 the Minister for Transport and Communications instructed his ministry to withdraw from committees discussing KCFC and ACFC. In effect, he was withdrawing the ministry from an interministerial approved programme. This was in breach of collective responsibility and government operational procedures.[86] This action highlighted serious operational weaknesses in government project management procedures. What is more, it advanced the cause of conspiracy theories[87] because the minister hailed from the central part of Kenya.

Amid this controversy, the government saw fit to improve its institutional knowledge. Officials were sent to Brazil in May 1980 to acquaint themselves with fuel ethanol production. They ascertained that Codistil had exported a distillery of capacity 240,000 litres a day to Costa Rica in 1978 at a cost of US$13 million. This verified Centre for Industrial Development (CID), ISPC and World Bank reservations on pricing of the KCFC plant. It contrasted with KCFC's capacity of 60,000 litres a day, which had cost Kenya US$67 million. A second group sent to Zimbabwe, now independent, in August 1981 recommended flexible feedstock, a suggestion the Ministry of Energy submitted for negotiations. But this proposal had no impact on events already in place.

The supportive interest of the Austrian embassy helped ACFC. Construction started in April 1981 and was completed in May 1982. Trial runs were conducted in June 1982 and commercial production was scheduled to start in July 1982 but was delayed by the oil companies. When ACFC faced closure, the Austrian embassy made it an agenda of Austro-Kenyan bilateral negotiations. The embassy expressed concern that ACFC might default on Austrian loans. This led to stronger government intervention, culminating in a series of directives that launched gasohol in Nairobi in April 1983. It took a foreign government's intervention to stiffen the decision process.

KCFC had no such powerful intermediary. By 1980, project costs had escalated from KShs 516,441,000 to KShs 952,598,000, but work was not yet complete. The cost of generating one job at KCFC averaged KShs 1.5 million compared to the then national average of KShs 120,000.[88]

When foreign loan syndication efforts to buy time failed, local creditors moved in. Solel Boneh ceased construction work in December 1981 because of non-payment. In April 1982, PEC notified its intention to demobilize operations since Deweto could not undertake further erection work because the civil contractor, Solel Boneh, had stopped work. PEC demanded payment of SFr 1.1 million as a demobilization fee. In May 1982, the Power and Lighting Company disconnected power supplies, claiming non-payment. In August 1982, Eximcorp resigned its directorship of KCFC because of non-payment of management fees. National attention was temporarily diverted in August 1982 by an attempted coup by the armed forces, which derailed government decision-making for several months. By this time total capital expenditure at KCFC stood at US$125 million compared with US$27 million for ACFC. This should be compared with the proposed US$67 million (Table 7.5) and US$18 million (Table 7.7) and the dates initially approved. The World Bank reported that in 1983 KCFC had become a 'subject of cabinet discussions regarded by the civil service as highly sensitive and confidential'.[89]

But KCFC had glaring and perplexing design and implementation faults. Even though the ethanol facility was 95 per cent complete, it could not come on stream until all other facilities (Table 7.9) were ready. But whereas the ethanol market was certain, the market for the other products was not known. In any case, they had not been priority areas. Madhvani had unilaterally expanded the parameters of the project and created additional problems. Otherwise, phased commissioning might have made it possible for earnings from ethanol to help fund completion of other units.[90]

The siting also entailed prohibitive molasses transportation costs. Located in a town and not near a mill, KCFC was designed to use bunker fuel and electricity rather than bagasse. This would have raised operational costs to three times those of ACFC.[91] Considering the pricing problems ACFC had to contend with later, this lends credence to questions about Madhvani's intentions.

In January 1983 the Ministry of Energy fixed the ex-factory price of ethanol on the recommendations of the Ministry of Finance. The Kenya Pipeline Company (KPC), a wholly owned government venture, agreed to store ethanol at a fee and to supply it to oil companies for blending. KPC also undertook to purchase blending facilities which would be installed on the premises of the oil companies.

After the blenders had been installed, the government in March 1983 directed the oil companies, by means of a legal notice, to start taking ethanol. It gave them four days to run down oil stocks and prepare to receive ethanol for blending from KPC. On the morning of 16 April 1983, motorists in Nairobi woke up to a new fuel on the market. A decree by the Ministry of Energy overruled the Traffic Act, which bars the use of any fuel other than that specified in a vehicle's licence. In 1985 the government directed that all petrol in Nairobi be blended with ethanol. This has permitted ACFC to attain 75 per cent capacity. All negotiations from 1978 to 1985 ended without an agreement.

CONCLUSIONS

The institutional management of the transfer of power alcohol technology to Kenya was characterized by weaknesses. These included weaknesses in documentation procedures which made operational diagnosis and accountability difficult. There were also weaknesses with operational guidelines which gave officers excessive discretion in interpretation and application of regulations, making the process unpredictable, subjective and susceptible to political manipulation. It also encouraged lax supervision of project implementation, which was abused by contractors.

There were cases of poor institutional memory that not only weakened the quality of decisions, but also undermined the ability of government departments to arbitrate. It contributed to poor preparation and bureaucratized decision-making on technology matters, and precluded the use of expert input and institutional learning. The fact that the government had no prior concept of the direction that the ethanol programme was intended to take made preparatory effort discretionary and undermined institutional competence. There was no transparent plan against which to evaluate proposals. This removed initiative and leadership from national institutions, forcing them to accept, without validation, data and proposals presented to them.

Discretionary use of expert input and poor documentation of events and decision-making processes weakened institutional memory, learning and the cultivation of expertise. The practice of not retrieving and using relevant past studies to inform negotiations and decisions encouraged a disregard for institutional learning and poor preparation before negotiations or arbitrations. This operational style could not nurture improved performance or transfer of experience between projects.

Bureaucratized evaluation systems are not amenable to review and do not take on board new developments and change. This is evident in the systems used to fix prices in the sugar industry and, later, to review KCFC.[92] Alternative broader, evolving systems are required for informed decisions that can manage change. Young economies like Kenya need to adopt, for example, diversified sources of commercial energy as a risk management strategy. Systems to evaluate such a programme would need to take into account local peculiarities. Such an approach is required when evaluating the sugar industry and the ethanol programme. Only the results of such a system would inform decisions. As it is, Kenya has integrated into its energy management plans little by way of lessons from the volatile events and experiences of the 1973 oil crisis.

Diversity and flexible specialization do not strictly conform to established economic and financial concepts of specialization, production efficiency, comparative advantage, international division of labour, economies of scale and opportunity cost. On this premise, there can only be one economically optimum form of energy generation or sugar processing, which becomes dominant. But this leaves vulnerable economies without autonomous contingency mechanisms or strategies.

Existing tools of evaluation aim to establish single, optimal ways of doing things. The case for diversity requires holistic cost–benefit approaches able to take into account the benefits of economic stability, regional integration and national synergy in wealth creation. This can be achieved only at some cost to short-term returns and immediate efficiency calculations.

Kenya's experience in this case points to weaknesses in the operational modes of national environment enabling institutions. Since the individuals in these institutions are as adequately trained as anywhere else, the problem must reside with the corporate operational styles. These styles preclude use of *in situ* expertise and prevent inventory of national capabilities even when necessary.[93] To manage change, institutions need to be coordinated and consistent in order to support informed decision-making, social learning and participative development. This has much to do with managing information flows.

National environment enabling institutions need to build a capacity for project management, including a capacity to define, identify, set up and enforce fallback positions. This would include setting maximum exit costs as benchmarks for declaring a project a failure and, therefore, best abandoned.[94] The failure to build this capacity has led to the state of limbo that KCFC remains in. Inability formally to declare the death of a project means that it lives in other planes. It is a failure to recruit the wider society to accept a scientific search for solutions, to underpin technology. Avenues for marrying Western science to indigenous ways are subverted when national institutions cannot scientifically deliver on expectations or account satisfactorily for failures, and therefore the burying of 'bad projects'. The subsequent political bad blood undermines fundamental national integrity and dissipates efforts and resources in unproductive directions.

NOTES

1 'Firms make alcohol', *Kenya Times*, 22 January 1990, pp. 20–2.
2 N. Clark and C. Juma, *Long-Run Economics: An Evolutionary Approach to Economic Growth*, Pinter, London, 1987.
3 C. Juma, 'Evolutionary technical change: the case of ethanol in developing countries', unpublished PhD thesis, University of Sussex, Brighton, 1986.
4 E. O. Awilli, 'Introduction to chemical processing technology', unpublished manuscript, Kenya Sugar Authority, Nairobi, 1989.
5 Interviews with the Production Manager, South Nyanza Sugar Mills (Sony). He is a chemical engineer and sugar technologist by training. Chemical engineering appears the common background of most sugar technologists in the industry, with postgraduate sugar technology training undertaken in the Indian sub-continent. Kenya sugar technologists have undergone periods of industrial attachments in both India and the Philippines.
6 C. Juma, 'Market restructuring and technology acquisition: power alcohol in Kenya and Zimbabwe', *Development and Change*, vol. 16, part 1, January 1985, pp. 39–59.
7 Interviews at the Kenya Sugar Authority (KSA) with the Sugar Technologist, Economist and Planner. The Sugar Technologist is a chemical engineer with sugar technology training while the others are economists by training.
8 'State takes over sugar company', *Daily Nation*, 30 June 1990, p. 12. This report illustrated the strained relations between the government and the Mehta Group at the termination of the management contract at EASI Muhoroni. A minister, in this case from the Office of the President, supervising the handover ordered the representatives of the Mehta team out of the meeting. The latter appear to have been taken unawares because signals from the Ministry of Agriculture had indicated that the contract would be renewed. The result is that for the first time since the inauguration of ACFC in 1979, the management of EASI and ACFC would be different. Both IIC at ACFC and Mehta at EASI were actually representatives of the same company. Strained relations between EASI and ACFC followed this change. ACFC then received 30 per cent of its molasses and all steam energy from EASI at special rates.
9 Interviews at Agrochemical Food Corporation with the Works, Production and Quality Control Managers. The Works Manager, a chemical engineer by training, is a former Production Manager at Miwani and an Indian citizen. Both Production and Quality Control Managers are Kenyans. The Managing Director is also an Indian citizen.
10 Interviews at Agrochemical Food Corporation with the Works, Production and Quality Control Managers.
11 KIRDI, Annual Report and Statement of Accounts 1985/86, Kenya Industrial

Research Development Institute, 1985; KIRDI, Annual Report and Statement Accounts 1987/88, Kenya Industrial Research Development Institute, 1987; H. N. Njenga, 'More energy, cheaper energy for faster economic development of Kenya', paper presented at the National Seminar on the Role of Research and Development Institutes in the Development of Kenya Industry, 2–3 July 1987, Nairobi.

12 R. Kaplinsky, 'Developing an appropriate policy environment: small scale sugar production', unpublished manuscript, 1989.

13 G. Hagelberg, 'The structure of world production and consumption', in *Cane Sugar: The Small Scale Processing Option. Proceedings of ITDG/IDS Conference on Small Scale Sugar Processing, Brighton, 1987*, pp. 41–50.

14 A. Bush, 'Introduction to processing techniques', in *Cane Sugar: The Small Scale Option*, op. cit., pp. 27–9.

15 Interviews with some farmers around the Sony factory.

16 The following reports covering a two-month period in 1990 are typical of the confusion in the industry: 'Imports have been haphazard and alarming as reports show: KPA to off-load sugar', *Daily Nation*, 27 March 1990 (reports on the arrival of 13,000 tonnes of imported sugar from Brazil); '180 million shillings vessel owners "not known"', *Sunday Times*, 25 March 1990; P. Mwangi, 'Sugar shortages: the key issues to examine', *Sunday Standard*, 4 March 1990, pp. 25–7; 'No sweet news for sugar industry', *The Standard*, 28 April 1990, p. 21. This confusion is borne out by the even more confusing official statistics given in the following table, which shows trends in the importation of sugar over the period 1984–9:

Year	Production	Consumption	Imports
1984	372,000	341,000	4,000
1985	345,000	376,000	41,000
1986	369,000	381,000	126,000
1987	390,000	400,000	49,000
1988	412,000	485,000	42,000
1989	475,000	—	22,000

The discrepancies in the figures are officially attributed to smuggling but are more a reflection of poor documentation despite a major government presence in this industry.

17 J. E. O. Odada *et al.*, *Incentives for Increased Agricultural Production: A Case Study of Kenya's Sugar Industry*, Friedrich Ebert Foundation, 1986.

18 E. O. Awilli, op. cit.

19 Republic of Kenya, *Development Plan 1974–1978*, Government Printer, Nairobi, 1974.

20 R. J. M. Swynnerton, *A Plan to Intensify the Development of African Agriculture in Kenya*, Government Printer, Nairobi, 1955.

21 D. Makanda, 'Sugar policy in Kenya: a farmer's dilemma', in *Cane Sugar: The Small Scale Option*, op. cit., pp. 94–104.

22 A. Bigsten, *Regional Inequalities and Underdevelopment: A Case Study of Kenya*, Gower, Aldershot, 1980.

23 T. Shaw, 'Ethnicity as the resilient paradigm for Africa: from the 1960s to the 1980s', *Development and Change*, vol. 17, 1986, pp. 587–605.

24 D. Hunt, *The Impending Crisis in Kenya: The Case for Land Reform*, Gower, Aldershot, 1984.

25 R. Kaplinsky, op. cit., p. 25.

26 Interviews at the Kenya Sugar Authority (KSA) with the Sugar Technologist, Economist and Planner.

27 R. A. Onyango, 'Strategic national information management and technology transfer', PhD thesis, University of Strathclyde, Glasgow, 1991, p. 166.
28 Interviews at the Kenya Sugar Authority (KSA) with the Sugar Technologist, Economist and Planner.
29 D. Makanda, op. cit., p. 98.
30 Interviews at Agrochemical Food Corporation with the Works, Production and Quality Control Managers.
31 C. Juma, 'Evolutionary technical change', op. cit., p. 75.
32 Republic of Kenya, *Sessional Paper No. 1 on Economic Management for Renewed Growth*, Government Printer, Nairobi, 1986.
33 Ibid., pp. 66–7.
34 M. Tribe, 'Scale considerations in sugar production planning', in *Cane Sugar: The Small Scale Option*, op. cit., pp. 53–60.
35 R. Kaplinsky, op. cit, p. 36.
36 H. Schmitz, 'Flexible specialisation: a new paradigm of small-scale industrialisation?', IDS Discussion Paper No. 261, Institute of Development Studies, University of Sussex, 1989.
37 D. Gachuki and P. Coughlin, 'Structure and safeguards for negotiations with foreign investors: lessons from Kenya', in P. Coughlin and G. Ikiara (eds) *Industrialisation in Kenya: In Search of a Strategy*, Heinemann, Nairobi, 1988, pp. 91–111.
38 Interviews at Agrochemical Food Corporation with the Works, Production and Quality Control Managers.
39 ISPC, *Pre-feasibility Study on Industrial Utilisation of Molasses for Manufacture of Power Alcohol in Kenya*, Industrial Survey and Promotion Centre, Ministry of Commerce and Industry, Nairobi, 1976.
40 F. Diouf, 'Information technology and development in Senegal: the importance of culture', in C. Chen (ed.) *NIT '96: Proceedings of the 9th International Conference on New Information Technology*, MicroUse Information, West Newton, MA, 1996, pp. 81–4.
41 ISPC, op. cit., p. 14.
42 D. Gachuki and P. Coughlin, op. cit., p. 97.
43 Madhvani Group, *Final Proposal for the Utilisation of Molasses in Kenya*, Madhvani Group, Nairobi, 1977; Vogelbusch, *Feasibility Study for Industrial Utilisation of Molasses in Kenya*, Mehta Group, Nairobi, 1977.
44 D. Gachuki and P. Coughlin, op. cit., p. 110.
45 'Madhvani seeks to complete factory', *Daily Nation*, 14 April 1990, p. 11.
46 O. Odidi, 'Financing of recurrent expenditure in Kenya's industrial sector', paper given at the Kenya Economic Association's Workshop on Recurrent Costs of Public Investment and Budget Rationalisation in Kenya, Nairobi, 27–29 April 1988, pp. 1–48.
47 D. Gachuki and P. Coughlin, op. cit.
48 O. Odidi, op. cit.
49 D. Gachuki and P. Coughlin, op. cit., p. 94.
50 C. Juma, 'Evolutionary technical change', op. cit., p. 131.
51 O. Odidi, op. cit., p. 36.
52 C. Juma, 'Evolutionary technical change', op. cit., p. 131.
53 O. Odidi, op. cit., p. 37.
54 Opinions expressed at the interviews with various Kenya National Chamber of Commerce and Industry (KNCCI) and Kenya Association of Manufacturers (KAM) representatives, including the chief executives.
55 C. Juma, 'Market restructuring and technology acquisition', op. cit.
56 Interviews at the Kenya Sugar Authority (KSA) with the Sugar Technologist, Economist and Planner.

57 ISPC, op. cit.
58 C. Juma, 'Market restructuring and technology acquisition', op. cit.
59 G. Hagelberg, op. cit., p. 47.
60 N. Clark and C. Juma, op. cit., p. 128.
61 Ibid., p. 129.
62 Interviews at the Kenya Sugar Authority (KSA) with the Sugar Technologist, Economist and Planner.
63 Interviews with E. O. Awilli, Sugar Technologist at the KSA.
64 A. Djeflat, 'The management of technology transfer: views and experiences of developing countries', *International Journal of Technology Management*, vol. 3, no. 1/2, 1988, pp. 149–65.
65 Interviews with the Production Manager, South Nyanza Sugar Mills (Sony), the Sugar Technologist, Economist and Planner at the Kenya Sugar Authority (KSA) and the Works, Production and Quality Control Managers at Agrochemical Food Corporation.
66 S. Lubbe, R. Eggert and N. Hawkes, 'Determining the significance of decision criteria in the selection of IT investment in South Africa', *Information Technology for Development*, vol. 6, 1995, pp. 125–38.
67 Interviews at Agrochemical Food Corporation with the Works, Production and Quality Control Managers.
68 M. Godfrey, 'Stabilisation and structural adjustment of the Kenyan economy 1975–1985: an assessment of performance', *Development and Change*, vol. 18, 1987, pp. 595–624.
69 Interviews at Agrochemical Food Corporation with the Works, Production and Quality Control Managers.
70 P. Bennel, 'Engineering skills and development: the manufacturing sector in Kenya', *Development and Change*, vol. 17, 1986, pp. 303–24.
71 R. Matthews, 'The development of local machinery industry in Kenya', *Journal of Modern African Studies*, vol. 125, no. 1, 1987, pp. 67–93.
72 N. Clark and C. Juma, op. cit.
73 Madhvani Group, *The Kisumu Project: Utilising Molasses to Meet Kenya's Needs for Energy, Food and Foreign Exchange*, Madhvani Group, Nairobi, 1981.
74 A. Djeflat, op. cit., p. 155.
75 Interviews at the Kenya Sugar Authority (KSA) with the Sugar Technologist, Economist and Planner.
76 C. Juma, 'Evolutionary technical change', op. cit., p. 169.
77 'Madhvani seeks to complete factory', op. cit.
78 Interviews at Agrochemical Food Corporation with the Works, Production and Quality Control Managers.
79 Ibid.
80 ISPC, op. cit.
81 KCFC press release, 2 July 1980.
82 Interviews with local authority staff in Kisumu.
83 KCFC press release, 2 July 1980, p. 5.
84 Ibid.
85 *The Standard*, 2 February 1982, pp. 18–19.
86 P. Anyang' Nyong'o, 'State and society in Kenya: the disintegration of the nationalist coalitions and the rise of presidential authoritarianism 1963–1979', *African Affairs*, vol. 88, no. 351, April 1989, pp. 229–51; C. Hornby, 'The social structure of the National Assembly in Kenya 1963–1983', *Journal of Modern African Studies*, vol. 27, no. 2, 1989, pp. 275–96; J. D. Barkan and M. Chege, 'Decentralising the state: district focus and the politics of re-allocation in Kenya', *Journal of Modern African Studies*, vol. 27, no. 3, 1989, pp. 431–53.

87 Interviews with local authority staff in Kisumu.
88 Republic of Kenya, *Sessional Paper No. 1 on Economic Management for Renewed Growth*, Government Printer, Nairobi, 1986.
89 See N. Clark and C. Juma, op. cit.
90 Interviews at Agrochemical Food Corporation with the Works, Production and Quality Control Managers.
91 'State takes over sugar company', op. cit.
92 O. Odidi, op. cit., pp. 36, 37; C. Juma, 'Evolutionary technical change', op. cit., p. 131; opinions expressed at interviews with various Kenya National Chamber of Commerce and Industry (KNCCI) and Kenya Association of Manufacturers (KAM) representatives, including the chief executives.
93 'Is this economic sabotage?', *Finance*, 15–30 September 1990.
94 T. Curtis, *Business and Marketing for Engineers and Scientists*, McGraw-Hill, Maidenhead, 1994.

8

THE KENYAN NATIONAL CAR PROJECT, 1984–1990

PREAMBLE

This is a study of Kenya's attempts to manage a project that was intended to result in a commercially produced home-grown car, the Nyayo Pioneer. It was a programme aimed at advancing the country's efforts at industrialization. It was, therefore, an opportunity to take stock of existing capabilities, identify capability gaps, initiate mechanisms to fill such gaps and then implement them with an eye on general multiplier effects in an economy trapped in commodity exports whose prices and markets are dwindling. It was an effort at economic diversification.

It is an important case study because diversification and industrialization are the objective of many a developing country, and lessons can be gleaned from Kenya's efforts. It is a case of a country managing a long-term project, and is therefore a test of the capability of national institutions as environment enablers. Most important, it is an evaluation of the information sensitivity of such institutions in their endeavours to carry out their responsibilities. It is an assessment of a less developed country's national institutions' capability to manage, in an age of information, and their abilities to take advantage of what the information age offers. Finally, it is a study of information management in the development process.

INTRODUCTION

On 27 February 1990, two saloon cars and a pick-up were unveiled before the President of Kenya at a public rally. They were prototypes for the National Car Project, which had started in 1984.[1] It was announced that the prototypes and components were designed, developed and built locally.[2] The vehicles were named 'Nyayo Pioneer'.

It was explained that developing the prototypes had cost KShs 66 million (then US$4 million). The saloon cars had an engine capacity of 1,300 cc, used premium petrol and had a cruising speed of 120 kilometres per hour (kph). The pick-up, with the same engine capacity, used regular petrol, and had a cruising speed of 100 kph. All had four-cylinder engines.

A complete set of parts for the vehicles was on display, imprinted 'Made in Kenya', including engine block, crankshaft, steering wheel, gearbox, electrical parts, cylinder head, carburettor, camshaft and pistons, among others. The components were, reportedly, based on specifications of the Kenya Bureau of Standards (KBS). It was also reported that international technical quality control procedures had been adopted and that tests confirmed the vehicles as equalling any on the market.[3]

The unit cost per prototype vehicle was put at KShs 160,000 (US$7,000). This was expected to rise with commercial production. It was, however, intended that Nyayo Pioneers be the cheapest vehicles on the Kenyan market.

The first report on the National Car Project (NCP) was made to a Nairobi University student audience on 23 February 1990. The next public comment, two days later, described it as an advance in Kenya's technological sector, the success being credited to the engineers in higher learning institutions. It was further described as an achievement 'unequalled in Africa'. The project brief was reported as being 'to produce a Kenyan car in the 1200–1600cc range with all parts designed and made in Kenya'.[4]

The project was conceived and launched on a political platform. It followed the President's challenge to national universities to produce a car, a challenge that must have been taken up by administrators of the University of Nairobi.

This chapter looks at how the national institutions set about defining and interpreting project mission, aims and objectives, and examines how they worked towards attaining them. It looks at the process of institutional and expertise identification and selection, information-seeking and use, the options explored, and the decision-making processes. It also examines levels of institutional awareness of concurrent or related activities on a regional and global basis; that is, the global reconnaissance capability of the national institutions is evaluated. The latter is dependent on the ability to exploit global information infrastructures and systems. The extent of goal and time specificity in the project and flexibility in implementation are assessed. Lastly, transfer of experiences and lessons between and across projects is examined in the context of institutional exploitation of memory and the learning-by-doing phenomenon. This chapter, therefore, examines instances of lessons transferred from other projects and sectors, the quality of information, documentation and records used, and how these affected decision-making.

EVOLUTION OF THE PROJECT

The project involved:

- the University of Nairobi as project head/leader and responsible for design work;
- Kenya Railways, where fabrication and assembly was done;
- the Department of Defence;
- the Kenya Polytechnic;

- the National Council for Science and Technology (NCST); and
- the Ministry of Industry.

The senior resource persons from these institutions made up the Advisory Committee of the National Car Project. In its launch report, the Advisory Committee expressed satisfaction with funding and support for the project. This, therefore, excluded finance as a possible project constraint.

An inventory of the landscape highlights the absence of the Ministry of Research, Science and Technology (MORST), the Ministry of Commerce and the Ministry of Finance/Treasury. Also missing from the reportage was representation from the local motor trade such as the Kenya Motor Industry Association (KMI) or the Kenya Vehicle Manufacturers' Association (KVMA). KMI membership includes assemblers, component manufacturers and general motor and parts dealers. KVMA is an umbrella for assemblers.

Plans to establish Nyayo Motors Corporation to oversee commercial production of the vehicles were announced at the unveiling ceremony. This was six years after project conception and after the production of prototypes. NCP had, therefore, operated as an *ad hoc* gathering for six years. As noted previously, such an arrangement deprives operations of an enduring focus and location for gathering and accumulating information, expertise and experience. Early availability of such a facility would have given NCP team leaders the line responsibility over its membership – a strategic requirement in any long-term project management.[5]

A 5 per cent equity in Nyayo Motors Corporation, it was announced, was being offered to Mitsubishi Motors Corporation (MMC) of Japan. External technical expertise was being sought six years into the project. Land for assembly and parts plant was to be located on the outskirts of Nairobi in an Export Processing Zone (EPZ).[6] It was made clear that Nyayo Motors was to produce most of its components, as was emphasized by the absence of components manufacturers at the launch and their non-participation in the designing of the parts put on display.[7]

Nyayo Motors' intended output was to be 3,000 units per year, and was to target domestic demand, then estimated at 10–12,000 units annually (Table 8.1). The President, in an off-the-cuff remark, expressed his preference for a capacity of 100,000 units per year and aiming for exports. This pointed to low goal specificity and poor preparatory groundwork. Such basic issues should have been sorted out and clarified at earlier stages of project definition.[8] In any case, the saloon car niche targeted and the internal system for components sourcing adopted would have led to serious diseconomies of scale at output levels below 100,000 units per annum.[9] This should have been ascertained by the technical teams assembled at project definition stage – not late in the day and not by a politician.

Suspicions of low goal specificity or poor outcome definition were confirmed by the Ministry of Education's description of NCP as a deployment of 'intellectual technical creativity' that put Kenya on 'the threshold of becoming

Table 8.1 Total vehicle production and passenger car share in some LDCs

Country	Vehicle output 1980	Passenger car percentage	Vehicle output 1987	
Kenya	—	—	10,758	(1990 – 12,000)
Nigeria	—	—	42,758	
Egypt	—	—	23,455	
Zimbabwe	—	—	3,000	(1990 – 10,000)
Malaysia	100,971	84.4	82,500	
South Korea	123,135	46.5	957,394	
India	113,326	26.9	287,813	
Brazil	1,165,174	40.4	1,069,000	
Argentina	288,917	70.7	193,316	

Source: P. O'Brien, *The Automotive Industry in the Developing Countries: Risks and Opportunities in the 1990s*, Economist Intelligence Unit Special Report no. 1175, 1989; and interviews and communications with the Kenya Motor Industry Association, May 1990

a high technology country'.[10] The ministry asked Kenyans to feel proud of this national effort that confirmed the country's scientific and technical research capability. This capability would now be used to turn idle industrial capacity to tangible gain.

An analysis in a daily newspaper at the time estimated that a production plant with an output of 100,000 vehicles a year and producing engine and transmission systems in-house would cost between US$300 and US$500 million. Therefore, with free land and tax concessions on machinery imports, a complete plant could cost around US$400 million (or KShs 9.2 billion at April 1990 exchange rates). Such investment demanded strong government support. But this was a time of public expenditure cutbacks and restricted international borrowing. Such large outlays would also have demanded high levels of installed capacity utilization to keep prices competitive against the internationally sourced vehicles assembled locally.

NCP reports make no suggestions on funding options or on how production levels are to be managed. Production and marketing failed to receive adequate attention in the first six years of NCP. These considerations would have suggested alternative approaches to pursuing the national car idea.

Insularity characterized the management of this project, and made it inflexible and unable to receive and ingest information. For instance, between 1983 and 1985, Mitsubishi Motors was a partner and co-financier in Malaysia's national car programme. The car came on stream within two years and the programme cost US$263 million. Mitsubishi had also been a partner in the realization of Korea's first local car, the Hyundai Pony, in 1976. It took two years. At this time, Mitsubishi was also collaborating in a project to develop a minicar with Hyundai Motors of Korea which was expected to take three years and cost US$373 million. Another then ongoing minicar project involved Korea's Daewoo Motors in collaboration with Japan's Suzuki Motors and was to cost US$219 million and take two years. These time-frames included getting the product on to the market.[11]

Information on such events and developments (past, concurrent and planned) questions the logic of spending six years on prototypes. It demands that NCP reports should have included clear indications on when and how commercial production was to commence and when and how the plant was to be set up.

NCP reports show that the exploration of production possibilities began only at the time of launch of the prototypes. This indicates that NCP had not kept abreast of relevant market developments and that its calculations had not taken account of market realities and changes. This indicates a weakness in project definition going back to the very beginning.

Keeping abreast with relevant developments might have suggested alternatives to the definition of the national car project or, at least, infused flexibility into it. Pemberton,[12] for example, reports that by the early 1980s the development cycle for new vehicle models, from conception to showroom, had dropped to under four years. The six years spent on NCP prototypes was thus unacceptable in this industry. The calculations by NCP were not in tune with the industry. But the project responsibility included steering the country's entry into the motor industry.

Other NCP calculations were similarly unrealistic. For example, the cost of 'developing a new vehicle from scratch' already approached US$1 billion in 1987. It was costing US$300–400 million to develop a new engine alone.[13] These were competitive costs in developed and more efficient locations. The costs were forcing the industry into collaborative schemes for product and parts development to cut costs and time, and ensure quality and price competitiveness. Such information questions the direction of a project launched on a one-off budget and its time feasibility. It emphasizes the critical need to have focused NCP on a clear industrial context. However, NCP reports do not justify its progress in the context of realities that underpin the motor industry. As a result, the reports did not inform projections or chart what was to be followed.

Instead, NCP reports urged 'those concerned to make appropriate arrangements for mass production of the Kenya car'.[14] This statement was directed at the government, which, in turn, extended the invitation to Kenya's friends abroad. Responsibilities were vague and no specific plans were set to inform subsequent discussions or negotiations.

NCP was financed through the National Universities Research Fund. This fund was raised from public donations and was intended to bridge the gap in research financing at the four national universities. After NCP, little remained in the fund. The fact that this was the source of funding, together with official statements, indicates that NCP was considered as being in part a research enterprise. It was thus described as a pursuit of research excellence and an application of findings to solve practical problems. But neither its approach nor its system of documentation adhered to known research tradition.

Poor definition of goals and objectives of NCP was encouraged by the insularity of participants. This was because the project was classified and therefore subject to government secrecy regulations. The participation of the Department of Defence further added to this mystery. However, even classifying NCP seems to have been an afterthought. For instance, an article in the November 1987 issue of *Science and Technology Newsletter*[15] reported that the National Council for Science and Technology (NCST) was 'fully involved in the ongoing research to produce a Kenya Car'. KIRDI (the Kenya Industrial Research Development Institute),[16] in its 1985/86 Annual Report, openly refers to the 'Engine Project', which faced machining problems occasioned by lack of proper machinery. These events were recounted, and thus confirmed, at the unveiling ceremony. KIRDI further reported that work on the 'camshaft design' had been handed over to a workshop in Nairobi for fabrication. This referred to the Railways Workshop. These references and reports stopped after 1986, and the decision to go secret must have been made then. Once the project was classified, documented reports and references on the national car disappeared. The subsequent insularity shielded the management of the project from peer evaluation.

NCP then evolved in an atmosphere of secrecy, insularity, and poorly defined goals, objectives and time specificity. This weakened the learning process and was exacerbated by the *ad hoc* system of committees and teams. The absence of a continuing corporate body responsible and accountable for project performance undermined the cultivation of the corporate loyalty required for such an undertaking. This is evident in the chronology of events.

INFORMATION, DECISIONS AND THE CHRONOLOGY OF DEVELOPMENTS

The car project was based on the premise that low labour costs, reduced foreign exchange input and increased use of existing industrial capacity would make the cars among the cheapest on the market. But this excluded other considerations which were brought to the fore soon after the prototype launch. The local press, for example, pointed to the 'unusual' design and appearance of the cars as limiting their appeal. This was echoed by KMI.[17]

As compared with the prototypes, additional costs would be incurred for production models which, eventually, would raise unit cost above US$7,000 and weaken price competitiveness. This should have been recognized. The reality was more complex than the NCP reportage portrayed – whether by design or from lack of information.[18]

The Advisory Committee held its major meeting in July 1986. This is the meeting that set out the criteria for design, provided indications on social utility, economic viability, use of locally manufactured components, and the aesthetic and external styling, and specified the engine capacity. It defined the project aim as to 'produce a vehicle with 100 per cent Kenya manufactured components'. It also selected the Technical Committee and set what it considered to be that committee's priorities, which covered policy issues, design criteria and Kenyan needs. The Advisory Committee drew up these parameters without the benefit of experiences from Kenya's motor industry. The Technical and Advisory Committees then drew up a Working Programme and terms of reference for Technical Committee Teams. They did not renegotiate the terms of reference of the Advisory Committee. Renegotiating missions for specificity and attainment focus is standard project management practice.[19]

The Technical Committee was divided into five Development Teams:

- the *Body and Superstructure Team*, responsible for design and development of exterior and artistic styling of chassis and superstructure;
- the *Engineering Team*, responsible for designing, developing and producing the engine;
- the *Transmission Team*, to design, develop and produce components of the transmission system, including gears, gear casing, the differentials and the flywheel;
- the *Suspension and Control Team*, to design the suspension system, beam axle and braking system; and
- the *Electrics Team*, responsible for developing a wiring harness system and designing, developing and producing electric items such as the starter, coil, alternator and wipers.

The emphasis was on independent design and development. As a result, teams replicated much from known models.[20] This emphasis on 'copying' without regard for production costs or intellectual property rights is what created friction with Associated Vehicle Assemblers (AVA), which, at the early stages, had a representative on the Technical Committee.[21]

The Technical Committee's brief was:

- to identify, mobilize and utilize available resources relevant to the project;
- to acquire and develop relevant expertise and technology;
- to design, develop and produce the Kenyan car; and
- to establish a bank of knowledge, specialists and facilities that would help develop a national industry and capacity to produce the Kenyan car.

This committee had the responsibility to constitute the required expertise within parameters set by the Advisory Committee. Identification, locating and requisitioning (or excluding) of relevant and/or known expertise resident in Kenya for (or from) the project was, therefore, the duty of the Technical Committee. The ultimate responsibility for exclusion of resident motor industry input from NCP thus rests with this committee. But also notable was its failure to address the mandate of enabling the country to 'develop a national industry and capacity'. In all the six years of its existence, building capacity for a sustainable national motor industry does not appear to have been addressed.

The prototypes used existing locally manufactured components such as tyres, tubes, batteries, radiators, leaf spring shock absorbers, exhaust systems and brake linings. These are based on KBS standards. But the teams developed their own 'standard part-numbering system' for identifying other parts, this 'standard' being developed without local industry input, which had immediate and future cost implications.

Designing the 'standard' without involving local components manufacturers made it difficult to contract work to them later. Collaboration in the drawing up of standards could have ensured input from existing practice and the benefit of that experience, and could have supported subsequent commercial production of components for the national car. As it was, the possible benefits of local components experiences were lost to the project. This vacuum affected decisions on how component kits were to be produced. NCP could not and, evidence shows, did not competently address this issue. But commercial realization of NCP was dependent on competitive sourcing of component kits.

The costs of insular operations included the team's having to carry out chemical and physical analysis tests internally and to source raw materials and end products locally. It is inconceivable that local component manufacturers were not already doing some of this. But this practical knowledge was not sought. Insularity and the emphasis on local sourcing, at any cost, led to wasteful duplications. The project team reported spending 20,000 person-hours designing, casting and moulding the engine block before subjecting it to trials. But the opinion in the industry was that the engine could not be adopted for commercial production if the vehicles were to be competitively priced.[22] The limited production runs made its production uneconomical and NCP did not suggest other markets. In any case, this engine had no special specified qualities that might have appealed to new markets. It is also possible that attempts at export might have met with industrial property questions.[23]

The team reported having to 'develop new processes' to harden material required for 'crankshaft, camshaft and connecting rods'. The Transmission Team reported having to design tooling from scratch and learning to harden gears. All development teams report 'considerable efforts' involving long hours with beds provided on site. But much of this effort was expended in pirating widely practised procedures, processes and tools. Justifying this is difficult in a project intended to produce a marketable, competitively priced product. NCP reports offer no justification. This emphasis on reproduction casts doubts about whether the commercial viability of the vehicles and the need to 'develop a national industry' ever received consideration.

The origins of the project idea in the political arena and subsequent government-imposed secrecy make a sequential study of institutional activities difficult. They certainly contributed to low accountability. NCP also illustrates weaknesses in goal specificity and points to excessive discretion accorded to project members, leading to poor project management.[24] By the conclusion of the pre-commercial phase of the project in 1990, the Kenya Industrial Property

Office (KIPO) had been established. But NCP spun-off no applications for patents, designs or marks for registration at KIPO. There have also been no professional seminars or workshops on the findings of NCP. It therefore failed as a research undertaking.

INFORMATION, DECISIONS AND INSTITUTIONAL PROJECT MANAGEMENT

The project brief, it was reported, was the challenge to the university community, by the President, to 'come down from the ivory tower and make a car, however ugly, and even if it did a mere five kilometres an hour'.[25] This is an unacceptable way to spend public donations intended to advance research. It reflects the latitude the Advisory Committee gave itself and the teams. It is, nonetheless, normal project management practice that converting 'broad, diffuse and ambiguous terms' of projects into defined project mission, and setting aims and specified objectives, is the responsibility of the project leader and his team[26] – in this case, the University of Nairobi. The retention of this ambiguity in the project is an indictment of the Advisory Committee and its technical teams rather than the political process that set the project in motion.

It has been pointed out that imprecise terms of reference contributed to the absence of informed debate on the project while secrecy shielded it from public scrutiny. The use of funds raised from public collections instead of specified allocations probably encouraged this laxity and non-accountability in the institutions and individuals involved in the project. The project was not pre-costed and there were no set ceilings defining the work of the development teams,[27] even though the setting of such ceilings is a basic project management requirement. The market price of components was not used to guide product development work. The project was not subjected to opportunity screening or business analysis, important steps in technical project definition. It is such considerations that inform decisions on whether to produce a component in-house or to source it externally.[28]

The absence of a permanent and accountable centre weakened the need for accountable decision-making procedures. The membership of NCP was temporary and *ad hoc*. The loyalty of team members remained with their original employers. Membership was institutional and no formal framework for the individual was built. This weakened continuity in the accumulation of expertise, interest and motivation. During the six years, some individuals changed employers or were promoted and left NCP. Coupled with poor documentation of decision processes, logical continuity and learning became difficult to sustain. Issues set aside for further review were naturally forgotten. Institutional memory could not receive adequate back-up without an accountable organization and individuals responsible for the running of the Project. Henley's[29] musical-chairs syndrome was played out in full.

For individual team members, NCP duties were part of other duties. It was a temporary assignment for both the individuals and the participating institutions. No secretariat was set up to coordinate this exercise.[30] As a result, continuity was not given adequate attention and nobody shouldered this responsibility. However, information on markets and future developments would have been difficult to acquire without the motor trade's input. No one in NCP had the relevant expertise and experience to address the future of this industry. Until the launch, there had been no efforts to create and build that 'outer group of supporting links' which would have remedied this.[31]

Such gaps are highlighted by the short-term goals set by NCP. Its reports argued that the prototypes confirmed the worth of Kenyan scientists and that it was now up to the government to conceive and set up the structures for mass production.[32] The implication was that the NCP team had successfully accomplished its tasks. But this is not correct, even by the standards of the terms of reference that it gave itself. NCP did not, for instance, leave informed proposals or considered options for developing the national motor industry and the national car.

NCP attempted to portray its efforts as an academic undertaking that highlighted the nation's potential for research and innovation. This underlines an inadequate definition of research parameters by the NCP teams, despite a good presence of academics. This group would, of course, have been aware of the accepted criteria of measuring research outputs such as patents, publications, seminars/workshops, and reports for peer review. None of this has been forthcoming. These gaps have created evaluation difficulties, and inadequate evaluation has undermined projections for the next phase of the programme. The NCP participants indulged in shifting the goal posts and evading objective performance evaluation on returns to input.

The non-participation of MORST (as it then was) contributed to gaps in the definition of project objectives as research enterprise. Whereas NCST advises on research, it was MORST, at the time, that administered and accounted for conduct, direction and adherence to procedures and standards in research in the country. MORST would have been required, by virtue of its portfolio, to ensure proper definition, interpretation and conduct of research parameters. Its absence contributed to a loophole in institutional accountability and weakened capacity for goal definition and attainment. This permitted extravagant claims of research achievements to be made in a political forum at which they could not be subjected to competent peer accountability.

The absence of the then Ministry of Commerce also precluded the potential to use accumulated institutional project management experiences such as those in the records at the Industrial Survey and Promotion Centre (ISPC) library. The absence of the Treasury and Ministry of Finance representation removed financial discipline from the exercise. This was particularly important because it was at a time when bilateral and multilateral donors and financiers had imposed strict financial operational guidelines on government which were being

130

administered by this ministry. The result of such a gap in crucial institutional representation is that the NCP objectives were not subjected to financial rigour. For instance, it was not deemed necessary to justify the need for three prototypes when the usual practice is to develop and test one. Thus NCP spent six years developing products of unspecified quality or destiny using public funds.

THE NATIONAL CAR PROJECT'S CONTRIBUTION TO NATIONAL CAR RESEARCH CAPACITY

A self-propelled vehicle cannot, as such, in this day and age, qualify as a researchable idea. It is not new. Pemberton[33] explains that development research in the motor industry now focuses on specific items or areas. These can include fuel economy, safety, cheaper production methods and processes, use of alternative substitute materials such as fibre optics, plastics and ceramics, pollution control, body styling, increased reliability or information technology applications. But even over such specificities, the costs and expertise required demand broad-based collaboration if commercial competitiveness is expected. The credited NCP institutions did not represent adequate broad-based expertise, nor did they seek to recruit it.[34]

The self-propelled vehicle is a researchable issue only when specific dimensions of it are to be addressed. Such was the case with, for instance, efforts to develop the minicar in the late 1980s. Major motor corporations in Korea were involved in efforts to produce a 600–1,000 cc small urban vehicle with a price tag of around US$3,000.[35] Similar efforts were taking place in Brazil, India, Taiwan and several other countries.[36]

Developing the minicar was a research effort that underlined and exercised the multi-faceted nature of this industry. It engaged several corporations, disciplines and independent research centres around the world. The concept developed from a realization that the motor industry, as structured, could not generate a product within the income reach of most LDC residents. It was a search for a cheap, reliable car with low fuel consumption and needing little maintenance. It was the result of surveys that had noted that Asia's crowded cities pointed to the need for small-bodied frames. It also recognized the lack of popularity of large American cars in Latin America. The minicar concept was a synthesis of observations from engineers, economists, environmentalists, anthropologists, designers and mainstream motor industry experts from several continents. This crystallization of ideas was traceable in papers, seminars, conference/workshop reports and proceedings, studies and other such known indicators of research activity. These are referred to in information science as the social activities of information generation.

NCP reports indicate little application to identification and definition of problem and niche, but much effort in building prototypes. A solution was being devised for a problem that was not clearly specified. But the gaps in institutional representation and documentation make it difficult to isolate the specific causes for this unusual order of priorities. It is difficult to decide whether it was caused by the absence of required expertise in the country or whether it was the way NCP was designed and managed that prevented the search for and use of existing available resources and expertise.

The NCP research status breached all known standards, definitions and procedures of research. But no explanation or justification was given. Questions include whether 'Nyayo Pioneers' qualify as original Kenyan inventions. One view is that they represent the ability to assimilate, utilize, adapt or imitate modern technology, but not new inventions. It is pointed out that the source of such inputs as dies, moulds and patterns was not credited or acknowledged. As Tsuma[37] stated, everything 'cannot have been manufactured by the sole use of Kenyan expertise and know-how'. 'Imported technology' used in the process needed to be indicated; in proper research, credit has to be awarded where due. But the broad claims made by NCP reports did not award credit, which makes their evaluation difficult.

It is also difficult to evaluate NCP's contribution to national skills inventory. It failed to identify gaps that might require the borrowing, or buying-in, of expertise to bridge. The technical skills gap is considered a major weakness in Kenya's industrialization efforts, and those of LDCs in general. But NCP failed to contribute to the understanding of the problem. Another suspected gap is the level of theoretical skills needed to unpackage, select and bargain for technologies required from a forest of patented technologies and packages around the world. NCP presented an opportunity for testing and evaluating national skills in this area that would support the search for alternative technologies required to activate Kenya's idle infrastructure. These important technological capability spheres remain undiagnosed.

Gaya[38] concluded that the criteria for NCP remain known only to participants, who are bound by an oath of secrecy under the Official Secrets Act and who, as interested parties, could not be expected to be impartial anyway. This has served to obstruct objective evaluation. Therefore, even reports of prototypes being '100 per cent local' cannot be accepted without tangible data and technical specifications, or without subjecting the claims to impartial evaluation. Gaya further reported that at the unveiling ceremony, access to parts and components on display was restricted and no questions were entertained. The Department of Defence personnel actively discouraged curiosity. He concluded that 'the research, design, production and future of Nyayo Pioneer remained a mystery' six years and US$4 million after it began.

The active and high-profile participation of the Department of Defence in NCP totally clouded it in mystery. This is now lending credibility to speculations that NCP was a smokescreen for an entirely military enterprise with participants sworn to higher than normal levels of government secrecy. No evidence is, however, forthcoming either way. We can, therefore, evaluate NCP only on the basis of what it set out to do. We must assume that the other issues are attempts to shift goal posts and evade objective and transparent evaluation of performance.

Whatever the case may be, secrecy contributed, to a large measure, to diversion of publicly donated funds for a purportedly technological project that, in the end, has contributed nothing to advancing national technological capability.

TERRAIN REALITIES ABOUT A CAR

If NCP was indeed what it was purported to be, there was no need to classify it. This was a time when Kenya faced spiralling vehicle prices, an unfavourable balance of payments, deteriorating exchange rates and an overstretched public transport system. This was adequate justification for a search for a cheaper national vehicle. The public were well-disposed, and a transparent and accountable system of project management would have mobilized active and participative interest.

To ensure this, public pronouncements on NCP needed to be accompanied by some technical specifications and sufficient information to inform and activate enthusiasm from potential buyers and public. Because NCP was locally and independently initiated and funded, a higher degree of accountability and transparency than is the normal practice was to have been expected. After all, the public had paid for it, over and above their normal tax obligations.

If it failed to reach the mass production stage, NCP served no purpose; the exercise had little value if the cars proved too expensive or uneconomical to run. What is more, the cars would not sell unless they were cheaper than foreign models. Such insights should have informed decisions on NCP. The project needed to be put in the context of transparent global realities.

Experience shows that, once produced, vehicle specifications cannot remain secret. The strategy should, therefore, be to emphasize strong points and to elicit and monitor public and industry reactions – which means subjecting the concept to testing. Concept testing is possible even without a prototype.[39] Such feedback is required for further refinements; the incorporation of proposals from potential buyers makes the product more acceptable to them. This is important because success in the domestic market would be required to support export initiatives. This is standard commercial project management practice despite risks of commercial leaks. Secrecy was harmful to NCP.

The project raised and left unanswered scientific and marketing questions of product price, suitability and accessibility. The economics of production needed consideration. This included calculations on the extent of losses per unit expected before the venture became viable and self-financing, estimates of break-even points and cash flows, and maximum exit costs. These would inform government decisions on subsidy levels expected and the search for external financing; after all, members of NCP were aware that this was a time of public expenditure cutbacks. They would also highlight early signals of possible project failure and therefore indicate when to let go.

Understanding the industry would have informed NCP of the need to consider alternative or novel funding schemes such as those that have been used elsewhere. One such example is a system of loan payments based on royalty per car sold. This was the method used to partially finance technology acquisition, plant construction and training for Malaysia's Mitsubishi-guaranteed national car programme.[40] The scheme gave Mitsubishi, the intellectual-property owners, the incentive to strive for the Proton's export success. In Latin America, debt–equity swaps and international bond issues have been used to fund such schemes. Using alternative financing facilities demands a more thorough and rigorous approach to project design and proposal. NCP lacked this.

Such information and knowledge would also have informed the later process of negotiating with Mitsubishi over participation in Nyayo Motors. There are no available reports on why Mitsubishi Motors failed to take up the invitation to participate in Nyayo Corporation. As it is, the project failed to address long-term realities and made no suggestions as to how they could be pursued. Mitsubishi's invitation could not, therefore, have been a product of considered, debated and informed institutional decisions. There is little likelihood that the best terms possible could have been exhaustively explored and negotiated for in this arrangement. As it is, nothing materialized.

An opinion survey by the local press found motorists supportive of NCP but critical of the prototypes' body design and styling.[41] They recommended the involvement of specialists from the motor industry to advise NCP on tastes, body aerodynamics and future development. This was considered vital if the product was to reflect particular Kenyan conditions. This survey exposed glaring market inexperience in NCP designs. This was a potential handicap in domestic sales which could have weakened niche realization in export markets. Ordinary motorists were aware that this sort of information and knowledge resided with the local motor industry. But this was the expertise NCP chose to ignore.

The body design of the prototypes showed scant resemblance to anything on the market. It displayed a 'uniqueness of design' with no attempt to imitate cars assembled or sold in Kenya or anywhere else.[42] The Superstructure Team must have interpreted the '100 per cent Kenya car' idea literally.

Car body designs reflect tastes and fashions, which are in a perpetual state of change. This is why body designing is a competitive business that has spun off international operations. Organizations such as Ital Design, Bertone, Lotus and International Automotive Design (IAD) are international corporate operations dedicated to motor body design work.[43] They testify to the critical role of body design in vehicle production. Ordinary Kenyan motorists recognized this. The NCP team of experts did not.

Fashion-oriented business is driven by currency and imitation. The 'uniqueness' of Nyayo cars could, therefore, only prove a hindrance. Replication in motor designs is now driven by CAD (computer-aided design) and CIM (computer-integrated manufacturing) developments, as is attested to by the apparent ongoing convergence of designs across makes, models and marques. This has contributed to shorter product body life cycles, a reality that must be reckoned with by new entrants to the industry.

It is the deployment of innovative approaches and technologies that has cut the time required for a model, from conception to production, to under four years in such leading centres as Japan. The approach adopted by NCP was going to take over ten years. By not considering realities such as the critical need for currency, the efforts of the Superstructure Team, and others, proved a waste of time in commercial terms. NCP could not have passed the commercial evaluation stage of product project management.

Exclusion of known resident expertise from NCP made many of its claims difficult to accept from a commercial standpoint. One such was the report that Kenya has the technical capability to produce the steel required to support motor manufacturing, a claim made despite the country's not having an operational steel plant. However, vehicle production is an integrated industry in which such specific capabilities require objective evaluation. O'Brien,[44] for instance, emphasizes that prices of key inputs such as steel must be kept to international levels if vehicles are to be competitively priced. He also emphasizes the need for production at full capacity.

An in-house steel mill capable of producing the special steel needed for motor vehicles would have been required for the new plant because Kenya does not have such a facility in place. Kenya also suffers from an industrial sector that operates below capacity and is not efficient and competitive in acquisition of inputs from external sources. This means that Nyayo cars would have had to carry costs of inefficiency not experienced in more technologically developed and efficient locations. The NCP team needed to realistically explore options available to the programme in the light of such arrangement. Alternatives to be explored should have included the appraising of every aspect of the production process and taking inventory of technology, skills and facilities in place. As it is, NCP assumptions of normalcy were unrealistic. This could only have hampered the further development of the programme.

Having to import sheet steel, for instance, requires advanced institutional global reconnaissance capabilities if competitive prices are to be secured. Observers of Kenya's motor industry scene continue to identify the absence of an established steel industry and overseas competition as the two major threats to its development. A considered evaluation of the required level of institutional capability should have been an integral part of NCP reportage. It was not.[45]

As we have seen, NCP fails as a purely academic or research invention. It also failed as an inventory exercise. As an invention, the car is not new. The original idea of a self-propelled road vehicle cannot even be attributed to any one individual or country. It was the culmination of many individuals working simultaneously in several countries.[46] As a result, this often led to intellectual-property disputes such as the one over the four-stroke principle.[47]

The modern automobile is now a complex technical system of more than 14,000 researchable parts. This reality argues against the '100 per cent Kenya car' principle followed by NCP. The aim should have been to conceive, design and bring on stream an affordable, competitive and reliable product that is cheap to run and within a time frame that considers competition and imitation.

A proactive search for globally available knowledge and information with the intention of applying it to competitively produce a car arguably constitutes innovation. Also innovative would be an exercise aimed at creating a car that addresses peculiarities of the Kenyan market better than any existing car. These are researchable objectives. The NCP reports, however, make no references to the state of either the domestic or the international motor industry. The absence of input from the local motor trade left NCP without the specialization to handle this issue competently. This is particularly so because motor industry skills are taught only peripherally by training institutions in the country.[48] This made the motor trade the only credible source of relevant expertise available in Kenya.

The 1,200–1,600cc niche targeted by the Advisory Committee has been described as 'choc-full of competition' among established models. The unit cost of US$7,000 was the going price for established and reputable low-cost vehicles in international and domestic markets. It was already being undercut by models like the then Yugoslavia's Yugo Florida, which entered international markets at around US$4,000. Price competition, therefore, promised to be a nightmare. But it received inadequate attention.

NCP reports refer to intentions to enter export markets. But Kenya lacks relevant industrial experience, and the reports do not elaborate on how this is to be addressed. The export situation is exacerbated by the fact of negligible intra-African trade. In any case, the experience of projects such as Malaysia's Proton indicate that acceptance in LDC markets depends on successful performance in developed markets. This is what bestows technological credibility on a developing-country product in the eyes of other LDCs. Nyago Cars needed to gain entry and acceptance in the developed markets before entering neighbourhood ones, despite the advent of trading blocs.

THE REALITIES OF KENYA'S MOTOR INDUSTRY SCENE

Kenya's position in the motor industry is marginal even by the standards of LDCs (Tables 8.1 and 8.2). Also, the country is located in a region of insignificant and falling production as well as falling per capita incomes (PCI). Kenya's vehicle production demand levels are well below scale economies of 100,000 units per annum, a fact that should inform the national car planning process.

Kenya suffers low PCI, high numbers of persons per vehicle levels (Table 8.2), a low parc (number of vehicles in use) and a low effective demand level of around 18,000 per annum. This number cannot support economic manufacturing at prevailing prices.

In 1990 Kenya was described as a small, sophisticated but opaque consumer market with a parc of 300,000. The country imported around 6,000 CBUs

Table 8.2 Indicators of vehicle use and demand in selected countries, 1987

Country	Vehicle parc (millions)	Population (millions)	Persons/car	Average per capita income ($)
Kenya	0.26 (now 0.30)	21.0 (now 22.7)	167	284
Ivory Coast	0.25	10.5	65	712
Nigeria	1.41	105.4	134	806
Zimbabwe	0.26	9.0	51	572
Egypt	0.67	50.5	118.6	1,154
Morocco	0.64	23.7	53.1	54.2
Malaysia	1.49	15.8	14.1	2,007
South Korea	1.11	43.3	77.8	2,104
Taiwan	1.34	19.6	21.4	—

Source: P. O'Brien, *The Automotive Industry in the Developing Countries: Risks and Opportunities in the 1990s*, Economist Intelligence Unit Special Report no. 1175, 1989; and interviews and communications with the Kenya Motor Industry Association, May 1990

(complete built-up units) annually. Local assembly production averaged 12,000 units annually from three operational assembly plants (Table 8.1). This market, however, showed a unique preference for luxury cars, which had given Nairobi 'a higher proportion of Mercedes-Benz in its traffic than any city outside Germany'.[49]

The supply side of the market is dominated by assembly and franchise-holding distributors who continue to lobby for bans of CBU imports even in this age of market liberalization.[50] They argue that imports of CBUs deny the industry economies of scale and undermine efforts to rationalize the range of models.[51]

The absence of transparency in the industry is attributed partly to the practice of 'deliberate over-invoicing and false records'.[52] The KMI admits to publishing statistics that are at best 'educated guesswork'.[53] This situation is exacerbated by the tendency of the local media to represent these 'guesses' as facts and by the absence of alternative verification mechanisms. Government departments then use this 'guesswork' to inform their decision-making processes. An unclear national car agenda was therefore being introduced into an already opaque environment.

Government equity in commercial operations in Kenya is presently fluid, owing to the World Bank/IMF-led privatization drive. However, in 1990 the following position prevailed. The motor trade revolved around three assembly plants: Associated Vehicle Assemblers (AVA), located in Mombasa, Kenya Vehicle Manufacturers (KVM), based in Thika, and General Motors (Kenya) Ltd (GMK) in Nairobi. AVA was the largest operator, with an output of between 50 and 60 per cent of national total. KVM came on stream in 1974 as Leyland (Kenya) Ltd. The name changed in mid-1989 following equity changes that admitted D. T. Dobie, local franchise holders for Mercedes and Datsun-Nissan, into the partnership.[54] It also reflected the diminishing fortunes of Leyland UK. The government is a dominating shareholder in the assembly operations.

For instance, AVA was founded in 1974 through a partnership between the Industrial Development Bank (IDB)(a parastatal), Inchcape East Africa (a subsidiary of Inchcape UK) and Motor Mart Group – Lonrho Motors since 1994 (Lonrho UK's local motor franchise traders) – as a multi-franchise contract assembler.[55] In 1975, a joint-venture agreement was signed between the Treasury, IDB, Inchcape and Lonrho. Assembly of Ford trucks began in 1977 and was extended to include Nissan-Datsun, Mazda, Peugeot, Toyota and Mercedes trucks. In 1983, Marshalls East Africa purchased Inchcape shares. Marshalls, the local distribution franchise holder for Peugeot and Volvo, is 85 per cent owned by Marshalls Enterprises Ltd, which is 100 per cent owned by Somaia Group (now Dolphin-Dubai), a family company.[56] This trading group bought Marshalls in 1989. Previously, Marshalls was owned by the Aga Khan. The Aga Khan had purchased the business from Marshalls Universal plc of the UK, which had first established the East African regional franchise network for Peugeot vehicles. AVA, therefore, lacked credible association with experienced vehicle manufacturing.

AVA undertakes contract assembly of completely knocked down kits. It is 51 per cent government-owned with Marshalls and Lonrho Motors holding 24.5 per cent each. What is significant is that no equity holder at AVA had relevant technical expertise or experiences to transfer. AVA, therefore, typifies poor selection of partnership in an assembly project that was intended to advance technology transfer to Kenya. That was the essence of government equity participation. Instead, AVA is tightly integrated into import franchise with assembly as a revenue catchment strategy. Improving technology to reduce costs, for instance, has not been a priority.[57] Therefore, technological evolution was never intended and has not taken place. The level of assembly technology and local component input at AVA has remained essentially unchanged since inception.

GMK operations in Kenya were also majority-owned by the government through the Industrial and Commercial Development Corporation (ICDC).[58] GMK started operations in Kenya in 1975. It was listed as a parastatal under the Ministry of Industry and as an ICDC share company,[59] which indicates state equity of 51 per cent or above. But the management and control of operations remained under General Motors Corporation of the USA, through a management contract. GMK reflected ongoing divestment trends by US corporations in Kenya through which they transferred equity to private and public local interests. This way they reduced exposure. They were, however, retaining control through management contracts.[60] This strategy had been repeated at Firestone, Union Carbide, Bank of America, First National Bank of Chicago, Mackenzie Dalgety and Mobil. The management contracts ensured that operational and technological control remained under foreign minority interest but permitted the firms to borrow locally to finance operations. It allowed a situation in which local funds were used to finance operations that passed for foreign direct investment. Little core technology was transferred in such arrangements and operations remained concealed from local experts, but the firms were able to make political demands for protection and monopoly status. Firestone Kenya, for example, successfully used this strategy to block licensing of competition or competing imports from the early 1970s onwards.[61]

At GMK, management, technological expertise and CKD sourcing were exclusively controlled by General Motors Corporation (GM). This was confirmed by the assertions of the then American Managing Director that GMK was part of the global operations of General Motors Corporation whose activities included collaborative arrangements in Japan, Canada, Europe and the USA. Therefore, strategic decisions on GMK operations could not be influenced by developments on the Kenya market – government equity notwithstanding.

GM Corporation's global strategy straddles big names like Isuzu and Toyota in Japan, Opel in Germany and Daewoo in Korea among others. However, GMK is not a technology or marketing partnership on the footing of these others. GMK is an assembly facility intended to integrate GM's distribution interests in a market with a marked preference for Japanese and European models. As a result, GMK assembles none of its world-renowned badges or marques in Kenya. It instead assembles Isuzu, old Bedfords and Opel saloons.

KVM (formerly Leyland Kenya Ltd) had an initial ownership structure of Leyland International 45 per cent, the Kenyan government 35 per cent and Cooper Motor Corporation (CMC), local franchise holders of Land Rover and Range Rover, 20 per cent. The 1990 structure was 20 per cent Leyland, 25 per cent D. T. Dobie, 20 per cent CMC and 35 per cent the government of Kenya. The government was a big player.

The need for integration was the reason D. T. Dobie gave for moving its CKD business from AVA to KVM. D. T. Dobie explained that 'developments in local assembly were important and the company needed equity interest in it'[62] because it had become the only large franchise holder in Kenya without a direct assembly stake.

This statement crystallized the basis of assembly in Kenya. It is intended to enhance distribution franchise operations and not to develop towards vehicle manufacturing. To develop manufacturing would have meant restricting franchises in order to advance scale economies in parts and components production and specialization. This, however, would have been in direct conflict with the prevailing mood and direction of assembly business, which inclined towards diversity in order to skim-off little niches. KVM production remained below the design capacity of 4,500 units per year, but this capacity was at the mercy of franchise and distribution business.

The vision that informed government's entry into assembly was that of 'progressive manufacture'. This was intended to enhance national technological capability and reduce dependence on commodity cash crops through export of high-value items such as cars. The assembly was to develop from semi-knocked down kits to CKD and generate its own foreign exchange.[63] No time specificity was imposed for this evolution, nor was a defined master-plan ever drawn up. The result is an assembly sector that became the most expensive foreign exchange sector in the economy. It remains so.

The striking feature of this assembly is the absence of emphasis on technology-based or manufacturing expertise. It is operated on the agenda of firms holding badge and marque distribution and service franchises. Even GM and Leyland, despite their vehicle production pedigree, tuned operations in Kenya to assembly purely in support of import distribution operations. KVM and GMK started as dedicated assemblers handling products of mother corporations. But this changed, and their assembly operations are now on a contract basis. AVA has complained about this as an encroachment on its portfolio and breach of market segmentation arrangements.

Local assembly continues to claim 'substantial export potential' and the intention eventually to enter regional export markets,[64] but in fact it remains focused exclusively on the domestic market. In any case, export ambitions would have to conform to the global market vision of source manufacturers which guides franchise holders. The statements are mere commercial posturing. However, they add confusion to the sector. What is more, the prices are so uncompetitive that local assembly survives on state protection, favoured status and import bans. This assistance cannot be secured in export markets.

Its high foreign-exchange content means that the level of activity in this industry depends on earnings from agriculture and tourism. It cannot sustain itself. Like Kenya's other manufacturing sectors, the motor industry is 'locked into a regressive spiral',[65] as is also true of Kenya's textile sector, also partnered by middlemen rather than reputable textile specialists. The result has been a perpetually ailing industry despite decades-long bans on the import of all fabrics, a ban even frequently extended to donations from charitable organizations of second-hand clothes intended to clothe the poor. These textile ventures too were intended to undertake exports and earn foreign exchange.[66] But they slid into the 'import replacement trap' with all the attendant problems.

The import replacement trap is a product of a faulty tariff regime that does not discriminate on local value-added, or remove tariffs when an infant industry should mature. It lacks time specificity. Without time specificity, this motor industry failed to nurture a viable local components sector that could have supported the national car ideal.

All participants in assembly (except the government) have distribution interests. They have no incentive to pursue improved technology as a means to enhance earnings. Therefore, they advocate measures that nurture technological complacency such as government protection. The emphasis has been on consolidating earnings; technology acquisition, adaptation and development are peripheral. To change this requires improved institutional information and knowledge on the sector and industry. The NCP was an opportunity to acquire such knowledge, but failed in this respect because it failed to evaluate the state of the sector through accumulation of information and knowledge on the sector. It therefore did not enhance the transparency of the sector.

An opaque sector becomes the subject of obstructive practices, as we saw in the sugar/power alcohol sector. Obstructive tactics require an opaque terrain in order to thrive. Here it led to intra-industry frictions. For instance, as at 1990, Legal Notices 22 and 124[67] listed all locally produced components that could not be imported. But assemblers and franchise holders often complained about the quality of local components as undermining their warranty commitments to source manufacturers. Their proposals often argued against these lists and, therefore, their own general protection.

Legal Notice lists could be suspended only with the approval of the designated component manufacturers through their having to admit inability to meet demand. On occasions when this happened, it was observed that importers flooded the market with cheap imports. Such acts then led to disputes.[68] Government tax concessions intended to nurture the local components sector[69] were often undermined by demands by assemblers to revoke parts of Legal Notice 22.[70] Although all the parties shared membership of the Kenya Association of Manufacturers (KAM) and KMI, they often strove to undo what they collectively lobbied for; they were victims of an opaque terrain. This fray could have been resolved by efficient administration of standards. However, the credibility of KBS remained low in all sectors of the industry and its seal of approval inspired little confidence.[71]

In this opaque terrain, statistics, studies and observations made by organizations like KMI and KAM needed to be subjected to alternative verification mechanisms. NCP should have explored possibilities for setting up and strengthening such alternative mechanisms, because its success depended on making this terrain transparent. But this was not done.

THE LOCAL COMPONENTS SECTOR AND THE NATIONAL CAR

A successful national car programme requires an efficient components sector. An expert is quoted as pointing to the initial failure to develop a viable components sector as a major weakness in Kenya's motor industry prospects.[72] However, in Kenya, assembly is the core of the industry. KMI admits that the 'local components sub-sector does not enjoy a high profile'.[73] This is the result of general emphasis on final products and technology packages rather than the constituents of technology and the learning process. The industry is trapped in the ISI strategy, which does not emphasize unpackaging of imported technologies. A strategy favouring unpackaging technology would emphasize component parts development as the motive force of the whole industry and therefore the means to nurture a national car programme.

Kenya's motor trade has not nurtured a self-sustaining components sector. Even government attempts to inject life into it have often failed. For example, in

1985, the government lowered customs duty and sales tax on locally assembled vehicles to try to revamp the industry and the local component manufacturing sector. Import liberalization measures were instituted to facilitate processing of import licences for CKD kits and raw materials for local component manufacturers. It was intended that assembly operations progressively replace CKD kits with local components. This would then allow manufacturers of components to improve economies of scale by supplying existing parc, the after-sales market and new-assembly output. But the strategy failed because the sector was unable to rise to the challenge. The industry continues to complain of 'the foreign exchange famine'.[74]

There are no incontrovertible standards guiding the sector. For example, KMI once reported that locally assembled vehicles 'contained up to 30 local components, representing local value added in labour, parts and materials of up to 50 per cent of ex-factory cost'. But this report did not use the known standards for measuring local content. This approach prevents comparison with similar sectors elsewhere (Table 8.3). It is difficult to devise ways of building the sector if objective evaluation is circumvented. In any case, 30 components in a unit with over 14,000 parts cannot amount to much. What is more, the KMI presentations of '30 local components' included consumables such as sealants, lubricants and glue.[75]

It is evident that KMI devises elaborate schemes to conceal the unimpressive state of the local components sector. This, however, obstructs objective assessment which could lead to constructive and progressive measures to develop the industry. It undermines the process of clarity required to conceptualize and realize a national car ideal.

As of 1990, local components production itself depended heavily on imported raw materials;[76] it was a sub-assembly operation dependent on foreign exchange. For instance, the then sole tyre manufacturer in Kenya, Firestone East Africa, a parastatal, had its products listed as '100 per cent local'. But it is the Firestone

Table 8.3 Local-content estimates for local car and commercial vehicle production, 1988 (%)

Country	Passenger cars	Commercial vehicles
Kenya	15	
Nigeria	30	
Egypt	40	
Morocco	50	60
Malaysia	18–22	
South Korea	95	70–90
Brazil	90	90
Argentina	90	90

Sources: P. O'Brien, *The Automotive Industry in the Developing Countries: Risks and Opportunities in the 1990s*, Economist Intelligence Unit Special Report no. 1175, 1989, p. 13; and interviews and communications with the Kenya Motor Industry Association, May 1990.

Corporation's international division that controls its operations.[77] There remains little local exposure to the core business. As a result, the supply of rubber and process technology is exclusively controlled by the Firestone Corporation, and Kenya's technological capability in rubber production has advanced little since it set up in Kenya in 1969.[78] To claim 100 per cent local content for tyres exclusively supplied by Firestone is therefore misleading. Similar definitions were applied to batteries exclusively supplied by the subsidiary of Chloride Industrial Division of the UK, and other component parts. Thus this sector, like the rest of the motor industry, is import-dependent without earning its foreign exchange upkeep, making it a burden on other parts of the economy.

The local components list, as of 1990, included batteries, interior trims, tyres, radiators, springs, wiring harnesses, exhausts, seats, paint, shock absorbers, windscreens, flat glass, brake linings, filters, U-bolts, O-rings, spark-plugs (Champion brand assembled in Kenya), lubricants from imported petroleum, sealants and adhesives.[79] This, together with local wages, was what KMI defined as 'between 35 and 50 per cent local value added'.[80] The actual local content percentage must have been very low (Table 8.3) to warrant this evasion.

The components sector is frequently attacked by the distribution and assembly interests. For these, technological development is not a priority for corporate survival. KBS standards have not supported the sector. Quality faults in KBS-certified goods tend to emerge late in production and thus cause costly disruptions which drastically affect input. The poor workmanship of local components has proved particularly costly to assemblers in cases of expensive units because of guarantee clauses. Assemblers, therefore, often press for importation of finishings for expensive units directly from source manufacturers. But such moves curtail the market for the components sector and stultify its development. It is notable that the option of collaboration between the assembly and components sectors to enhance quality has not appeared on the agenda.

Improving the local components sector's 'learning curve' is not favoured by the structure of assembly, in which original model owners define requirements to which assembly and franchise operations must conform. These requirements are normally based on their global strategic considerations and are not empathetic to weaknesses specific to small locations such as Kenya. They cannot make the temporary allowances necessary to remedy weaknesses and enhance learning. In addition, the many models in the country work against the potential benefits of standardizing components and improving 'learning by doing'. For instance, standards on fuel tanks could bring down the cost of the item immensely, but the number of models in the country and the various specifications of manufacturers work against this.[81]

Innovative measures addressing local peculiarities, such as power alcohol engines, which could give local components a niche specialization are blocked because the industry is not structured to make local-specific decisions. The ground rules are quite unspecific. AVA, for example, believes that such a decision would depend on KBS providing the standards for power alcohol engines and forcing the requirements on franchise-holding importers.[82] But KBS claims to draw up standards at the request, and with the help, of the industry responsible.[83] It is a situation that perpetuates indecision.

Other than the large players like Firestone Tyres and Chloride Batteries, themselves multinational operations, the component sector is dominated by small family concerns. These often resort to political lobbying to get listings in Legal Notices rather than use quality and pricing competitiveness. There is limited competition, contrived obstacles to entry, little drive for excellence, and a rush for quick returns on investments. Much enterprising skill and energy in the sector goes into lobbying for protection against competing imports.[84] The resulting assembly–component intra-industry frictions prohibit possible cooperative ventures that might remove known problems and create an efficient, integrated and competitive terrain. Government protection has created a component sector whose products are regarded by local motorists as of poor quality, expensive and often unavailable.[85] The market is thus willing to pay a premium for 'any import'.

The informed view is that a successful components sector offers the most realistic avenue for LDCs to gain competitive entry into the global motor industry.[86] The reason is that enormous and risky investment is required for full-scale motor manufacturing, and such investment is difficult to come by in most LDCs, more so now than ever before. Second, limitations on availability of public capital call for an option capable of attracting joint-venture private funds (local and foreign). This means an option with export prospects. Components production offers the best export prospects in the motor industry for LDCs. Third, components production consists of a wide spectrum of manufacturing activities that can open up opportunities for an underindustrialized country. It allows countries and entrepreneurs with different levels of technological sophistication to find and develop a niche. This conforms to the 'progressive development' that the initiators of Kenya's motor industry may have envisioned in 1974. However, they chose an inappropriate route and wrong partners.

O'Brien[87] points out that in seeking a competitive niche in components, differences are only in specifics of participation. An advanced country, for example, would sell more to domestic and foreign users, rely more on technological collaboration rather than simple contracts, have a broader mix of domestic and foreign capital, and larger firms. But an LDC could create a sector tied to two or three export markets where its source of contracts is located and use that to build capability to compete in the wider components trade. It is all about being adequately informed about the sector and being able to disaggregate it.

O'Brien suggests that the emphasis should be on entering and staying on the global stage. This is the way to ensure maintenance of high quality standards through the pressure of open competition. It is also the avenue that addresses balance of payments. A focus on domestic markets conceals inefficiencies that eventually become difficult to identify and costly in subsidies. O'Brien believes that maximum benefits depend not on a complete domestic motor industry, but on an ability to respond quickly to, and take advantage of, developments. This favours small operations in LDCs. But even widening operations is only realistically attainable under such a framework.

Such informed propositions contradict the posture of Kenya's motor industry, but they do not contradict the national car ideal. In fact, O'Brien's proposal is a realistic avenue for 'progressively' pursuing the national car ideal. As such, the entry of Mitsubishi Motors in NCP was potentially beneficial. It would have depended on the terms negotiated and how informed the negotiators were. Japanese corporations have a track record of contracting components production to suppliers and partners in LDCs. What is more, Mitsubishi would have injected new experience, knowledge and expertise into this closed, opaque terrain. It would have gradually improved the quality of discussions and debates towards advancing the national car programme.

But progress depended on a clear policy framework. A scheduled master-plan, for instance, even if tentative, could have better informed future negotiations, agreements and proposals than nothing at all. This is what nurtures an institutional culture of preparation and information-seeking before negotiations in government. It could have nurtured symbiotic and synergistic cooperation in this industry.

O'Brien's[88] studies of components sectors forecast growth only in an arrangement in which LDC components producers collaborate directly with manufacturers with the aim of supplying their global requirements. The intermediary presence of local-assembly lock-in arrangements restricts components suppliers in this direction.

O'Brien further points to a trend away from in-house production of components by major vehicle manufacturers. They are opting for collaboration with independent component manufacturers across the world. These specialized operations are better able to take advantage of new technologies, materials and processes. This development is referred to in the industry as 'responsibility transfer'. It is difficult to see how Kenya's component suppliers can enter this new wave of long-term buyer–seller collaboration relationships with vehicle manufacturers if assemblers such as AVA are allowed to demand lock-in arrangements of components suppliers on behalf of distribution franchise holders.

If the components sector is to grow, it needs to develop direct links with franchise holders and source manufacturers. Relations transacted through AVA hinder, rather than improve, the links. This undermines the potential development of the whole national motor industry while giving assemblers the illusion of being major players, whereas the reality is that assembly is made up of peripheral technological skills. Only improved links between manufacturers and local component producers could build the required technological skills.

A terrain study by NCP should have sought to explore ways in which the local components sector could be strengthened and integrated with the assembly sector. The national car would have been more dependent on this arrangement than the foreign models assembled locally. Only a successful, competitive and quality-conscious local components sector could give the national car competitiveness. For this, it required an expanding assembly and services sector and export opportunities.

The absence of an objective study of the area in NCP reports left serious knowledge gaps, which undermined the credibility of the projections for the next phase of the programme. The lack of confidence in the projections could have undermined prospects for informed investment in this strategic undertaking. At a time of public expenditure cutbacks this was a serious oversight.

In Kenya's assembly sector, selection of partnership was not appropriate. The whole motor industry needed the injection of more dynamism and competitive spirit. In this the arrival of the Mitsubishi Corporation would have been, probably, the most positive development in the industry since 1974, but did not materialize. The sector also needed greater transparency to make future entry for others easier and to eliminate the culture of obstruction. A six-year study by NCP should have raised the level of sectoral transparency and built a database of corporate profiles of operators. This was not addressed, but the success of the next phase required it.

The culture of complacency is entrenched in this industry. It explains the predominance of franchise distribution instead of technology licensing to manufacture parts and components. An official at the Chamber of Commerce and Industry[89] explained that licenses are more demanding to administer and require a capability Kenyan enterprises have not been given the incentive to build. What is more, the dangers and costs of infringing patents and licences are higher. Franchising is thus indicative of limited technological and entrepreneurship sophistication in the industry and country. The recent admission of Hyundai Motor Corporation assembly in the EPZ in Nairobi confirms the complacency. Hyundai's products, instead of being exported, have entered the local market. The EPZ concept has been interpreted to mean Kenyans with access to foreign exchange. The other assemblers are now clamouring to be accorded similar status.

CONCLUSIONS

There are no collaborative arrangements between the motor trade and local research.[90] Assembly plants do not, for instance, turn to Kenya's centres of research for potential solutions when faced with technical problems. They resort to equipment dealers who operate parts and service maintenance contracts. These are local agents of MNCs and, in turn, turn to the mother company in case of complications. But complications are rare because operations take the form of a simple service and replacement arrangement.

This is the set-up that surrounded NCP. AVA reports early involvement in NCP but left because of 'poor communication' between it and, particularly, the University of Nairobi team[91] which was coordinating the exercise. NCP reportage does not refer to this at all. The assemblers' association, KVMA, admits to closely monitoring developments of NCP.

GMK reports 'neither being approached or consulted' over NCP, but it expressed a willingness to link up with the project.[92] KVM was not approached, nor was KVMA as an association. KMI reported that its membership was supportive of the 'Kenya vehicle logic' and that the industry, in general, and assembly, in particular, was committed to the idea of 'progressive manufacture'. KMI argued that local assembly had been 'moving steadily towards a wholly Kenyan vehicle' and that local industry 'lacks neither the inclination nor the capability to progress along this line'. KMI asked for the 'political and economic chance' to pursue this ideal. It reported that individual members 'repeatedly offered assistance and co-operation' to NCP but were snubbed.[93]

Others have suggested that NCP would have gained little from the participation of the local motor trade.[94] This view argues that the national car was a threat to existing arrangements and that this sector could have sabotaged it. A government official opined that 'ideas created by the team' could have been stolen by representatives of the local motor industry. It is, however, difficult to see how the outdated replications could have benefited this sector's currency-inclined niche market. In any case, turning ideas to products is something this sector had no experience of.

This camp has further argued that the technical expertise of this industry was not relevant.[95] KMI[96] lists the skills of the sector as including 'high quality welding, metal finish, metal pre-treatment, spray painting, precision tool construction and maintenance, motor vehicle mechanics, engineering and repairs, clerical, administrative and salesmanship'. These are not necessarily motor vehicle-specific skills and were not exclusive to the sector, but its pool of cumulative experiences cannot be ignored offhand. This sector naturally possessed insights unknown to the teams and which could have been put to good use. In any case, its presence could have aided efforts to isolate and specify sectoral weaknesses. This is particularly important because this industry does not publish true accounts of its state.

The absence of this representation, therefore, contributed to NCP weaknesses in niche-targeting. These feature in reports that do not indicate specialized or outstanding qualities to be emphasized or local advantages expected to accrue from realization of the project to, for example, the local components sector. Nor do these reports specify weaknesses the national car is to address. In failing to tap the only locally available source of, albeit limited, expertise, the Team was unable comprehensively to define the problem at issue. This weakened the search for solutions. The NCP reports, therefore, carry no inventory of locally available expertise, do not take account of, or acknowledge, any previous studies of this sector,[97] and fail to specify trends in the motor industry that made NCP necessary. To effectively inform its decision process, the team needed an information reconnaissance and processing back-up. It had none.

Membership of KMI includes importers, service and sales agents, assemblers, local component manufacturers, ancillary services[98] and leading insurance and finance companies with substantial motor business interests. Such diversity is a good source of industry information to tap into. It has shortcomings. For instance, at the time, it had no databank to inform the sector and thus eliminate the commercial posturing that characterized the terrain opacity. KMI itself argued for studies to enhance terrain transparency. Its ideas and opinions could have constituted part of the preliminary surveys required to inform preparations. Such a survey, early in the day, might have changed project focus and specificity.

KMI has Technical Committees that represent all sectors of the industry and address specialist matters. It admits that local componentry has a marginal profile in its operations. Since local componentry has been identified as the core framework for a viable and competitive motor industry, NCP could have nudged, through collaboration, KMI to adopt a constructive stand in relation to componentry to support the national car.

Informed intervention in the sector would have been timely and legitimate because of government equity in assembly and also as an environment enabler. But its effectiveness would have depended on the instituting of alternative mechanisms to improve sectoral transparency. Such mechanisms could, for example, involve creating affiliated, but parallel, indigenous technology-building institutions. These would help build an impartial picture of the industry and improve government institutional knowledge and decision-making processes on it. This is crucial for success of a national car programme and has policy implications for national information and knowledge management. An example of such a parallel impartial institution would be an affiliated technology or policy analysis centre at one of the public universities with a membership in KMI or one of its affiliates. This would serve as a bridge between the industry, the national enabling institutions and the economy.

This bridging is important because KMI has not set up a technology research and development portfolio despite the entrenched sectoral problems. Its attitude to national research institutions and arrangements remains unflattering. Like other MNC-dominated sectors, the leadership of KMI prefers to import solutions rather than seek to create them from local resources. This system prevents the development of indigenous technological capability and weakens national understanding of the industry. Local relevant research could activate the participation of national enabling institutions and emphasize the importance of components development to the industry. Only an independent study focused on the development of the national industry can reach such a conclusion. Currently, KMI conclusions are a summation of wide corporate interests. Such compromises, inevitably, address the wrong sectors and issues of the industry.

Constructive proposals could have arisen from a broad-based dialogue, and NCP offered such an opportunity. Exclusion of the motor trade prevented the evolution and development of such a dialogue. KMI could have brought crucial industry insights into the dialogue. In fact, general KMI statements go some way in isolating some problems. Actively seeking views on the industry would have only further informed discussions by NCP teams.

For instance, KMI reports that 'there are no specific and official figures on the national fleet size or model mix' and that its own figures are estimates based on 'street observations'.[99] It admits that market figures are difficult to reconcile because a large proportion of vehicle registrations occur outside the formal motor industry and because figures are distorted by commercial posturing.

With KMI figures the only ones available, questions about NCP assumptions on, for example, the state of the market became valid, which casts doubts on the institutional competence and foresight that introduced assembly into Kenya's motor trade. It raises doubts about the credibility of government policy statements based on KMI data. It suggests an absence of a defined vision or masterplan for the industry that would have required the instituting of mechanisms to monitor progress and development. This raises questions about the data management capability and role of the Registrar of Motor Vehicles and other related government departments. Correcting measures would have included the need for creating and building the ability to gather and interpret data on the industry and building appropriate databases.

The foregoing indicates that the National Car Project may not have been conceived as a 'progression' from assembly to an integrated industry. An informed dialogue would have suggested the need to set up a framework and mechanism for improving understanding of the sector and designing its development within the framework of a national car. As it is, NCP reports do not show this inclination. The role of institutions as environment enablers cannot be effectively and competently carried out in such an uninformed and opaque environment.

NCP suffered from a serious lack of information gathering and processing back-up. Coupled with insularity and secrecy, this undermined progressive learning. For example, media reports on concurrent programmes elsewhere in Africa, discussed in the next chapter,[100] did not attract NCP reportage. NCP even ignored local-specific studies of Kenya's motor industry.[101] What is more, lessons from neighbouring Tanzania, then reportedly pursuing a 'national tractor' idea, did not exercise NCP interest either. NCP did not scour the region to apprise itself of related activities, experiences and lessons. NCP tried to 'reinvent the wheel' without the benefit of existing stocks of information, knowledge and experience. It did not bother to create a supportive information-processing capacity and capability. No legacy library, documentation or information centre or database has been spun off by NCP. There are a few personal computers and some CAD (computer-aided design) and CAM (computer-aided manufacturing) software at the University of Nairobi's Faculty of Engineering reportedly acquired and used for NCP. But no information content collection exists (unless it was transferred to the Department of Defence). NCP was institutionally insensitive to external stimulus. In information management and systems terms, survival of a project with such a posture is always doubtful.

NOTES

1 'Kenyan cars for you', *Industrial Review*, April 1990, pp. 4–5.
2 'Cars that are made in Kenya', *Weekly Review*, 2 March 1990, p. 29.
3 'President launches Pioneers', *Kenya Times*, 28 February 1990, pp. 1, 13, 19.
4 'The Kenya car revving to go', *Kenya Times*, 26 February 1990, p. 1.
5 T. Curtis, *Business and Marketing for Engineers and Scientists*, McGraw-Hill, Maidenhead, 1994.
6 'Kenya pioneers local car industry', *African Business*, May 1990, p. 35.
7 Interviews and communications with the Kenya Motor Industry Association (KMI), May 1990.
8 T. Curtis, op. cit., p. 270.
9 P. O'Brien, *The Automotive Industry in the Developing Countries: Risks and Opportunities in the 1990s*, Economist Intelligence Unit Special Report no. 1175, 1989.
10 'President launches Pioneers', op. cit.
11 MIRU, *Into the 1990s: Future Strategies of the Vehicle Producers of South Korea and Malaysia*, Motor Industry Research Unit, Norwich, 1990, pp. 1–181.
12 M. Pemberton, *The World Car Industry to the Year 2000*, Economist Intelligence Unit, Automotive Special Report no. 12, 1988, pp. 1–109.
13 Ibid., p. 16.
14 'President lauches Pioneers', op. cit., p. 13.
15 NCST, *Science and Technology Newsletter*, National Council for Science and Technology, November 1987, pp. 1–12.
16 KIRDI, Annual Report and Statement of Accounts – 1985/86, Kenya Industrial Research and Development Institute, pp. 1–32.
17 Interviews and communications with the Kenya Motor Industry Association (KMI), May 1990.
18 Interviews, Kenya Industrial Research Development Institute (KIRDI), March 1990.
19 T. Curtis, op. cit.
20 Interviews with a former member of the Transmission Team of the National Car Project.
21 Interviews with personnel officers of Kenya Vehicle Manufacturers (KVM), Thika, and Associated Vehicle Assemblers (AVA), Mombasa, March 1990; interviews at AVA, Mombasa, March 1990.
22 Interviews and communications with the Kenya Motor Industry Association (KMI), May 1990; interviews at AVA, Mombasa, March 1990; interviews at General Motors Kenya, Nairobi, January 1990.
23 Interviews with a former member of the Transmission Team of the National Car Project.
24 T. Curtis, op. cit.
25 E. Omari, 'What it took to make local Pioneer cars', *Daily Nation*, 28 February 1990, p. 3, quoting the Vice-Chancellor, Nairobi University, and head of the Advisory Committee of the National Car Project at the launch.
26 T. Curtis, op. cit.
27 Interviews with a former member of the Transmission Team of the National Car Project.
28 T. Curtis, op. cit.
29 J. S. Henley, *The State and Foreign Investor Behaviour in Kenya: Capitalism in a Mercantilist State*, Department of Business Studies, University of Edinburgh, 1989, pp. 1–35.
30 Interviews, Kenya Industrial Research Development Institute (KIRDI), March

1990, and with a former member of the Transmission Team of the National Car Project.

31 T. Curtis, op. cit.
32 'Cheers as President launches Nyayo cars', *Daily Nation*, 28 February 1990, p. 1.
33 M. Pemberton, op. cit, p. 16.
34 Interviews and communications with Kenya Motor Industry Association (KMI), May 1990; interviews with a former member of the Transmission Team of the National Car Project; and interviews at the Kenya Association of Manufacturers (KAM), Nairobi, March 1990.
35 P. O'Brien, op. cit., pp. 47, 70, 72; MIRU, op. cit., pp. 84, 109.
36 P. O'Brien, op. cit., pp. 47, 70, 72; MIRU, op. cit., pp. 84, 109; M. Pemberton, op. cit., p. 53.
37 G. K. O. Tsuma, 'Next step after the Nyayo Pioneer car', *Daily Nation*, 1 March 1990, p. 7.
38 H. Gaya, 'Nyayo Pioneer cars take the industry by surprise', *Daily Nation*, 6 March 1990.
39 T. Curtis, op. cit.
40 MIRU, op. cit., p. 154.
41 H. Gaya, op. cit.
42 'Kenya made beauties', *Daily Nation*, 22 March 1990, pp. 18–21.
43 MIRU, op. cit., p. 30.
44 P. O'Brien, op. cit., p. 14
45 Interviews with a former member of the Transmission Team of the National Car Project.
46 R. Kahaso, 'Origins of motor cars', *The Standard*, 14 March 1990, pp. 24–5.
47 J. M. Hawkins (ed.) *The Oxford Reference Dictionary*, Clarendon Press, Oxford, 1986, p. 596.
48 Interviews at the National Council for Science and Technology (NCST), March 1990, and at Kenya Polytechnic and Mombasa Polytechnic Motor Vehicle Sections. The two polytechnics offer the highest level of motor vehicle training in the country, but it consists of small units in mechanical engineering departments.
49 Communication from G. Bennet, Executive Officer of the Kenya Motor Industry Association (KMI), February 1989.
50 M. wa Ngai, 'Proposed boost to CKD is two decades overdue', *Sunday Nation*, 10 November 1996, p. 7.
51 G. Bennet, 'Sparks of change', *Executive*, May 1989, pp. 9–21.
52 'The man and the vision of GM Kenya', *Daily Nation*, 13 March 1990, p. 16.
53 Interviews and communications with the Kenya Motor Industry Association (KMI).
54 'D. T. Dobie to buy shares in Leyland Kenya plant', *The Standard*, 18 May 1988, p. 16.
55 AVA, *AVA Review, 1989*, Associated Vehicle Assemblers, Mombasa, 1989.
56 'Somaia denies he is selling Marshalls', *Kenya Times*, 18 April 1990, p. 10.
57 Interviews at Associated Vehicle Assemblers (AVA), March 1990.
58 'The making of Titan truck', *Daily Nation*, 1 March 1990, pp. 15–18.
59 O. Odidi, 'Financing of recruitment expenditure in Kenya's industrial sector', paper presented at the Kenyan Economic Association's Workshop on Recurrent Costs of Public Investment and Budget Rationalisation in Kenya, Nairobi, 27–29 April 1988, pp. 1–48.
60 S. K. Adalja, 'Moi bids to plug the leaking ship of state', *South*, June 1989, pp. 29–30.
61 Interviews at the Kenya National Chamber of Commerce and Industry (KNCCI), Nairobi, February 1990.

62 'D. T. Dobie to buy shares', op. cit.
63 G. Bennet, op. cit., p. 9.
64 'Major contribution to the economy', *Weekly Review*, 8 June 1990, p. 57.
65 J. S. Henley, *The State and Foreign Investor Behaviour in Kenya: Capitalism in a Mercantilist State*, Department of Business Studies, University of Edinburgh, February 1989, pp. 1–35.
66 S. Langdon, 'Industrial dependence and export manufacturing in Kenya', in J. Ravenhill (ed.) *Africa in Economic Crisis*, Macmillan, London, 1986, pp. 181–212.
67 H. Gaya, 'Industry must be kinder to motorists', *Daily Nation*, 6 February 1990, p. 11.
68 P. Warutere, 'Motor parts importation hurts local industry', *Daily Nation*, 12 January 1990, p. 10.
69 H. Gaya, '1989 Budget a landmark in the vehicle industry', *Daily Nation*, 20 June 1989, p. 12.
70 'Local motor assemblies are full of promise', *Kenya Business Directory 1986/87*, pp. 39–42.
71 Interviews with personnel officers of Kenya Vehicle Manufacturers (KVM), Thika, and Associated Vehicle Assemblers (AVA), Mombasa, March 1990; also interviews at the Kenya Association of Manufacturers (KAM).
72 P. Warutere, op. cit., p. 10.
73 KMI, *KMI Bulletin No. 2*, Kenya Motor Industry Association, April 1990, pp. 1–4.
74 G. Bennet, op. cit., pp. 9, 11.
75 Interviews at Associated Vehicle Assemblers (AVA), Mombasa, March 1990.
76 B. Njururi, 'Sales are on the up and up', *African Business*, June 1988, pp. 43–4.
77 S. K. Adalja, op. cit., p. 29.
78 Interviews at the Kenya National Chamber of Commerce and Industry (KNCCI), Nairobi, February 1990.
79 P. Warutere, 'AVA: shining example', *Financial Review*, 21 September 1987, pp. 18–20.
80 'The motor trade transformed', *Weekly Review*, 19 May 1990, p. 24.
81 Interviews at Associated Vehicle Assemblers (AVA), Mombasa, March 1990.
82 Ibid.
83 Interview with the Deputy Director, Kenya Bureau of Standards, March 1990.
84 Interviews at Associated Vehicle Assemblers (AVA), Mombasa, March 1990.
85 H. Gaya, op. cit., p. 11.
86 P. O'Brien, op. cit., p. 32.
87 Ibid., p. 32.
88 Ibid., p. 7.
89 Interviews at the Kenya National Chamber of Commerce and Industry (KNCCI), Nairobi, February 1990.
90 Interviews at the National Council for Science and Technology (NCST), March 1990.
91 Interviews at Associated Vehicle Assemblers (AVA), Mombasa, March 1990.
92 *Wheels*, April 1990, p. 29.
93 Personal communication from G. Bennet, Executive Officer, Kenya Motor Industry Association (KMI), February 1989.
94 Interviews at the Office of the President, February–March 1990.
95 Interviews with a former member of the Transmission Team of the National Car Project.
96 KMI, Position Paper, the Kenya Motor Industry Association, Nairobi, April 1990, pp. 1–26.
97 Z. Murage, 'The vehicle assembly industry in Kenya: an economic evaluation',

unpublished MA research paper, Economics Department, University of Nairobi, 1983. Quoted in P. Coughlin and G. K. Ikiara (eds) *Industrialization in Kenya: In Search of a Strategy*, Heinemann, Nairobi, 1988.

98 G. Bennet, 'Focus on the Kenya motor industry', *Weekly Review*, 21 December 1990, pp. 34–6.

99 KMI, *Passenger Car Rationalisation: Facts and Forecasts*, Kenya Motor Industry Association, March 1990, pp. 1–19.

100 'Nigeria makes engine block', *Kenya Times*, 22 January 1990, p. 10; J. Miller, 'A car for all seasons', *South*, October 1987, p. 71; 'Mazda in Zimbabwe', *Industrial Review*, December 1989, p. 23.

101 Z. Murage, op. cit.

9

PARALLEL ACTIVITIES IMPORTANT TO THE NATIONAL CAR PROJECT

INTRODUCTION

Institutional sensitivity to stimulus can be measured through capacity to pick relevant signals from the environment. The National Car Project reports confirm a disregard for parallel activities that are a learning opportunity and the means to gather information on possible competition. This is a basic project management requirement.[1] A programme such as NCP, with its decidedly preferential trade authority (PTA)-focused overtones, needed to build capability for monitoring competitive events and reading the mood in the region.

This is important because economic and social strategies have a tendency to appear simultaneously in sub-Saharan Africa. For instance, plans to set up export processing zones (EPZs), manufacturing under bond (MUB) and one-stop shop licensing and capital markets[2] featured in Development Plan documents from Kenya, Zambia, Botswana, Zimbabwe, Ghana, Nigeria and others at around the same time between 1980 and 1990. Privatization, public-sector expenditure cuts, free markets, financial and monetary discipline and economic diversification are common agendas that have featured in the 1990–2000 development plans across Africa. The reason for this is that Africa gets ideas, advisers, packaged solutions and funding from similar sources, institutions and countries. This leads to concurrences of ideas and programmes. An awareness of developments in the region is thus an important and immediate source of information on lessons and experiences, and particularly so for a commercial venture. It is basic to product development project management. As Tony Curtis[3] explains, such an awareness allows decisions on whether to adopt, create or clone. This depends on market information-gathering and analytical capability. He explains that products are rarely new to the world, only to the firm. This is particularly true in LDCs.[4]

What is more, what appears as 'new' in the region's development plans will normally have already been operational somewhere else. For instance, there have been EPZs in South America, the Far East and the Indian Ocean islands since the 1960s. Ironically, they were gaining currency in Africa in the late 1980s when other regions were already becoming disillusioned with them. The MNCs that EPZs are designed to attract are instead relocating production facilities to developed countries because cheap labour is becoming less important in the production equation owing to technological and organizational changes.[5] What is more, even at the height of their popularity, EPZs had structural problems[6] not currently referred to in the African plans. In any case, the indications are that the flow of investments is away from this region and towards the Far East. These complications cannot be addressed by the introduction of old initiatives, but EPZs continue to be presented as novel means of diversifying economies, earning foreign currency, gaining technological capability and reversing economic decline in Africa. It would, therefore, have been strange for the idea of a national car to dawn only on Kenya. In any case, the idea is not, in itself, new and has been pursued in various ways by LDCs since the 1950s.

PARALLEL AFRICAN ACTIVITIES

It was reported in a Kenya daily in January 1990 that Nigeria had removed the obstacle to a 'wholly made-in-Nigeria car' by building an engine block locally.[7] Olympic Technical Works, a commercial parts manufacturer, had sourced the required 'raw materials locally'. According to the report, Olympic, formed in 1987 and based in Anambra State, boasted one of the largest foundry and machine shops in West Africa and laboratory facilities of international standing, and specialized in spare-parts production. Olympic had built the engine for Volkswagen Nigeria Ltd, a commercial enterprise.

It was explained that the engine was a product of coordinated effort. The work was supported by the Projects Development Authority in Enugu, the Ministry of Trade and Industries, the Raw Materials Research Council, and by research programmes at the universities of Nigeria-Nsukka, Benin and Ahmadu Bello. Such links between national research and industry were, of course, absent in the Kenyan case.

In another development, in February 1988, Nigeria's Ministry of Industry gave N 500,000 to the Project Development Institute (Proda) to be used in developing the prototype of a four-wheel drive vehicle for use in rural communities and urban centres[8] and to be ready by December 1989. The 'made-in-Nigeria' four-wheel drive vehicle was demonstrated in public at the Science and Technology Exhibition Week in Lagos in March 1990. It cost N 700,000 to build, had a net weight of 450 kilograms and a gross weight of 1,000 kilograms, and was capable of doing 100 kph. The pre-production model was expected to be an improvement on the prototype. Notable here is that the deadline was adequately achieved.

This prototype was, however, faulted for having small tyres, low headroom, a crude steel roof, low ground clearance, a fuel tank located directly under the back seat, a heavy net weight and questionable silencing. The Project Team complained of shortage of tools, inadequate staff, lack of raw materials, inadequate flow of funds, lack of technical information, and 'lack of exposure to modern automotive technologies'. A technician referred to 'occasions on which they had to bend metal with bare hands'.[9]

It was suggested that the design had been determined by cost, and showroom prices set at between N 15,000 and N 20,000. The team complained of having to apply engineering to cost in order to design something within this price range. This is what made 'the vehicle short horizontally and high vertically'. It was emphasized that 'most developed nations whose products we admire today, and rush to buy at the expense of others, had humble beginnings'. This was an appeal to patriotism. But a notable feature was the price specificity.

The prototype had a local content of between 65 and 75 per cent, which the team considered appreciable since 'some vehicles in developed nations have less than 40 per cent local input'. Local content here had included arrangement of body system, design of drive arrangement, front-wheel drive, springs and suspension, brake system, steering mechanism, exhaust, transmission, fuel line and clutch. A Fiat 126 23-horsepower engine was bought-in and 'modified to requirements'.

Commercial production was intended to reach 500 cars a day for a national demand estimated at 100,000 per year (Tables 8.1 and 8.2). It was estimated that, when operational, the plant would employ a workforce of about 75,000.[10]

There are similarities and differences between this Nigerian project and NCP. Except for the Olympic's engine, both were politically, not commercially, initiated. But the Nigerian project shows a deliberated and considered approach to implementation. It was launched at a scientific forum and the team had rational answers to criticisms. It had deadlines and fixed costs which shaped decisions. For example, having to buy-in the engine was a decision influenced by cost and price, and by technological capability. The cost of developing a new engine to be produced in limited quantities for the domestic market would have pushed up the price of the final product. This showed greater commercial realism than NCP. Producing 3,000 engines annually for the Nyayo cars would push unit costs of the vehicles well above the hoped-for US$7,000.

The Nigerian project also paid attention to the future direction and phase of the programme. Ongoing work to complete the pre-production prototype, which accommodated noted criticisms, was announced. But NCP remained politicized and secretive, and responsibilities were not specified. The Nigerian project addressed production plant requirements. The NCP reports did not. The Nigerians achieved within a time span of two years what NCP could not accomplish in six years. This project also underlined the superfluous nature of NCP's two extra prototypes and the failure of NCP to address production requirements.

But the Nigerian project also showed weaknesses. Why, for instance, were Olympic's experience and facilities not used on the project? Was it necessary for the team to 'bend metal with bare hands' when the Olympic Technical Works, and probably other firms, boasted modern facilities? And why was the Olympic's Volkswagen engine not used in order to save on the costs of having to 'modify' the Fiat 126?

This Nigerian team also considered only the facilities on site. They did not search wider afield for expertise, facilities and information – locally or regionally. A national project should, however, be an occasion to evaluate national facilities, institutions and skills.

Like NCP, this team makes no reference to concurrent activities in neighbouring regions or countries and does not try to pool such experiences. This must have contributed to some of the project weaknesses. For example, complaints of lack of information and exposure to automotive technologies are vague. Such gaps can be bridged by co-opting or buying-in requirements once they are specified.

This failure to explore around is particularly strange because Africa has, over many years now, put in place institutions intended to administer science and technology information exchange, including the OAU–UNECA-established African Regional Centre for Technology (ARCT), located in Dakar, Senegal. With a membership of over thirty states, including Kenya and Nigeria, ARCT runs Technological Consultancy and Advisory Services and Information and Documentation Divisions to which members can refer. These divisions monitor new global and regional technological developments and activities, and make observations and interpretations available on request. ARCT collects industrial and technical information from a wide catchment area and carries out global state-of-the-art searches when asked to. Expert joint facilities and institutions such as ARCT are costly, and are intended for use by such projects to justify the costs and to ensure the upkeep of the facilities. Their use would also help diagnose weaknesses in the facilities and help improvement efforts. There is also the UNECA's Pan African Documentation and Information System (PADIS), intended to support information provision.[11]

During this period, Zimbabwe adopted a different approach. In 1989, it instead launched a collaboration project with the Japanese Mazda Corporation. Mazda boasts partnerships with the US Ford Corporation and is involved in a joint venture with Kia Motors in Korea to produce the new-concept minicar with a 500–800 cc engine aimed at low-income consumers in LDCs.[12] Mazda was, therefore, expected to bring to Zimbabwe useful collaboration experience with large and small vehicle operators. This knowledge enriched Zimbabwe's efforts and influenced the definition of its programme.

The Zimbabwe car project was a tripartite venture agreement between Mazda, the Japanese trading firm C. Itoh and Willowvale Motor Industries (WMI), Zimbabwe's motor vehicle assembler.[13] It involved Z$5 million (US$2.5 million) worth of investment from Mazda and Itoh to strengthen Willowvale's manufacturing base. It also involved technology transfer arrangements through which Willowvale would increase local content from 34 per cent to 62 per cent over three years and reduce its production costs. It further involved automotive design and management training for Zimbabwean staff in Japan.

At half the cost and time of NCP and with foreign money, Zimbabwe was to get a ready and marketable product under tutelage of an experienced and reputable partner. In addition, local manpower would be trained in a leading motor vehicle-producing location. The Zimbabwe programme included a locally experienced vehicle assembler for which this venture promised advanced corporate capability. WMI was to be the focus and location around which to accumulate motor expertise, experiences and capability.

These dimensions were missed in the Nigerian and Kenyan programmes. They were the kinds of considerations that arise from having the input of motor vehicle industrialists in such a project. Both the Kenyan and the Nigerian projects excluded industrial input and gave the responsibility for realizing the projects to an *ad hoc* grouping whose loyalty and accountability lay with their permanent employers. What is more, the Kenyan and Nigerian programmes did not seriously address motor industry training, a serious oversight that undermined future capability development.

The priority in Zimbabwe was to set up an engine and transmission assembly operation at WMI and gradually phase in more locally manufactured engines parts. The second phase was to set up a press shop at WMI's subsidiary, Deven Engineering, to press non-critical body and chassis parts such as floor pressing, reinforcing panels and the chassis itself. As technological expertise improved, more sophisticated pressings would follow. Running parallel was another project to make electrical wiring harnesses. Timetabling was emphasized, unlike in NCP, and 'all was to be in place in three years'. As argued before, time specificity advances performance, supports objective reviews and ensures accountability.

The Zimbabwe programme recognized the value of a successful components sector. To develop the expertise of local component manufacturing, Mazda had agreed to extend the life of its existing models in Zimbabwe. This was to allow local component manufacturers to tool up, provide spares competitively locally and gain the necessary experience through specialization. In Kenya, local component development was never considered, nor was the centrality of the sector to the success of the programme recognized. Without a focused model to specialize in and sharpen skills through adequate economies of scale, private-sector investment in equipment and skills becomes difficult to attract and encourage.

Zimbabwe illustrates more exhaustive preparatory work and a greater sense of realism as compared with the Kenyan and Nigerian projects. Preparatory groundwork involves information-gathering and information reconnaissance. If exhaustively executed, it enhances terrain transparency and makes subsequent steps easier to plan and undertake. The lack of references by the NCP and Nigeria to local, national, regional or global endeavours and experiences indicates a disregard for such preliminaries and accounts for duplications of efforts and errors. For instance, both suffered design weaknesses. In the case of Zimbabwe, the presence of an experienced local assembler and an international manufacturer brought into play pools of information and knowledge that bridged the critical knowledge gap.

Replicating a car should not, in an age of increasingly transparent technology, information and skills exchange, be considered a scientific attainment. India, for instance, produced its first 'home-grown car' in 1988, years after independently launching Indiasat, the national satellite, into outer space and confirming its credentials as a leading scientific state.[14] The patriotic rhetoric and claims of NCP were, therefore, inappropriate and misplaced.

The goal of such projects should be to bring the enterprise successfully into commercial and export markets. A national car offers a potential niche for entering technology-based international commerce, for reducing dependency on commodity trade and for integrating the national industrial base. To attain this calls for objective scientific, technological and commercial considerations to inform decisions. O'Brien[15] points out that the attraction of the motor industry is in its being a 'technological bridge' for commodity-trapped LDC economies. Sectoral bridging and integration are difficult to achieve in an opaque terrain. Efficient information flows across sectors and, when managed by information-sensitive institutions, can raise terrain transparency and enable the fruitful technology transfer of such ventures.

First, the market size and distribution channel which this industry requires can create a basis for export-oriented manufacturing which, if competitive quality is attained, would carry manageable risk. Second, the industry permits a mix of techniques which allows a developing country to cash in on low labour costs while opening up a number of avenues for technological learning. Third, the scope for pursuing exports in this industry does not rule out a simultaneous pursuit of import substitution in the sub-sectors. And finally, this industry uses a wide range of metalworking skills, closely related to craft skills of LDCs, and is also a pioneer in use of microelectronic skills that are defining the future. A successful local motor industry will put integrating pressures on sub-sectors while positioning an LDC's economy to start exporting manufactured goods. Identification of the national car idea as an enabling technology niche is logical. But if the pursuit of that objective is uninformed, it becomes unattainable.

Pemberton[16] states that this industry demands total interdependence and availability of thousands of items at exact moments of need. For it to be successful and competitive, this industry puts pressure for total transparency in acquisition, production and distribution on most sectors of a country's industrial base. It is this goal for which the national car idea is important in economic and technological terms. Such realities needed to be accommodated by NCP.

The Nigerian project brief was specific. It required a four-wheel drive rural vehicle with a projected price. The NCP brief was not; it only required a 100 per cent Kenyan vehicle. However, a technological venture intended for commercial goals needs to bring something new into the market, something that becomes the basis for its competitive edge.

When KMI refers to local assembly products as 'extra-tough',[17] this is in fact the beginning of an attributes analysis.[18] It implies market peculiarity and a potential for niche-targeting. Because Africa produces no vehicles of its own and is relatively insignificant as a consumer, it does not develop products ideal for its needs. Local assembly patches around this inadequacy. It is the implications of such features that, once gathered, can constitute a design brief and help isolate the niche. In this, assemblers have accumulated knowledge that can inform discussions and decisions on the idea of an African car. The Zimbabwean programme was better designed to benefit from such stocks of knowledge and flows of information.

The pursuit of an African car ideal is not new. British Leyland's Land Rover was designed to address this market in the 1950s,[19] and this attributes niche continues to receive implicit references in reviews of new models. For example, Bennet's[20] evaluation of a newly launched Honda model in 1990 carried such a message. This model had won reliability surveys in Europe and was a best-seller in the USA, but it was found wanting in Kenya in terms of ground clearance, ride height and suspension. For example, the double wishbone system, which allows for a lower bonnet line, good looks and aerodynamics and is intended to improve handling on smooth roads, made the model a 'high-speed road grader' in Kenya. Such observations can be crystallized into a design brief.

A practical example of this was the Africar project in 1987. This was an attempt to address the niche. It considered the skills shortages, poor roads and extreme climates that characterize the African market. It was conceived by a British-based company, Africar International, set up by a British engineer, Tony Howarth, in the early 1980s. Africar aimed to produce a car of low cost using appropriate and readily transferable technology. It was designed to eventually replace the foreign-exchange-consuming kit assembly industry common across Africa.

The body and chassis were to be built from plywood-reinforced plastic (PRP), a tough, cheap, lightweight and rustproof material. PRP is 30 per cent lighter than steel and 15 per cent lighter than fibreglass, and has a high energy absorption on impact. The mechanical components were to be based on diverse design features ranging from the Model T Ford to the 1935 Citroen 2CV, probably to avoid proprietary design costs.

Howarth's mechanical refinements considered the constraints of Africa's motor industry. Therefore, and in order to avoid the foreign-exchange costs of licensing components from other companies, which would push up manufacturing price, Howard designed and built his own engine, transmission and suspension systems.[21] The PRP chassis frame was made rigid, durable and easily repairable, and the galvanized steel components made rustproof.

The engine was to be virtually maintenance-free with an air cooling system designed to accommodate extreme temperatures. It was designed as a modular system, with two- and three-cylinder versions that could be tailored to local needs. The suspension system was designed to allow for fast driving over rough ground while maintaining a smooth ride. Africar was to be offered in ranges from four-wheel saloons to pick-ups, six-wheel vans and eight-wheel, three-tonne trucks and tankers.

It was calculated that production of 5,000 mixed models a year could save up to US$30 million a year in foreign exchange as compared to CKD kit assembly. The Africar was expected to retail for US$6,500 and the plant to cost around US$20 million.

Africar addressed a functional niche, but the editor of Kenya's *Autonews* argued that it did not address 'the social status functions of the car' in Africa. He considered it 'admirable but unmarketable', 'what Africa needed but not what it wanted'.[22] Others argued that what Africa needed was 'tough utility vehicles for rough roads'. The Africar and such debates point to the complicated nature of niche-targeting and the need for realistic discussions, compromises and informed decisions.

The goal appears to be to competitively design a low-cost, low-technology product. This could open up access to 75 per cent of the world population's motorized transport needs. It is efforts to meet this need that characterized the formerly ongoing pursuit of the minicar car idea in India, Korea, Taiwan and Brazil.

Such technical and commercial realities need objective considerations. To do this, existing lessons need to be taken on board. Zimbabwe opted to be led and nurtured by a successful and experienced company. Kenya believed it could go it alone, and collaboration with Mitsubishi came only as an afterthought. In the event, six years produced prototypes that never saw commercial production. Zimbabwe's was, therefore, the realistic route.

Africar's conception brought something new onto the technology market. It was designed to support the technology learning process in countries pursuing a national car ideal. Africar's modular system, for example, allowed for parts of its technology to be purchased in 'unpackaged' form and repackaged in the country together with ideas developed there or anywhere else. It was intended to facilitate indigenous technology learning. Not selling Africar as a technological package, as is the prevailing practice in the industry, constituted a radical approach to technology sale. It was based on an information concept of a car and its manufacturing process as a package of information. It indicated a new avenue that may commoditize technology trade in the future. It represented the ideal in technology transactions that LDCs should be striving to attain or have adopted in such trade regulatory fora as the World Trade Organisation (WTO).

Information on these concurrent or parallel ventures and institutions could have reduced duplications in literature searches, materials-testing, market surveys and other activities that NCP had to undertake. It would have removed the need for NCP teams to spend nights redesigning existing tools and processes or for the Nigerian teams having 'to bend metals with bare hands'. An efficient information search would have revealed cheaper and tested existing alternatives successfully being deployed elsewhere, thereby saving money, time and energy. This is the economic value of information management.

It is the need to avoid duplication costs that has led countries with more advanced technological capabilities to avoid the path of independent design and production of '100 per cent home-grown' vehicles by seeking collaboration with established reputable operators. This is the option Zimbabwe took. It is also the option that has nurtured all successful motor industries in LDCs, including Korea and Malaysia. What is more, it is the way in which this industry is globally structured and designed to operate.

THE PARALLEL GLOBAL PICTURE

The global motor industry is dominated by MNCs from Europe, Japan and the USA (Tables 9.1 and 9.2). This was also the case in 1990, except in the specially protected markets of Eastern Europe, but these collapsed along with the Berlin Wall. However, Eastern Europe was not a major player and its departure did not change the global equation.

Increased sophistication of the car and competitiveness of markets has led to shorter model life cycles and increased development costs to levels not sustainable by single companies. The result is joint ventures in design and manufacture of major components such as engines in order to spread costs and risks. This has led to increased numbers of similar vehicles being produced in many countries

Table 9.1 Regional shares of world production of motor vehicles (%)

Region	1946	1970	1985
USA	79.2	28.2	26.0
Western Europe	13.4	39.9	28.2
Eastern Europe	2.7	5.1	7.5
Japan	0.4	18.0	27.4
Others	4.3	8.8	10.9
TOTAL	100.0	100.0	100.0

Source: M. Pemberton, *The World Car Industry to the Year 2000*, Economist Intelligence Unit, Automotive Special Report no. 12, 1988, p. 11.

Table 9.2 Regional shares of world sales of passenger cars (%)

Region	1960	1965	1970	1975	1980	1985
North America	58.4	54.1	41.1	36.9	34.4	38.4
Western Europe	29.9	33.3	36.3	34.1	35.3	33.8
Japan	1.2	3.2	10.8	11.1	10.1	9.9
Eastern Europe	2.3	2.2	3.3	6.1	7.1	6.7
Rest of the World	8.2	7.2	8.5	11.8	13.0	11.2
TOTAL	100.0	100.0	100.0	100.0	100.0	100.0

Source: M. Pemberton, *The World Car Industry to the Year 2000*, Economist Intelligence Unit, Automotive Special Report no. 12, 1988, pp. 1–109

around the world and MNCs owning several marques and using badge engineering to differentiate products.[23] For example, the Mazda 121 was being sold in the USA in 1990 as the Ford Festiva and in Korea as the Kia Pride as a result of collaboration between the Ford, Mazda and Kia motor corporations. The Opel Kadette was sold as the Vauxhall Chevette, the Maepsy-Na and the Isuzu Gemini in various parts of the world through collaboration between Opel, GM, Isuzu and Daewoo. This is the reality of the industry.

Product developments focus on specific items such as gearboxes or body design, and allow a particular type or model of component to be installed in more than one manufacturer's product. The increased sales reduce unit costs of such components. With costs approaching US$1 billion (1987 figures) to develop a new vehicle from scratch, and US$300–400 million needed for a new engine alone, the trend is 'collaboration and mutual assistance'.[24]

These trends contradict the autonomous philosophy of NCP. But collaboration and assistance has been forced on the industry by pressures of the market. For instance, in 1990 annual global sales of cars totalled over 35 million units. These came from fifty major manufacturers in twenty different countries, with widely differing technical and other specifications and in a host of colours. They were shipped round the world and built from components scheduled up to 12 months prior to production. Added to this was the interest on borrowed money used to finance production, distribution and selling. This is an industry that stretches technological and logistics capability. This is what creates demand for cooperation and the need for competent partnerships. The result of this is an industry that proactively seeks and uses new ideas. NCP was not proactive. It lacked the posture to cope with the realities of this industry.

In 1989, for example, the Economist Intelligence Unit (EIU)[25] advised LDCs against trying to build autonomous motor industries because these would not be viable. It recommended cooperation with top-league producers while keeping a keen eye on possibilities for exports in both CBU vehicles and components. In components, EIU identified Japanese vehicle producers as showing a greater tendency to transfer responsibility to partners for parts component supplies. But US and European companies were also moving in the same direction. Technological advances and cost minimization pressures were forcing MNCs to rely on creative contributions from specialized component producers. Such a landscape needs a capability to gather profiles of players and their partnership track records when one is seeking a collaborative partner.

The complexity of many new components, especially those relying on microelectronic technology, and the multinationalization of components firms themselves, is stimulating sharing of responsibilities, and opening up the path for longer-term buyer–seller relationships. LDCs were being advised to seek a niche amid these changes and to use local content regulations to persuade local affiliates of foreign producers to increase exports.

This EIU approach could lead to a sector able to earn its own foreign exchange upkeep and contribute to the balance of payments. It could create an impetus for inter- and intra-industry linkages and cooperation that would strengthen and upgrade the national industrial base.

The EIU survey points out that success is likely to be attained in a strategy that strives for a foothold overseas while simultaneously widening domestic demand. It emphasizes entering export markets through links with successful MNCs which support expansion of parts and CBU production. This strategy would demand improved technology to sustain the export drive and to build a strong base for local content.[26] It points to the need for LDCs to search for and negotiate beneficial partnerships. The success here is based on being well-informed about the industry and the players.

To gain a place on the international motor industry scene requires the negotiating of agreements acceptable to MNCs. This is possible only if negotiations are founded on realistic ambitions, which depends on LDC governments being informed on the realities of this industry. Although MNCs are likely to be better aware of what is feasible than most LDC governments, real success depends on the negotiating capabilities of LDC government institutions as environment enablers. These institutions need a good base of information and knowledge of this industry. The interests of both parties are best served by well-negotiated terms that allay future suspicions, doubts and frictions, even when the going gets rough.

This EIU survey underlined the importance of effective negotiating capability as the basis for a successful entry into the international motor industry trade. By inference, a successful national car programme would depend on the negotiating capacity of the responsible institutions, which requires good institutional information management. This survey argues for beneficial collaboration based on informed negotiations. For export success local skills must keep pace with what is happening in key overseas markets, and local product standards need to be comparable. This requires enhanced institutional global technology reconnaissance capability and the acquisition of best-quality technology at the most competitive prices. It argues against the emphasis on second-rate or 'intermediate/appropriate' technologies that has informed previous theories and studies of technology transfer. Such technologies can only increase production costs and undermine price and quality competitiveness. But without competitiveness, export strategies cannot be pursued. This is the reality that escaped previous industrialization strategies in LDCs generally and in Africa.

Informed realism includes acknowledging and adapting to the inequalities in the industry and the insignificance of LDCs in the global production and consumption equation (Table 9.2). For example, in 1988, all LDCs contributed about one-sixth of Volkswagen's global production and about 9 per cent of Fiat's total output. The loss to such MNCs from cutbacks in LDC outputs is insignificant and from any one country negligible, and this is even more so for other MNCs. It is important to note that the continued presence of MNCs in LDC markets is based on the long-term notion that LDCs represent a demand potential for the future. This reality must inform the negotiating posture of developing countries *vis-à-vis* these MNCs. This is because to most LDCs these 'insignificant' operations – including assembly operations – are of vital national economic importance.

Reality should inform the negotiation process and lead to a concurrence of views and avoidance of confrontation. Reaching the right conclusions requires local institutional capability to draw up correct corporate profiles. It is also important to be able to keep track of the global performance and competitiveness of corporations responsible for guiding entry into export markets through distribution channels and networks they claim to control. Many MNCs have made commitments they cannot deliver. Kenya's textile industry was a victim of such a situation,[27] and others, like that of Botswana, appear to have suffered similar fates.[28] Informed negotiations and corporate profiles would make it possible to preclude potential partners that cannot deliver on agreements or have a track record of failures in their wake. Such partners can be a costly obstacle because they obstruct change and transfer an inordinate burden to enabling institutions to lead whole sectors and industries.

Fortunately for LDCs, this is one instance when there may be no need to reinvent the wheel. Such a capacity exists in the global operations of many commercial information vendor organizations or databases. These supply important commercial and scientific information for a fee. Such vendors need to be identified and exploited. Credit bureaux, such as the South African-based Information Trust Corporation (ITC) presently operating in Botswana, Swaziland and Lesotho, can, through their international affiliations, such as Dun and Bradstreet (UK) and Trans-Union (USA) in this case, provide access to corporate profiles of major technology players on a global basis. They make commercially available important global corporate performance ratings in addition to their local credit-rating activities.[29] Such databases are updated regularly and are an important means with which to evaluate potential partners for joint ventures. Access to such facilities through, for example, inviting such information vendors will deliver access to exhaustive studies for the national institutions and improve their decision process and ability to verify reports and claims by potential partners. This is an avenue to realistic partnerships. In fact, credit bureaux, local and international, have the potential to bring transparency to the commercial and industrial terrain of LDCs and to the global landscape. Transparency, in turn, makes flexibility possible.

In Malaysia, for example, Mitsubishi's partnership role in the Proton project changed from that of equity partner and technology supplier to that of project manager when the civil-service-trained local management proved incapable of responding to international commercial realities.[30] This was a case of tempering nationalism with commercial realism, possible only in a transparent terrain where it is difficult to shift goal posts. But Mitsubishi was also required to train and devolve responsibility within a transparent time-frame.

TERRAIN MANAGEMENT AND THE
NATIONAL CAR

Pragmatism, realism and flexibility need to inform the process of terrain management. This is the responsibility of environment enabling institutions and whatever support they can garner. The Korean performance in the international motor industry illustrates the benefits of flexible policy adjustments by the government on the instigation of environment enabling institutions and the motor industry.[31] It is a case of flexible terrain management. In the 1980s, this industry retained a flexible local components policy that varied depending on whether cars were destined for the domestic market or for export. By the end of 1988, for example, cars for the domestic market contained a localization ratio approaching 100 per cent (Table 8.3), but those for export markets possessed about 70 per cent local content. Manufacturers used imported components such as carburettors, automatic transmissions and spark-plugs for export vehicles because local components suppliers had not attained the desired standards of quality. This is a case of commercial realism and a pragmatic national car ideal. It demands transparent standards and a transparent terrain.

Korea's car industry was built by indigenous commercial firms and based on a locally designed agenda. Its spectacular success is a credit to indigenous initiatives,[32] and carries important lessons for a national car ideal. It is informed initiatives that made it possible for local organizations to select beneficial partnerships and negotiate the best terms. Korea's strategy was based on identifying and exploiting new investment and technological developments. It was informed by a clarity of purpose sharpened by clear national priorities supported by a transparent environment.

For instance, Hyundai Motors opted to perfect manufacturing, rather than seek all-round motor vehicle capability. This was a step-by-step capability-building strategy. It therefore rejected the traditional packaged recipes used in most collaborative programmes with MNCs then, which were based on subservience. Although part of an import substitution policy, exports were envisaged from the beginning. Because of this, international assistance was actively sought, rather than invited, starting with technical help from Ford UK and, later, Mitsubishi. The initiative was backed by a government determined to develop the industry and also competent enabling institutions ready to learn in the process.

Hyundai bought in technical, managerial and design expertise from abroad and licensed technology from Mitsubishi, which, in 1990, had a 15 per cent equity in the company. It employed experts such as John Turnbull of British Leyland and Talbot UK and Giorgio Giugiaro of Ital Turin designers.[33] This team was able to bring on stream the first Korean car, the Pony, within two years, in 1976.

The Pony sub-compact was developed with foreign design and technology help, and some components were imported, but it was nevertheless regarded as a Korean car. This was a realistic, cheap, fast, competitive and commercially viable avenue for attaining the national car ideal. It is the path that takes advantage of relevant global stocks of knowledge, information and experience. This path was vindicated by the speed with which the product came on stream and the global export success that has followed.

Government policy management included an industrial promotion plan which gave incentives for raising and improving local content. Measures included preferential allocation of foreign exchange, investment funds for developing components industry and special low-interest loans. Technology transfer agreements signed with foreign manufacturers were certified as being intended to improve quality. They were negotiated under government scrutiny, and with the support and advice of experts from government institutions.

In 1974, the government had changed strategy and decided to promote car production as an export industry. This was aimed at escaping the foreign exchange trap of traditional assembly and also at coping with the post-1973 oil crisis and its demands on the economy. This involved switching from assembly to production of 100 per cent local content. It also involved restricting the assembly plans of other car companies in order to create the required economies of scale for Hyundai Motors.[34] Foreign funding was sought and negotiated for under government supervision and support. The management of the terrain was flexible, informed and holistic.

The growth of Hyundai thus vindicates evolutionary capability-building, commercial realism, effective flexible terrain management and the ability to react to, anticipate and cope with change. It illustrates intelligent government interventions coupled with transparent and adequate notice to industry of duration and measures intended. Such government notices were adhered to. This consistency contributes to terrain transparency and predictability, and encourages the informed participation of organizations. It results in sectoral and industry learning and contributes to the process of change. Good terrain management enhances sectoral social intelligence.

The result was that Korean companies were able to succeed without command of the fundamental areas of the motor industry production technical chain. They reaped profits from mastery of manufacture and marketing, but without, for instance, mastery of design. This niche realization enabled Korea to competitively enter top-rank production without a grip on all the basics.[35] It lit a path showing what is possible even with partial competence but full information. It illustrated possibilities and benefits that can accrue from the systematic unpackaging of industrial and technological concepts and structures, and from identifying a niche that is compatible with a country's capabilities. Such entry is an important learning phase that is useful in nurturing total capabilities.

The need to buy in capability was caused by an awareness of the need for price and product competitiveness. It required a recognition that, for example, design capability can, for some time and within modest industrial ambitions, be hired, and need not be located at the plant or at a controlled dedicated facility. This is the *raison d'être* for independent operations such as Ital and Bertone of Turin, Italy, the Motor Industry Research Unit Ltd (MIRU), the Motor Industry Research Association (MIRA), Ricardo Consulting Engineers, and Lotus and IAD of the UK. These organizations offer independent commercial, research, testing, design and development facilities and expertise for hire. They offer access to the latest developments as well as accumulated industrial experience, skills and information. Such organizations constitute a pool of independent capacity to be tapped into at conception, negotiation or production points. They are a part of the global information industry, which includes commercial information vendors and databases, that LDCs can exploit to gain international transparency and then a foothold in world operations.

It is important to have the ability to make objective self-evaluation and isolate corporate and institutional capability gaps. Only then is it possible to effectively employ bought-in expertise. The failure of NCP to carry out an objective inventory of relevant national capabilities and identify gaps that might require the buying in of capability weakened the national car programme. Uncorroborated claims of capabilities made by NCP undermined the programme by putting forward misleading possible projections for implementing the next phase.

The development of the Korean motor industry was not left exclusively to market forces.[36] The terrain was managed. It is, for instance, the lack of innovative terrain management that undermined Brazil's motor industry around this time. Despite the promise of the early 1980s, it became a victim of a national 'profligate attitude to external borrowing' which undermined export flexibility.[37] Poor terrain management led to an erratic, uncertain and opaque environment which derailed investment planning. The result has been wasted capacity and stagnation.[38] Terrain management cannot therefore be taken for granted and bears no relation to technology capacity. But it has a good deal to do with information management.

Uninformed government involvement in major investment decisions in the industry contributed to Brazil's problems. In Brazil, this industry was a partnership between the government, the largely foreign-owned vehicle manufacturers, and a largely Brazilian-owned components sector. It was a larger and more entrenched version of Kenya's motor industry scene. Such systems quickly cultivate domestic political skills at the expense of entrepreneurial sensitivity to market trends. In Brazil this industry became adept at manipulating govern-ment favours and at portraying itself as an instrument of government policy because of government equity. This ear for domestic political nuances rather than business acumen is the sort of culture evident in Kenya. It is the route with the least prospects for growth and success in technologically based pursuits.

Flexibility and adaptability are also what characterized Malaysia's national car programme. This had political overtones similar to Kenya's NCP. The programme was described as being the result of the 'foresight and bold decision' of the Prime Minister. The Prime Minister described the occasion of the launch as a 'milestone in Malaysia's advent into heavy and high technology industry'.[39] But partnership with Mitsubishi was considered important, and when problems later set in, Mitsubishi was asked to take over the management. This was nationalism coupled with realism.

Malaysia's programme was not secretive and Mitsubishi's participation was recruited early. Mitsubishi was involved in training staff at its plants in Japan from the time the national car company, Perusahan Otomobil Nasional Sdn. Bhd. (Proton), was created in May 1983. The technical assistance agreement signed required Mitsubishi to 'provide training and progressive transfer of technology' that would enable Malaysia to become self-sufficient in all aspects of vehicle manufacturing.[40] The timely creation of the company ensured a corporate location around which to accumulate loyalty, information, knowledge, expertise and skills, unlike the *ad hoc* committee system for NCP. This became the national focus around which to gather related information and expertise on a permanent basis.

Proton was an exercise in collaboration. The Proton Saga was to be based on Mitsubishi's Fiore model and featured Mitsubishi Magma single overhead camshaft engines with the intention of moving to a gradual increase in local content levels. The joint-venture agreement with Mitsubishi provided for 'adequate technology transfer to Malaysians'.[41]

Construction work on the plant began in August 1983. Production began in September 1985, followed by the government's instituting of a 'rationalization process' to prevent dealers importing or assembling competing models.

When management problems surfaced, the Malaysian Finance Minister asked Mitsubishi to take over the management of Proton in mid-1988. Mitsubishi set up a task force and sent several of its own executives to the Proton plant. They identified the problem as 'management by ex-civil servants'.[42] Mitsubishi's senior management stepped in to help with the running of Proton, an instance of buying-in appropriate expertise.

Mitsubishi instilled a more professional style of management in the Malaysian management team. Proton made its first profit in the 1988/89 financial year. The improvements in finances were such that repayments for loans were made ahead of time. Bringing in foreigners to manage a national capability show-case illustrated flexibility in terrain and project management. Proton ceased to be a national technology capability show-case and became a commercial venture. Patriotism was tempered with realism. Pragmatism serves the cause of patriotism better because the collapse of high-profile national projects can undermine national pride and reputation.

In 1989, Proton hired Stamford Research Institute of California, worldwide management and engineering consultants, to advise on competitive sourcing of parts for the car. Proton, acknowledging its inadequacy, bought-in reconnaissance capability. On the basis of the Stamford Report, fifty high-value components

Table 9.3 Proton's projected production volumes

Production period	Projected output	Actual output
July–December 1985	8,290	7,484
Full year 1986	40,250	24,148
Full year 1987	67,600	24,858
Full year 1988	84,400	42,500
Full year 1989		65,700
Full year 1990 (MIRU forecast)		80,000

Source: MIRU, *Into the 1990s: Future Strategies of the Vehicle Producers of South Korea and Malaysia,* Motor Industry Research Unit, Norwich, 1990, pp. 1–181

sources were selected from Canada, the USA and South Korea. Proton intended that the Japanese content of the car should be reduced to less than 20 per cent in two years and be replaced by either Malaysian or alternative sources. Diversifying sourcing reduces dependence, builds technology-unpackaging skills, advances reconnaissance capabilities and permits regular stock-taking of corporate or national capabilities. This need to cultivate independent decision-making and selection capability is the cornerstone of development in the wider and true sense of the word. It is information management-based capacity to define and select one's perceived best options. It is not the independent ability to re-create technological artefacts that is important. What is required is the capacity to make informed independent and competitive decisions on the choice of technology, partners and the negotiation process. It is the foundation for technology transfer management.

Pragmatism was vindicated by Proton's export success. Exports were scheduled to start in 1990. But because of the unexpected shrinkage of the domestic market, an export drive was launched in 1986. The successful entry into the UK, under a generalized system of preferences, and managed through the 180 outlets of the British importer, Proton Cars (UK), was recognized by the award of the title of the UK's 'Best Value for Money' car in 1991.[43] This export success to an OECD country conferred technological acceptance of Proton among other LDCs. African countries, specifically Kenya, Zambia, Malawi and Tanzania, were reported to have shown keen interest in the Proton following its success in the UK. The cost of the Proton investment was put at about US$263 million as of 1984 (Table 9.4).

Flexibility in Malaysia has been backed by transparent plans and holistic implementation. For example, the 1990 operational Industrial Master Plan[44] focused on the growth of the local components industry. It was supported by a request to Proton to work closely with local suppliers to help accelerate the development of the sector. It was also accompanied by a notification to other assemblers of a forthcoming requirement to raise local content above the then levels of around 30 per cent. The plants therefore embarked on a process of raising local content levels in anticipation of a planned government move about which

Table 9.4 Proton's investment costs, 1984–8

	US$(millions)
Land (donated by Hicom)	30
Building and equipment	137
Dies, Jigs, etc.	96
TOTAL	263

Source: MIRU, *Into the 1990s: Future Strategies of the Vehicle Producers of South Korea and Malaysia*, Motor Industry Research Unit, Norwich, 1990, p. 154

they received adequate notice. This illustrates the advantages of a transparent and documented master-plan as a means of serving industry with ample notice.

In Kenya, the unveiling of the national car took the industry by surprise. Subsequent announcements were similarly sporadic, unpredictable and arbitrary. This included the announcement of Mitsubishi's partnership in Nyayo six months after the unveiling of the prototypes. Such a style of terrain management increases unpredictability and opacity. In the long run it keeps potentially beneficial capital and partnerships out of the sector.

CONCLUSIONS

There are various avenues for capability acquisition. What is important is the need to keep developments in perspective. The fact that large Korean corporations, with resources and established technological capabilities in heavy industry, shipbuilding and electronics, felt the need to seek guidance from established MNCs in the motor industry indicates a recognition of the intricacies of this sector. It points out that there is more to this industry than fabricating a self-propelled road vehicle. This was not recognized by Kenya's NCP team.

Parallel projects addressed special engineering attributes and accumulated information, knowledge and experience that could have informed NCP's niche-targeting decisions. Learning from such efforts would have saved on duplications of effort and advised on alternative avenues to attaining the national car ideal.

NCP preparatory groundwork was poor. It did not seek for or build the information-processing capacity required to define issues at this level. It was run without an information management back-up and capacity and without the ability to monitor or reconnoitre relevant developments. This undermined continued awareness and institutional learning. Moreover, the insular orientation prevented it from maintaining a learning posture. Without such a posture it lacked flexibility and adaptability. When AVA made representations that suggested a possible need for change in direction, the project found this difficult to accommodate.

NCP adopted a system of low documentation, as reflected in its sparse reportage and in the manner in which conflicting suggestions were shelved and forgotten rather than resolved. Without emphasis on documentation and activation of institutional memory, decision processes became arbitrary and accountability was lost. Poor documentation prevented NCP from being run as a learning and adaptable exercise. It became entrenched in its terms of reference and interpreted them to the convenience of the membership. The Official Secrets Act and the inclusion of the Department of Defence in NCP undermined documentation and accountability in decision-making. Reports at the launch show no evidence of an improved learning curve in the six-year period. The team, for instance, did not state why it had found it necessary to produce three prototypes when one pre-production unit, as in Nigeria, could have sufficed, and is normal practice. It did not justify the dropping of AVA, a government corporation, from the project, or the exclusion of other members of the motor industry.

The absence of balanced representation contributed to problems. Without finance, marketing and project management experience or expertise, NCP had no commercial bearing. The technical teams operated without budget ceilings. This allowed resources to be spent on developing two extra prototypes and 'reinventing the wheel' without cost considerations. This was not a sensible commercial decision. Nor was it viable to define the '100 per cent Kenyan car' brief without the benefit of industry experience. The seniority of the Advisory Committee and the powers it bestowed on itself also obstructed avenues for injecting realistic ideas into NCP.

The absence of an identifiable accountable organization also contributed to the problems. It encouraged short-sighted planning because no one held long-term responsibility and accountability for decisions and actions taken. For instance, no note was taken of the absence of appropriate training facilities in the country and the need to start accumulating this expertise early. There was no focus around which to collect the experts and the information they would need to carry out their duties. There was no employer to plan and project training and manpower needs. These oversights were the product of there not being an organ responsible for continuity, or what Curtis[45] called a management framework.

NCP was unable to recognize and respond to changes. In this, the project confirmed that there were entrenched problems in Kenya's institutional decision-making processes. This prevented the country from reaping potential macroeconomic benefits that could accrue from having successful institutions and corporations in the country.

Correct institutional arrangements can create beneficial spin-offs, increase domestic competition and generate further improvements. In Korea, for example, the success of the motor industry attracted many organizations that found it beneficial to locate there. These firms wanted to exploit the cumulative national technical and commercial expertise and to use the country's established reputation for quality to enter export markets. These potential spin-off benefits can be undermined by ill-defined national projects. High-profile national failures ingrain a culture of incompetence and weaken transfer of best practices by not attracting dynamic organizations. This is costly to a country's long-term reputation and productivity performance culture. It is illustrated by Kenya's textile, sugar and motor industries.

This study underlines that with the onset of mass production, the role of artisan and craft skills, emphasized in both the Kenyan and the Nigerian projects, became less important for the success of technological enterprises. As the MIRU report[46] emphasizes, 'engineering a car for mass production is quite a different matter from building a few by hand'. Mass production requires collaboration, and this demands negotiation skills and being informed about the latest developments. By demonstrating and emphasizing artisan and craft skills, NCP failed to address the requirements for setting up a mass production industry. In not addressing themselves to the wider issues of the project, its personnel wasted time and money, and damaged the reputation of the country as a technological location. By portraying NCP as a university research undertaking, the failed exercise undermined public confidence in the capacity of national universities to manage research and, by inference, to search for and deliver solutions to national problems.

It is recognition of the dwindling role of artisan and craft skills and the primacy of information-based mass production requirements in all technology products that made the inventive Koreans start their industrial programmes with foreign designs, as had Japan earlier. It is the route that NCP would have chosen if the team had developed an information management capacity and kept abreast of reality. It is the route that has driven the motor industry towards collaborative research, product development, production and marketing and created an enormously dynamic global industry. This industry offers a platform and opportunity for LDCs to enter the industrialization momentum if they can seek to be adequately informed about it and to manage their entry in a similarly informed manner.

This is the avenue that involves buying-in expertise, hiring well-qualified staff or commissioning reputable research centres. It is the route for competitively building technological capability. It is the avenue that exploits the opportunities presented by new communication and information technologies which are increasing global transparency. It argues for exploitation and support of commercial information vending and databases. It is an avenue that requires transparency in project design, management and implementation.

NOTES

1 T. Curtis, *Business and Marketing for Engineers and Scientists*, McGraw-Hill, Maidenhead, 1994.
2 Republic of Kenya, *Development Plan 1989–1993*, Government Printer, Nairobi, 1989.
3 T. Curtis, op. cit.
4 S. Goonatilake, *Aborted Discovery: Science and Technology in the Third World*, Zed Books, London, 1984.

5 M. Beirne and H. Ramsay, 'Manna or monstrous regiment: technology control and democracy in the workplace', in M. Beirne and H. Ramsay, *Information Technology and Workplace Democracy*, Routledge, London, 1992.

6 ILO, *Economic and Social Effects of Multinational Enterprises in Export Processing Zones*, International Labour Organisation, Geneva, 1988.

7 'Nigeria makes engine block', *Kenya Times*, 22 January 1990, p. 10.

8 'Nigeria gears up for the first homeland vehicle', *African Business*, May 1990, p. 34.

9 Ibid., p. 4

10 Ibid., p. 35.

11 N. M. Adeyemi, *Reader on Information Management Strategies for Africa's Development*, UNECA/PADIS, Addis Ababa, 1995.

12 MIRU, *Into the 1990s: Future Strategies of the Vehicle Producers of South Korea and Malaysia*, Motor Industry Research Unit, Norwich, 1990, pp. 1–181.

13 'Mazda in Zimbabwe', *Industrial Review*, December 1989, p. 23.

14 'India's Model-T Mercedes', *South*, November 1988, p. 7.

15 P. O'Brien, *The Automotive Industry in the Developing Countries: Risks and Opportunities in the 1990s*, Economist Intelligence Unit Special Report no. 1175, 1989.

16 M. Pemberton, *The World Car Industry to the Year 2000*, Economist Intelligence Unit, Automotive Special Report no. 12, 1988, pp. 1–109.

17 'Extra tough', *Executive*, May 1989, p. 15.

18 T. Curtis, op. cit.

19 J. Miller, 'A car for all seasons', *South*, October 1987, p. 71.

20 G. Bennet, 'Honda Civic: the fastest Kenya made car', *Kenya Times*, 15 March 1990, p. 17.

21 J. Miller, op. cit., p. 71.

22 Ibid.

23 M. Pemberton, op. cit., p. 15.

24 Ibid., p. 16.

25 EIU, *Automotive Prospects in Leading Developing Countries*, International Motor Business, Part 137, Economist Intelligence Unit, London, January 1989, pp. 36–52.

26 Ibid., p. 52.

27 S. Langdon, 'Industrial dependence and export manufacturing in Kenya', in J. Ravenhill (ed.) *Africa in Economic Crisis*, Macmillan, London, 1986, pp. 181–212.

28 J. Senabye, 'Atlas textile firm collapses in Selebi-Phikwe', *Daily News*, 7 May 1996, p. 1.

29 ITC, *The Clear Picture on the Credit Bureau*, Information Trust Company Botswana (Pty) Ltd, 11 November 1995, p. 3; Association of Credit Bureaus, pamphlet.

30 P. O'Brien, op. cit., p. 150.

31 EIU, op. cit., p. 50.

32 M. Ford, 'South Korea: drive to succeed', *South*, March 1990, p. 16.

33 MIRU, op. cit., p. 19.

34 EIU, *Update on South Korea*, Economist Intelligence Unit, International Motor Business, Part 138, April 1989.

35 P. O'Brien, op. cit., p. 49.

36 MIRU, op. cit., p. 60.

37 EIU, *Short-term Prospects for the Brazilian Motor Industry*, Economist Intelligence Unit, International Motor Business, Part 135, July 1988, pp. 40–65.

38 Ibid., p. 64.

39 *New Sunday Times*, 1 September 1985, p. 3.

40 MIRU, op. cit., p. 142.

41 'Revving up for localisation', *New Sunday Times*, 9 July 1989, p. 24.

42 P. O'Brien, op. cit., p. 150.
43 J. Currie, 'It's Proton power', *Evening Times*, 29 March 1991, p. 40.
44 MIRU, op. cit., p. 159.
45 T. Curtis, op. cit.
46 MIRU, op. cit., p. 126.

Part III

POLICY IMPLICATIONS AND TACTICS FOR CHANGE

INTRODUCTION

Development needs to be reconceptualized, a process that requires an attitude change among development thinkers, planners and implementers. This attitude change should perceive development as stemming from, and in part comprising, the advancement of capabilities in decision-making and productivity in a competitive global village. Information resources must be optimized so as to enhance internal and external transparency – which is what is meant by information management.

Development thus calls for institutional reorientation. Those organizations and individuals responsible for environment enabling need to see terrain transparency as their fundamental responsibility. Terrain transparency supports development possibilities, as the necessary agents are able to choose informed options and make informed decisions, and thereby enhance productivity and capabilities.

Capability enhancement as a fundamental goal in the development process needs the participation of private- and public-sector organizations. In this way information provision can be moved out of the welfare and training enclave into competitive production. The training of information human resources is important as an aspect of advancing infrastructure, and physical infrastructure too needs to be prioritized, but these aspects must be coordinated with changes in the regulatory and policy infrastructure; that is, the 'soft' infrastructure.

The participation of the private sector will include the improvement of physical infrastructure, input into the designing of the regulatory infrastructure, and provision of commercial information (partly obtained from government-held sources). The private sector will also be involved in activities concerned with environmental transparency, in the provision of credit bureaux and in the assessment of global corporate players such as technology suppliers and potential venture partners.

10

INSTITUTIONAL REORIENTATION AND ATTITUDE CHANGES

The case studies demonstrate that technology transfer and industrialization depend on improved capabilities on the part of institutions to enhance internal and external terrain transparency. This is information management.[1] Information management is central to advancing the capability of environment enabling institutions involved in managing technology transfer, industrialization and development. It is also central to enabling them to exploit the developments generated by new information and communications technologies,[2] thereby assisting economic players and agents to interact optimally. Investing in advanced information processing hardware without institutional reorientation is unlikely to give adequate returns. All it does is advance processing and storage capacity. The contribution of the information sector to technology transfer and to development efforts in LDCs centres on enhancing transparency in these economies. This is where skills, resources and technology generated in the information industry need to focus. This is because LDC terrains are afflicted by a high degree of opacity, resulting from the remoteness of the locations, poor infrastructures, and the multiethnic and multilingual nature of these countries. Coupled with poor documentation, information flow, critical to transparency, is severely impeded. Development institutions need to reorientate themselves and give terrain transparency priority.

Institutional reorientation is also necessary if developing countries are to benefit from the global information revolution and the information economy. Real gains from adopting new information technologies will depend on *appropriate organizational environment*.[3] This argues against conceptually equating technology, in the hardware sense, with information content and its use. It is information content and its use that define organizational and institutional posture.

If enabling institutions do not incline towards disciplined, informed corporate (not individual) decision-making, intended 'national information and informatics policies' being considered[4] will have no beneficial impact on LDCs' economies. Information availability is inadequate without the right organizational attitude. Such an attitude requires more than just access to information. In the cases covered here, available information and expertise was neglected. The

180

problem was one of organizational attitude, and exists in other LDCs too.[5] In such circumstances, having up-to-date technology and infrastructure makes little difference. Adopting new computer technology only raises potential information-processing capacity while having adequate infrastructure improves access to global databases. It does not ensure the optimal use of the technology in informing decisions concerning an economy (which is subject to a number of compatibility issues[6]). Kenya, for instance, cannot reap the benefits of new information technologies until the corporate culture concerning information use is changed.

Bringing about such change is not simple. Appropriate measures involve, for example, rebureaucratizing many decision processes to instil accountability while at the same time instituting mechanisms that curtail 'passing the buck'. This could go some way in reducing incidences of continuing failure to use existing information and expertise in preparing for negotiations and in decision-making. Ignoring local accumulations of experiences, expertise, information and knowledge undermines learning. The cost is particularly high for economies with limited resources trying to catch up with the rest of the world, which is constantly on the move. Decisions reached without the advice of designated specialized institutions or known local expertise undermine the development as well as the accountability of such costly resources. This has a ripple effect on the whole economy and its sub-sectors.

There is need to enforce existing regulations guiding the conduct of nego-tiations. Only under such circumstances can any weaknesses be identified and remedial action taken. The practice of negotiating without a prepared agenda upon which to base negotiations, ignoring local specific expertise that might have informed the negotiation process and known government guidelines, needs to be penalized. This is a way of institutionalizing bureaucratization that LDCs such as Kenya appear to have abandoned under the illusion that they were cutting red tape. What was gained, instead, was a haphazard system of corporate decisions and actions that are unaccountable and have led to opaque processes.

As part of a disciplined corporate decision process, investment practices of institutions need to conform to original policy. Only then can policy objectives be evaluated. This involves fitting project to mission. When projects and mission prove to be in disharmony, then transparent measures to change the mission should be instituted. The alternative would be to market or transfer the project to a more suitable institution. In the cases we looked at, organizations were loaded with projects they lacked competence to manage as the projects were not what the bodies were set up to pursue. Instead of relocating projects to appro-priate institutions, *ad hoc* arrangements were designed without there being the competence, vision or accountability to make them work. This culture of pursuing objectives by *ad hoc* arrangements leads to pursuit of directly conflicting goals and undermines development objectives. Thus NCP undermined support for the growth of the components sector, and the sugar factories actively under-mined the national alternative energy programme. Both are glaring examples of national institutions subverting national efforts at advancing indigenous techno-logical capability, technology transfer and industrialization.

National institutions need to proceduralize inventory of local expertise as a preparatory step in technology project planning. This involves an inventory of information and knowledge in all forms – physical, electronic, human, current and past. It requires that whenever the necessary expertise proves absent locally, responsibility needs to be transferred to the next suitable level with guidance on seeking and bringing in the most appropriate and competitive information and knowledge within available resources. The power alcohol programme was designed without input from resident sugar technologists and chemical engineers. These skills were long resident in Kenya and were the closest required for the programme. This is what was required to inform discussions and decisions. Decades of relevant sugar technology experience was ignored. The oil companies were not invited to provide input to plans, although it must have been envisaged that they would be expected to blend and distribute the product. The national car programme was similarly designed without the local motor trade, despite its being the only source of resident expertise in the country.

The culture of ignoring local expertise sabotages local capability-building. It undermines the evolution of the national learning curve. It prevents existing industry from contributing to the creation of new projects and benefiting from multiplier effects. Broad, informed contribution, especially in industrial undertakings, is important if sectoral segmentation is to be avoided. In Kenya, there was already in existence a poorly integrated motor industry. Designing a national car programme without addressing avenues for integration could not deliver positive results.

Ignoring local resident expertise generates ill feeling at inter- and intrasectoral levels and between professions and individuals. It undermines the confidence-building necessary if a nation is to take charge of its destiny. It transfers respon-sibility away from informed, qualified and, therefore, accountable individuals, institutions and locations, even though the advancing of autonomous decision-making processes is central to development.

This practice of ignoring local experts in technology projects is not usually a result of considered institutional perceptions of local capability. It is not a reasoned, balanced decision. The National Car Project did not exclude the local motor trade after evaluating its potential to provide input. The approval of KCFC and rejection of the Okeyo proposal was not a considered and informed decision. These were symptoms of institutionalized arbitrary decision-making practices. Such practices prevent the necessary processes of national capability inventory that are essential for identifying gaps that may need remedies such as the buying-in of capability or the provision of training. Documenting, and thus bureaucratizing, such decision processes could help curtail the tendency. This is the route to building national capability. Without this, technical training will bear no relationship to the requirements of existing industries. In Kenya, we witnessed testimony to the dangers of institutionalizing practices that ignore existing local information, knowledge, skills and expertise. The sum result is that all those involved are confronted by an opaque and bewildering terrain. Such a terrain elicits irrational behaviour.

As the case studies demonstrated, Kenya was not short of environment enabling institutions that could manage technology transfer. They were simply weak and did not pursue clearly defined objectives. Poor definition of objectives characterized the two cases studied. Because objectives were not specified and recorded, the programmes lost direction. The national environment enabling institutions should have guided the process to ensure the existence of statements of mission, aims and objectives and the resources required. Without documentation based on exhaustive informed preparations, subsequent discussions used various and differing sets of criteria. Lack of specificity led to a situation where, five years into the power alcohol programme, it was being argued that its price was higher than that of petrol. But this was always the case. Without the benefit of the *threads* of previous decision processes, the programme was now being abandoned, probably by entirely new faces, on grounds of income generation. Such systems are unscientific and unsuitable for the management of a modern state seeking a foothold in the fast-changing information-driven competitive global economy. Documentation and the accountability it engenders is critical to the creation and management of such a state. It is what makes it possible to tap effectively and creatively into pools of global knowledge and information to support one's development ambitions.

Lack of documentation back-up in deliberations allows individuals, institutions and organizations to apply discretionary interpretations to issues. Coupled with the culture of poor goal specificity, this 'serious failure in industrial policy'[7] makes Kenya continually dependent on foreign enterprises to conceive, initiate and manage industrial expansion. It illustrates the surrender of the thinking process central to development management. This dependence is illustrated by projects in the sugar and motor industries, funded and guaranteed by government, under open foreign management contracts without a clear training element. It is responsible for the peripheralization and stunting of indigenous technological and entrepreneurial capacities. Here, we witness a national technology agenda designed for the convenience of foreign corporations. This is why organs such as KMI come into existence but are unable to conceive agendas that can support a local components sector, despite its having the potential to power the industry.

Such a framework leads to the irrelevance of national planning systems. Ignoring local expertise and importing packaged solutions has, in the case of Kenya, led to decades of training of engineers, technicians and craftsmen on the basis of a critical-mass ratio formulated and designed as an imported package. There are always, however, local peculiarities. When, in addition, the industrial terrain is defined by foreign firms seeking protected locations, no link can be forged between training and skills deployment. In Kenya it led to a situation where industry does not need the all-round trained manpower which happens to be what national training institutions are designed to produce. Such firms, of course, also have few skills to impart.[8]

The result is national planning that is out of tune with reality. Plan documents forecast large demands for engineers while industry seeks skills acquired on the job and complains of inappropriateness of attitudes and skills from graduate engineers. Industry, in fact, considers local training facilities to be 'of dubious quality and relevance'.[9] In Kenya, it was further observed that the sugar, power alcohol and motor industries paid scant attention to government planning documents in their decision-making processes. Authors of these documents also, by not making reference to past documents in subsequent issues, demonstrated their own disregard for the documents. The whole purpose of documentation in planning is thus unclear.

The subsequent opacity that such a terrain nurtures obstructs the exposure of human resources to best practices. This is because this terrain attracts and nurtures individuals and organizations with neither the ability nor the inclination to build and pursue competitive practices. This is illustrated by practices that avoid objective performance evaluation through adopting unique terminologies and standards to circumvent comparisons with other industries, sectors and countries.

This was evident in Kenya's motor industry, where unique measures for local content were adopted. It was why NCP reported that it was formulating new parts-numbering standards and creating new tools and processes. It is why assemblers, like AVA, refer to their models portfolios as the widest in the world. It is also why Nittin Madhvani referred to KCFC as a project comparable to none other in the world and actively diversified product range to obstruct logical comparisons.

A terrain where goal-shifting operations thrive keeps out competitive and efficient operators. This deprives the locals of the opportunity of exposure to alternative good and competitive practices.

The responsibility for setting and enforcing transparency standards and benchmarks should rest with national environment enabling institutions. These are the institutions with the responsibility to call in support from other specialized commercial agencies such as global information vendors, consultants or credit bureaux, should the need arise. In Kenya, this failed to occur.

The study of Kenya's industrial terrain over a period of two decades from 1975 shows a preference by national institutional processes for low-performance organizations and individuals. When the government funds and guarantees borrowing for such poorly defined projects, it permits them to turn to patriotic appeals in order to circumvent performance criticisms. In government equity, they get the protection of secrecy under the Official Secrets Act. This reinforces uninformed decision-making and the unaccountable disregard for existing information and expertise. The sequential transfer of this persistence in folly from KCFC to NCP testifies to lack of learning from experience across national institutions and projects.

This institutional trait is encouraged by a system of administration that demands little documentation. Lack of documentation can only prevent lessons from being transferred further afield. NCP was designed and undertaken without the benefit of Kenya's experiences in project management. This was so despite its being conceived soon after the collapse of KCFC. Poor documentation also encourages poor project definition and implementation because decision sources can be made difficult to trace, which makes decision-makers unaccountable. Thus no one is accountable for the faulty definition of NCP parameters and no reason is given for making more than one prototype. Madhvani felt at liberty to obfuscate the project by converting it from the intended goal – that of addressing energy needs – into emphasizing citric acid production. Poor documentation makes it difficult to isolate sources responsible for such action. In such a situation, KMI and NCP could claim non-existing capabilities without being required to deliver. Not being required to deliver on commitments and contracts encourages incompetence and undermines professionalism at individual and professional levels. Nationally, it prevents the evolution of a culture of achievement because achievement cannot be recognized. This does not encourage the development of indigenous technological capability.

This practice can be quite widespread. In Kenya, it is evident in government documentation procedures that often make unattainable projections. Nor are the projections reviewed in subsequent documentation. This makes even documented plans fictitious, and has contributed to a loss of confidence in documented government planning. Keeping tabs on government thought has thus entered the alternative and unpredictable domain of rent-seeking insiders and influence peddlers. Government documents cannot inform industrial decisions. Potential entrants into the economy are not encouraged by such practices. Government documentation is perceived as posturing for donors and lending agencies, rather than statements of policy and goals to be met and against which national performance is evaluated. For example, despite the high political profile involved, neither of the cases studied were preceded by references in government plan documents such as development plans. Neither the country as a whole nor sectors within it, therefore, was given notice of government plans. Nor has anything followed the intended information and informatics policy which was to be implemented in the 1989–93 plan period.[10]

This system affects the design and style of management in national organizations: participative management is precluded; government actions become capricious. The cost of listening to the pulse of government rises as influence peddlers take centre stage. In the cases looked at, the result was that existing industry did not welcome the new projects and perceived them as threats to be obstructed at all costs. But these were projects that would have advanced national sectoral integration, which could only have been good for all players.

Arbitrariness protects government institutions from having to account for poor decisions, thereby further entrenching bad practices. But it also makes the whole system unpredictable and conducive only to organizations and individuals that are uncompetitive. To widen participation in development efforts requires giving ample notice and invitation. The successful car projects from the Pacific Rim were all nurtured by transparent national planning based on giving industry adequate notice and eliciting and gaining its full participation.

The practice of arbitrariness can be infectious. In the cases studied, the assembly sector used it to reject and undermine local components suppliers and roll back local content levels. The assembly sector drew up conclusions without the participation of local component manufacturers in a way that was intended to ambush rather than remedy through cooperation. National institutions can therefore contribute to transfer of bad industrial practices and undermine indigenous technological capacity and industrial development.

Without a system of transparent notice, the government cannot recruit the best partners or negotiate the best terms. Both ACFC and KCFC were approved without overtures to local industry for input or participation. They were, therefore, in no way the best projects that could have been designed locally. They were not a measure of national capability. Nor were Mehta and Madhvani the best choices of partner entrepreneurs. The Advisory Committee of NCP was not chosen on the basis of any transparent system or competence criteria. Permitting it, without strict guidelines, to define objectives and select partners did not encourage use of the most capable individuals and organizations in the country. Opaque selection systems can prevent countries from using national projects as an opportunity to take inventory of existing capabilities. The practice also prevents the selection of best foreign partnerships; the partners in the sugar and power alcohol programmes and motor assembly could not deliver the technology transfer ambitions required by Kenya, which illustrates weaknesses in partnership selection. The cost to the country of this poor choice has been demonstrated.

These are the sorts of arrangements that cannot support transfer of competitive practices into the economy. But no economy can survive nowadays without competitiveness. Instead, such arrangements perpetuate and intensify technological dependency that undermines price and quality competitiveness. Therefore, the products of the assembly and components sectors are uncompetitive on both counts; they cannot enter export markets without subsidy. As we saw, the textile sector is similarly afflicted. These practices have nurtured industrial sectors whose ability to survive, especially in these times of privatization and government cutbacks, is seriously in question.

Opacity and unaccountability of terrains permits masquerade. The operational weaknesses of environment enabling institutions fail to make organizations deliver the expertise and terms of their contracts. They encourage organizations to make commitments they do not intend to, and cannot, deliver. Both Mehta and Madhvani took on projects in areas where they had no experience. In a costly exercise for the country, they used taxpayers' money to fund their learning. They were not even required to deliver on deadlines and costs. They could claim unsubstantiated export potential without being held to account or being able to deliver, fully aware that down the road they would be able to shift the goal posts once more. There were no penalties in place for non-delivery on contracts. Thus local assembly boasts export potential without being required to deliver. This culture of unaccountability also infected NCP, which reported potential in areas not studied by anyone, including, for example, steel production and the production of kits.

Without accountability and penalties, existing institutions have no incentive to perform or build capabilities. Instead, many evolve negative traits that ripple throughout the economy. For example, the science officers at Kenya's National Council for Science and Technology (NCST) have been accused of not disseminating information as required. They conceal it. Officers in the Ministries of Commerce and Industry do not circulate sectoral study reports to industries concerned. They file them. Researchers are reluctant to register proposals with NCST, which is a legal requirement, or approach it for advice on funds, which is one of its responsibilities, for fear of their ideas being pirated. Commercial and industrial associations are reluctant to approach government departments with proposals because they do not perceive them as being impartial, reliable or competent. There were suggestions, surrounded by the high political temperature that continues to dog KCFC even today, that the Okeyo proposal details may have been leaked to a Madhvani official by a government functionary, as no clear reason for its rejection had been forthcoming. The potential of organizations such as the Bureau of Standards to arbitrate on quality and performance issues is compromised by their credibility position with manufacturers.

Terrain management is important and cannot be taken for granted. It does not just happen. Transparency is integral to this management process. It involves ensuring information flows across sectors. It is about information management practices. Poor terrain management practices will not support new projects and, therefore, growth. They do not nurture excellence, professionalism, accountability and performance evaluation, which are crucial to the development of indigenous technological capability. The absence of a transparent peer review mechanism in the country undermines pursuit of excellence because performance cannot be openly evaluated, which encourages claims that cannot be substantiated.

In the long run such unsubstantiable claims undermine the confidence of nationals in the ability of their institutions to manage their destiny. When a nation's universities, for instance, begin to participate in projects such as NCP that end in unexplained fiasco, confidence in capability-building is seriously eroded. Such national centres of thinking are what a nation relies on when faced with the unusual. Their public display of incompetence symptomizes cessation of the thinking processes.

A lack of confidence in a nation's ability to decide on and pursue its development is the root of dependency. This is a serious handicap in an age of rapid and continuing change. Collective learning must be instituted and monitored so that the national learning curve can be enhanced between and across projects.

What is required is the setting in place of databanks of joint-venture corporate profiles identifying partners. These are formal and institutionalized systems of accumulating and activating national stores of experience for decision-making, and they concern national information management at operational, tactical and strategic levels.

Without an institutionalized system of memory to inform government departmental decision-making, that decision-making can have little impact on existing practice. It cannot prevent recurrence of joint-venture fiascos in which taxpayers bear the costs of incompetence and inefficiencies. Bringing in more institutions may not be the answer. The answer is in attitude change and in the reorientation of these institutions so they can see their role as, first and foremost, working to enhance terrain transparency. This is what environment enabling in LDCs should first be all about. The degree of opacity in LDCs can be formidable and its reduction cannot be taken for granted. Its extent makes possible the pursuit of conflicting goals, inadvertently or by design, without the irony being clear to all.

Institutional memory gaps can be improved by encouraging private-sector participation. Much government documentation and information is difficult to activate when required. Transferring much of this to private and commercial information and database vendors is one way towards efficient access. Economic agents would then be directed to these vendors, and the costs of inefficiencies and incompetence would be more transparent and opportunities for correction improved. In this direction, the invitation of foreign participants such as credit bureaux, with enhanced portfolios that include global performance reports, is long overdue in many LDCs, as is encouragement for the setting up of local initiatives. Transparency creation needs to be pursued as a business venture to curtail the hidden costs of influence peddlers.

As we saw, Kenya does not mobilize its institutions when addressing a new project. The result is that government institutions set up to address specific issues of information management quickly atrophy and wither away. This was the case with the interministerial New Projects Committee (NPC) and the Industrial Survey and Promotion Centre (ISPC), reported to 'have died natural deaths'.[11] These were institutions central to the decision-making processes over the power alcohol programme. ISPC was an attempt at institutionalizing learning in project implementation. Its legacy is an impressive case library that has been abandoned. The records have not informed subsequent projects, including the NCP. Staff at later institutions like IPC (the Investment Promotion Centre) are unaware that it once existed. What is more, they have no equivalent facility of their own. This, and others of its kind in various government departments, is the kind of database and library that can be farmed out to private information vendors as part of an ongoing, but better-informed, privatization drive. It is the way to invite wider participation in the advancing of continuity in learning. Without learning, indigenous technological capability cannot develop.

New ICTs are spinning-off yet more avenues for commercial information provision that can advance indigenous technological capability, learning and terrain transparency. The Internet service providers in LDCs, for instance, have great opportunities and potential to expand into specialized regional technical, scientific and commercial information provision business. Government-collected data and information, plus guidance and initiative, would be the core of this area of potential commercial growth and transparency enabling. The governments can be seen as co-opting the private sector in environment enabling transparency efforts as well as supporting economic growth activities. Singapore is already, as usual, blazing the trail in this direction, closely monitored and followed by other Pacific Rim nations.[12]

The practice of using formal institutional memory mechanisms remains alien to formal decision-making procedures in Kenya, as we saw. For example, the Kenya Association of Manufacturers (KAM) admitted losing negotiating capability following the departure of its Director of fifteen years' service when he moved to IPC in 1986. But KAM records, information, documentation and files and operating systems remained haphazard.[13] It still relied on the memories, experience and initiatives of individual members of staff and board. This cannot support institutional learning.

This practice was repeated in other institutions surveyed in this study. Existing information and expertise was not sought as a procedural preparatory step in project formulation, and this contributed to poor project and objectives definition. Poor documentation exacerbated matters. The faults were repeated in government centres of excellence such as research institutions. Private-sector entry and participation in national institutional memory support efforts, via commercial storage and provision of information, as explained above, can trigger this long-overdue improvement in information management in LDCs. The lethargy in national information practices needs such infusions.

Inter- and intrasectoral cooperation is caused by a need to share strengths and subsidize weaknesses. The potential benefits of cooperation cannot be realized if claimed capabilities cannot be verified or do not exist. The result is fights within, and between, sectors, departments and industries. Conflict characterized the components, assembly and distribution sectors in the motor trade. It was evident among government departments and ministries over the KCFC controversy. It exists in the relationships between KAM, dominated by MNC representatives, and its views of the Kenya National Chamber of Commerce (KNCCI) as a grouping of 'small traders' with little capability to share.[14] It exists in KAM/KNCCI perceptions of local research efforts at the Kenya Industrial Research Development Institute and national universities, considered as unimpressive, irrelevant and inapplicable.[15] Verifying capabilities requires objective arbitration based on transparent and accepted benchmarks. If, as in the case of Kenya, potential arbiters like KBS are too compromised in the eyes of industry, and other government departments lack the right inclination, then invitations to the private sector to step in and arbitrate would be timely, and in tune with moves towards the privatizing of government business. But privatization of such critical responsibilities needs to be especially informed, because in many LDCs the private sectors also harbour distorted and incompetent practices. Institutional reorientation and attitude change is a social engineering undertaking in LDCs and needs prioritization, clarity of purpose and resources. It needs to be a very well-informed process based on adequate knowledge of existing global practices as well as internal experiences. It would be the right foundation for the reconstruction and development phase of LDC development and the stepping-stone into the new millennium.

NOTES

1 A. Taylor and S. Farrel, *Information Management for Business*, Aslib, London, 1994; J. R. Beaumont and E. Sutherland, *Information Resources Management*, Butterworth-Heinemann, Oxford, 1992; B. Cronin and E. Davenport, *Elements of Information Management*, Scarecrow Press, New York, 1991.
2 R. A. Onyango, 'Information, the nation-state and democracy: an African perspective', in C. Chen (ed.) *NIT '96: Proceedings of the 9th International Conference on New Information Technology*, MicroUse Information, West Newton, MA, 1996, pp. 187–97.
3 H. A. Engelbrecht, 'A comparative analysis of the use of information inputs in the manufacturing sectors of Korea and Japan', *World Development*, vol. 18, no.1, 1990, pp. 77–89.
4 M. Lundu, 'The formulation of a national information policy (NIP) in the context of an African environment: issues and strategies', in N. M. Adeyemi (ed.) *Reader on Information Management Strategies for Africa's Development*, UNECA/PADIS, Addis Ababa, 1995, pp. 25–42.
5 I. Paez-Urdanate, 'Information in the Third World', *International Library Review*, vol. 21, 1989, pp. 177–91.
6 F. Diouf, 'Information technology and development in Senegal: the importance of culture', in C. Chen (ed.), op. cit., pp. 81–4.
7 S. Langdon, 'Industrial dependence and export manufacturing in Kenya', in J. Ravenhill (ed.) *African Economic Crisis*, Macmillan, London, 1986, pp. 181–212.
8 P. Bennel, 'Engineering skills and development: the manufacturing sector in Kenya', *Development and Change*, vol. 17, 1986, pp. 303–24.
9 Ibid.
10 Republic of Kenya, *Development Plan 1988–93*, Government Printer, Nairobi, 1988.
11 Interviews at the Investment Promotion Centre, Nairobi, February 1990.
12 E. O. F. Reid, 'Internet developments and government diffusion: case of Singapore', in C. Chen (ed.), op. cit., pp. 219–30.
13 Interviews at the Kenya Association of Manufacturers (KAM) secretariat, Nairobi, February 1990.
14 Interviews at the Kenya National Chamber of Commerce and Industry (KNCCI) secretariat.
15 Interviews at the Kenya Association of Manufacturers (KAM) and Kenya National Chamber of Commerce and Industry (KNCCI) secretariats.

11

ISSUES OF TERRAIN
TRANSPARENCY

National information policy and its implications form an old agenda of LDC governments, and have exercised interest among information professionals since the 1980s.[1] The focus of this book lies within the general framework of information policies. Information policy has implications for infrastructures and technologies as well as for training. This book is in a similar vein, but here, the focus is on organizations and institutions as information-utilizing enablers of development. The concentration is on the process of development and the contribution of national institutions to the process through the advancement of environment transparency for development agents. In this, the institutions are pushing forward the cause of technology transfer, industrialization and development.

Transparency is critical to development. The cost of opacity is confusion, conflicts and loss of direction at individual, organizational, institutional and social levels. The ensuing threats to stability can be costly.

In a transparent terrain, it is possible to keep sight of objectives and the criteria for evaluating success or failure despite environmental changes. It is possible to effect continuing learning through awareness of relevant developments and the making of appropriate changes. Transparency also makes it possible to define fallback positions and maximum exit costs. These support logical and informed project demobilization: the letting go and graceful burying of dead projects. Projects remain important to development management processes and need refining.

Without adequate transparency, policy aims such as science and technology, training, technology transfer and industrialization become elusive, and evaluation and accountability impossible to institute. At the level of national project management it becomes impossible to declare a project a failure and to let go gracefully in order to direct energies and resources to new ones. In Kenya, for example, KCFC and the Nyayo Pioneer Corporation remain on government books, are the subjects of litigation, and generate heated political acrimony that continues to threaten social order. The government refuses to admit the death of the projects and to let go gracefully because of uncertainties as to what may follow once control is surrendered. These are consequences of opaque

191

management. These cases demonstrate existing failures in immersing Western science in indigenous practices and perceptions. This science remains alien and cannot be mobilized in the arbitration of disputes.

Shifting and discretionary objectives, as characterized NCP and KCFC, coupled with an opaque terrain, give a high profile to politics in what should be a reasoned, realistic and informed learning process. An informed community learns to respect and accept rationally deduced decisions, however unpalatable. Informed argument can then be used to diffuse social tensions. A politicized terrain doctors deductions to suit the moment. This was evident in attempts to present NCP both as scientific research and as a product development enterprise. NCP teams found it politically inconvenient to admit that the country lacked the ability independently to pursue any of the avenues it set, so it fudged the agenda. However, an information search to enhance terrain transparency would have shown that the global and intricate nature of this industry did not permit independent pursuits. It would have enabled a transparent and graceful acceptance of reality and opened the way for a more profitable direction and pursuit.

Without the cultivation of a culture of informed rationality, trained scientists and engineers, for example, cannot be beneficially deployed in informing national decisions. This has implications for national training policy. It underpins the basis for husbanding science and technology in the cause of technology transfer and development, including the deploying of institutions of higher learning to search for and deliver solutions to national problems.

Kenya, like other LDCs, continues to plan for expansion in training and educational facilities[2] despite reduced public expenditure. The Ministry of Education sees the avenue for effective use of diminishing resources as lying in greater emphasis in science in schools, colleges and universities. But this cannot lead to much if the national terrain as a whole is not considered. As it is, Kenya could deploy existing scientists and engineers better. The pursuit of numbers cannot remedy the absence of linkage between terrain requirements and training output. Nor does such a link come about naturally;[3] it has to be worked at. This is the lesson from both case studies, and from parallel ones in other parts of the world.

Not all science graduates are deployed in science-related work, and even if they were, this on its own would not lead to self-sustaining scientific and technological capability. The aim should be to ensure that scientifically founded skills are applied to decision-making and the administration of resources. Both Kenyan case studies demonstrated the national tendency to ignore existing expertise and its sciences, and this is something that will not change purely as a result of there being increasing numbers of scientifically trained people. The objective of increasing the number of scientists cannot influence this arrangement.

Informed decision-making measures have organizational and reorientation implications. They demand that decisions be grounded in the logic of science.

They demand back-up institutional memory-building and procedures that inform and make national decision-making mechanisms logical and accountable. Only then can the policy of training more scientists and technologists have an impact on the economy. It will enable the propulsion of the economy in a specific and agreed direction. The failure by Kenya, for instance, to admit formally that KCFC and NPC are dead projects attests to the dominance of unscientific thinking in the country's landscape. This could also be the prevailing situation in many LDCs and the source of their many energy- and resource-sapping contradictions.

An administrative system founded on exhaustive preparations and informed decision-making, which is a scientific approach, would have led to the redefining of the goals of the cases looked at in this book. The car project would not have been presented as a piece of scientific research. The power alcohol programme would have been redefined within the framework of the sugar industry and national energy needs, and it would have led to the introduction of mechanisms to censure or penalize organizations such as Advait International and some NCP participants for non-delivery and obfuscating of contracts, among other things. This is the basis for building transparent performance and accountability consisting of accepted benchmarks and yardsticks. It would widen participation, as the rules of the game would be clear and predictable to all entrants. If the institutions entrusted with the management of the benchmarks feel inadequate, then they could buy-in expertise – but in a transparent manner.

An important and necessary part of evolving these mechanisms and systems is being objectively able to highlight and then de-emphasize powerful institutions that buttress declining but costly economic niches, despite global signals to the contrary. In Kenya these included the assembly, coffee and tea sectors.[4] Institutions supporting declining vested interests are capable of obstructing necessary change because of the political and societal clout that they accumulate over the years. They can misinform decision-making. Imposing change on such institutions can be difficult because they are often adept at political manipulation. Although prime candidates for 'gales of creative destruction', they can put up costly rearguard resistance. Implementing alternative, less popular but necessary strategies would require well argued and verifiable proposals and solutions, and these in turn need consistent and transparent rules in order to build predictability and inject stability into the process of change. If well cultivated and nurtured, this approach could bring more participants on board, and help the process of letting go and healing as sacred cows are allowed to wither away. Change needs to be accepted as a necessary and integral part of development and growth.

Without institutional and organizational changes the attainment of human, institutional, expertise and organizational 'critical mass' will remain elusive. Justifications for increasing, for example, the amount of training and the number of places in science and technology will remain hollow until such training can be

193

applied and held accountable to national needs. This should constitute the basis of national science and technology policy, and it requires a transparent terrain.

In an opaque and unchallenging terrain, attainment of educational quali-fications becomes an end in itself. It becomes the means to enter a static, though privileged, station, rather than the means to support society in identifying and solving problems and meeting needs. Unapplied skills, however, atrophy because application nurtures learning, innovation, dynamism and transparent competitiveness. The ensuing productivity justifies further investment in training and capability-building. In this way, national capability is advanced and development takes place. This is what advances the culture of attainment and creativity. It is the way to weaning society off dependency on fortuitous gifts of nature and aid or grants and on to the creation of wealth.

Without challenge, the rules and standards of attainment become unpre-dictable and subject to political tinkering. This nurtures conflicts as competition for sharing limited and dwindling resources (the 'national cake') heats up. It allows unverifiable claims of the kind witnessed in the cases studied. Such culture does not nurture competitive practices, but obstructive practices and influence-peddling, whereas indigenous technological capability and technology transfer depend on competitive practices applicable in the global village.

The alternative, as we have seen, is a technological terrain marred by contradictions. It is a terrain of qualified and informed individuals associated with institutions that display appalling incompetence in decision-making and action. Knowledge and technological capability do not reflect the resources put into undertakings. Such are the gaps that undermine advancement of national capability.

In an opaque terrain, contradictions and gaps in the economy prove difficult both to identify and to bridge. For instance, it is thought that in Kenya, those with the means to venture into technology-based enterprises lack the technical, and entrepreneurial, capability and inclination to do so, whereas those with capability lack the resources. In the prevailing opacity, however, the country cannot devise bridging mechanisms because the extent and nature of this gap, if it exists at all, are indeterminable as individuals and institutions persist in making claims which, without accepted mechanisms for evaluation and arbitra-tion, cannot be verified. The opacity obstructs possibilities for arbitrating this terrain.

Transparency can contribute to such bridging. It would make possible communication and cooperation across capability gaps. Observations from the Pacific Rim, for instance, highlight innovative ways of bringing capital, skills and needs organically and synergistically together. Such engineering requires a transparent terrain.

Information on terrain realities encourages the practice of informed preparation. But informed preparation requires being apprised of the latest developments. This calls for the service of expertise, which must be immediately available in order to identify and highlight the gaps. Cultivating such expertise is one way of allowing experts and specialist institutions, for example, an entry into Kenya's technology transfer equation. It is an avenue that requires knowledge to be informed and constantly updated. It is based on continuous learning and would, therefore, support the development of indigenous technological capability.

Kenya exemplifies a commercial terrain dominated by import/export licences and replication of consumer goods. Institutions that should guide and lead change towards technology-focused ventures have not cultivated the capability or orientation to do so. The NCP illustrated this lack of inclination. The result is technically capable individuals underutilized or misdeployed and their expensively acquired skills wasted. Until a bridge can be engineered between capacity and resources, this vicious circle will continue.

This is the vicious circle that directs pent-up entrepreneurial energies and skills towards political intrigue instead of the designing of competitive products and services. When entrenched, these skills become obstacles to change and the evolution of a transparent and competitive terrain. Transparency becomes a threat to the *status quo*. Signals and information on markets, for instance, become deliberately distorted so as to enhance opacity and, therefore, fees for delivering a degree of transparency through contacts. This is the basis of influence-peddling. Obstruction and distortion of information flow become the means to serve vested interests. Rent-seeking for terrain transparency services becomes the occupation of the well-connected. This is influence-peddling. The economy becomes unproductive, stagnates and then declines. It is the recipe for the social disquiet and internecine conflicts marking much of sub-Saharan Africa's entry into the next millennium.

Inventing opacity is illustrated by the way in which the sugar and oil industries misinformed negotiations with KCFC, by the way in which KMI distorted signals on the motor trade, and by the way in which NCP reportage evaded market issues that would have cast doubt on the project. National institutions set up to transact information and signals between markets, consumers and industry have failed to correct these signals. Bringing in more experienced commercial information vendors into this equation could curtail and roll back the momentum of this opacity, and would be a positive step.

For instance, import/export commerce depends on government licences. Information barriers have become a means of raising revenue through economic rents. The opacity generated by government bureaucracies has created enterprising middle-men who 'raise' terrain transparency for a fee. This is not a simple case of corruption. It is the result of a stagnant and closed terrain in which the absence of challenge leads to misdirection of energies and skills away from the generation, and towards the skimming, of surplus. This is the spirit that is captured in the motto of 'sharing the national cake'. It underpins the decision of the clerk in a government department who conceals applications and files or a science secretary who refuses to circulate UN reports. They are the results of an unchallenging, unrewarding and opaque terrain that has failed to call its institutions to account and does not inspire the active participation of its skilled and specialized manpower. This tendency can be curtailed only by introducing more arbitration in the terrain, which can be brought about by having more information vendors, supported and supplied by data collected and held by government department and institutions.

The alternative is that one risks perpetuating an environment that does not inspire institutions to nurture the conceptual skills required to unpackage technologies. The Pacific Rim illustrates the benefits to industry that can accrue from institutions that inspire and effectively deploy its specialized personnel.

The Africar project demonstrated technological possibilities opened by conceptual skills that unpackage technology and that can back negotiating for technology purchases. The absence of this conceptual ability undermines possibilities for commoditizing technology trade. But it is only under such a framework that the various unpackaged parts of a technology can be identified and negotiations for the best terms for the parts considered. Bargaining capability and its development need to be founded on competence. But competence can only be cultivated in an inspired and purposeful workforce, which can be achieved only in a transparent terrain with clear rules of recognition and reward for exertion and excellence. This is the basis for arguing that effective technology transfer in LDCs will depend on each country's ability to mobilize and inspire its information workforce, institutions and organizations (private and public) to perceive terrain transparency as a priority in the pursuit of development.

NOTES

1 M. C. Lundu, 'The formulation of a national information policy (NIP) in the context of an African environment: issues and strategies', in N. M. Adeyemi (ed.) *Reader on Information Management Strategies for Africa's Development*, UNECA/PADIS, Addis Ababa, 1995, pp. 25–42; K. J. Mchombu, 'The cultural and political dimensions of information resources management in Africa', in N. M. Adeyemi (ed.), op. cit., pp. 103–24.
2 'The numbers crunch', *Weekly Review*, 27 April 1990, pp. 4–16.
3 S. Goonatilake, *Aborted Discovery: Science and Technology and the Third World*, Zed Books, London, 1984.
4 'Focus on coffee growing: the most valuable of our exports', *Weekly Review*, 3 August 1990, pp. 41–3.

12

TACTICS FOR CHANGE

INTRODUCTION

The cost of underdevelopment is high. Other than the pain and misery of deprivation juxtaposed against global wealth, there is the hopelessness and perplexity of the perpetual decline that faces regions like sub-Saharan Africa. This despair is spinning-off new trouble-spots that threaten to afflict it into the new millennium, including Liberia and Sierra Leone in West Africa and the Horn and Great Lakes region in East and Central Africa. Such trouble-spots could multiply unless hope can be reclaimed. They are the result of economic decline speeded up by the disappearance of the Cold War dividend that succoured these uneconomic entities and inept systems of government.[1]

The end of the Cold War and the onset of multi-party democracy exposed the illusions of capability. Over a generation has been wasted in pursuit of various development mirages.[2] Regions like this illustrate the need for autonomous decision-making capability in defining development options and direction. This is not autarky. It refers to the capability to address one's options realistically, and select and adapt what relates best to one's circumstances and sustainable capability-building. It therefore requires an objective evaluation of abilities as well as of what the world offers. Such an undertaking depends on objective, consistent and transparent mechanisms for measuring abilities and similar mechanisms that enhance the transparency of the landscape being dealt with. To develop such mechanisms requires information management skills, in order to support the ability to competitively identify and navigate entry into one's niche within the global village.

The global development agenda faces urgent and distracting problems. These require autonomous decision-making capabilities, as no two communities can be replicas of one another. Development needs to be viewed as the process in which a society or nation-state undergoes *change* in its structures by quantitative and qualitative improvements through promotion of higher levels of capabilities on the part of its peoples, institutions and production units.[3] Change is occasioned by internal and external realities and the need to be productive and competitive. It is about advancing the capacity of the society or nation to enable it to enjoy autonomous participation in the productive activities of the international community, which enables it to benefit from the international division of labour. This division is founded on comparative advantages, both natural advantages and those resulting from human activity. It is at the level of the latter that autonomous decision-making and creativity are called for. It is also the point of realistic competitiveness as natural advantages are frequently overtaken by new entrants and players, alternative substitutes, and changing demands and tastes. Therefore, the development process and capability of nation-states will be determined by their capacity to identify, acquire, assimilate, adapt, improve and contribute to the creation of scientific and technological information and knowledge, and to use it efficiently to further productive activities. This is the realistic landscape that LDCs have to reckon with. This landscape demands constant internal changes and adaptations, the decisions concerning which must be based on a realistic assessment of capabilities. It is also a landscape whose future is increasingly being determined by the ability of nation-states to exploit the opportunities being opened up by new information and communications technologies (ICTs).[4]

EXISTING REALITIES

Most LDCs, especially those of sub-Saharan Africa, have to reckon with social heterogeneity which, unless creatively addressed, may obstruct the capability to exploit the opportunities of the new ICTs. Poor information and communications infrastructures are another problem. They include the physical and the regulatory and procedural (policy) aspects. The emphasis on the hard (physical) without concurrent emphasis on the soft, or policy, aspects has led to sub-optimal exploitation of the former. The two need adequate attention and resources.

In sub-Saharan Africa, for instance, the emphasis on physical infrastructure failed to cement a heterogeneous society because the soft and intangible infrastructure was not given adequate attention and resources. It never developed to the extent and degree required to enable it to deliver the necessary creativity of commonness and unity in diversity that hold together socially diverse nation-states. Much that was assumed did not take place. Sophisticated systems of policies, procedures, rules and information, and human resources are required to hold together a society that has glaring differences and that is now at liberty to express such differences. This is more so than with authoritarian or conqueror–subject arrangements.

LDCs' efforts at capability-building must also reckon with the potential devastation of HIV/AIDS. Whereas the resources necessary for a curative solution are beyond the reach of most LDCs, the social engineering responsibility required to curtail the spread must rest with each state and its enabling institutions. There is, however, a noticeable tendency for many LDCs to leave the responsibility for conceiving and designing safe social behaviour strategies to developed-country institutions from which blueprints are traditionally sourced. Such dependency, even in the face of a life-threatening phenomenon, reflects a serious dereliction of responsibility on the part of national environment enabling institutions.

This posture is dangerous because of the challenges yet to be faced. These challenges include the advent of multi-party democracy which dawned with the end of the Cold War. Expressions of alternative views and articulation of differences (ethnic, religious and race) are now *de rigueur*. National environment enabling institutions have to design ways of dealing with this. Past methods of denial and coercion failed. Nation-state survival will depend on innovative solutions. In this, the centres of national thinking will need to be recruited. Institutional memories in the search for solutions will need to look at experiences and experiments far and wide.

The end of the Cold War has also brought a unipolar global power structure. Closely related to this are falling levels of grants and aid, tighter public-sector spending, rigorous financial discipline and, generally, cash-strapped governments. Waiting for blueprints to adopt, as is now the case, does not augur well in such a landscape. The ongoing World Bank/IMF-led and -funded public-sector retrenchments may not be the cure for institutions that were never designed or oriented towards enabling development. Containment is not development because it obstructs possibilities for necessary change. Change will call for internal engineering within a context of existing realities. Packaged solutions of retrenchments can only sow seeds of future social problems.

Another closely related reality is the entry of non-governmental organizations (NGOs) in the development arena as alternative conductors (alternative to government, that is) of development.[5] Governments addicted to aid or grants have reacted unhappily to this new competition for development funding and orchestration. But this should be a period of creativity and innovation on the part of national enabling institutions, especially as autarky, now more than before, is not a viable alternative for most. New infusions are an opportunity for exchange, learning and improvement.

It is in this landscape that we need to place the potential of the new ICTs and what they can deliver. It holds promise for those able to be creative, and willing to reconceptualize development as change made possible only by enhanced internal and external transparency. This is information-based development.

We look at some of the possibilities opened and relate these to the under-development peculiarities brought out by the cases studied.

SOME CANDIDATE ISSUES

New ICTs are opening up the world and bringing home the reality of the interdependent global village. This requires that internal strategies take on board concurrent and parallel developments on a global level. It is a reality that needs to be addressed, and it demands an attitude change among environment enabling institutions. But these institutions are directed by political structures. Therefore, the three decades of wasted effort in regions such as sub-Saharan Africa must be visited on the political corridors. The waste is attributable to poor politics and government. This is where the 'xenophilia' illustrated by the enthusiasm for everything imported was conceived. Either by design or default, it served to curtail room for transparency and accountability because foreign packages remained mysterious. It created dependency. But dependency is addictive and gained a momentum of its own. It eventually became necessary to obstruct national and indigenous thinking processes. Censorship, proscriptions of professional and academic associations, and propaganda and media control followed. These were short-sighted efforts at denial, and failed. In this phase of multi-party democracy and reconstruction, it is important to reinstate the culture of autonomous thinking and free expression. It is coming in as part of multi-party democracy. The journey, however, is a slow and painstaking one because the institutions of containment find it difficult to change and mend their ways.

As the processes of legislation to institutionalize change crank sluggishly into motion, it is important to take advantage of new ICTs formally and informally to open up space for free and constructive expression in the search for solutions. Resistance should be expected and taken on board.[6] But there is a positive global movement and a concurrence of opinion in business, science and academia that can overcome such hitches. Facilities such as the Internet will need to be exploited by the better-endowed centres and organizations to engineer innovatively, and in a multidisciplinary way, alternative paradigms of development. This is because, at the immediate level, they are a means to transcend censorships and restrictions on travel and gathering,[7] as well as the prohibitive costs of coming together caused by the declining economies. This can be achieved through such arrangements as informal or invisible colleges and campuses, and the Internet and World Wide Web (WWW).

Multi-party politics is bringing in its wake a new breed of politician. Although still sensitive to public criticism, the WWW on the Internet offers a forum for exchange of views between politician, senior civil servant and others away from the direct glare of publicity that politicians in LDCs prefer to hog. The enthusiasm with which, for instance, political parties and provincial and local governments are setting up web sites in the new South Africa illustrates possibilities for wider dialogue among LDCs using ICTs. This facility away from immediate public attention is important. In the past, alternative ideas have been nipped in the bud before they could be nurtured, tested and rounded off. This could be an opportunity for wider recruitment into the exchange of ideas, especially before the other avenues of multi-party politics become a normality. ICTs are thus an opportunity to expand space for the thinking process as well as widening recruitment into participation.

On the immediate front, NGOs are, if they can stay on course and immune from the infection of incompetence and capricious decision-making processes, a potential source and forum for demonstrating good practices in project development and management. Unfortunately, many are already showing symptoms of authoritarianism, simplicity and the culture of hoodwinking donors that characterizes government methods.[8] However, such symptoms are not widespread as yet. Many NGOs are able, for instance, to inculcate in young graduands the sort of culture of accountable and responsible decision-making and actions that has long been stunted by the anonymity of the public sector. What is more, new graduands are called upon to apply their skills before they atrophy. Training institutions thus have an opportunity to evaluate the competence of their output early enough to take remedial action if required. In the public sector, people reach decision-making positions long after their professional skills have atrophied.

NGOs can also contribute to advancement of alternative thoughts regarding the development process. Alternative thinking has been penalized through programmes that deprived non-conforming regions and individuals of resources. This still happens. If NGOs can pursue development programmes based on need alone, and resist government pressures to follow their cue, they could water down the intimidatory posture that has been so effective in snuffing out alternative thinking processes. But this will require that they be weaned off the prioritizing of high-profile locations and programmes that impress donors – because this is what governments did. Already much NGO activity is restricted to urban centres where their personnel can be at the 'right cocktail parties and next to the right people'.[9]

NGOs have potential as environment enabling institutions. They gather important data for their projects which, if shared, can support terrain transparency. Governments of LDCs have tended to distort data to suit political ends. This has added to the opacity of terrain. It is no wonder therefore that across the breadth and width of sub-Saharan Africa, no valid census data have been forthcoming for the past decade and a half. Census data are, however, critical to basic planning. To be partners and alternatives in the transparency efforts of national environment enabling institutions is a big responsibility. It is particularly so now because cash-strapped governments perceive NGOs as competitors for donor resources. It is therefore tempting for NGOs, and donors, to placate governments by accommodating demands by administrators to conceal data. A number are acceding to these pressures as a small price to pay for completing projects. But this is a myopic convenience. It is in everybody's interest, including governments', that single-solution approaches be done away with. Three wasted decades is a high enough price to pay. It is now of utmost importance that there be more than one player in the environment enabling plane and especially in the advancement of transparency.

This has wide implications. It includes avoiding cosy lock-in arrangements into 'good projects' or 'good consultants'. Innovation demands open minds and the constant search for new ideas and alternatives. In this, NGOs represent an opportunity for alternative technology acquisition and adaption methods and procedures. NGOs, as a result of the size of their projects and resources, have the incentive to unpackage technologies, source them widely and take inventory of local capabilities for installation, maintenance and sustenance objectives. Through their global network of associations, NGOs can access various well-inclined technology vendors such as the Intermediate Technology Development Group (ITDG) and others. As enablers, NGOs are well placed to support technology diffusion processes using SMMEs (small, medium and micro enterprises) as vehicles for the process. Many have SMME development in their portfolio. SMMEs are, at least for the moment, the only viable means for supporting efficient and competitive technology diffusion in LDCs. In this endeavour, NGOs have a great potential role to play in technology transfer and economic development of LDCs if they can evade the pervasive, infectious pitfalls.

Attitude change is also important at the level of donors, multilateral and bilateral agencies and financiers. This includes the Bretton Woods institutions (the World Bank and IMF). An opaque terrain confuses everybody and allows claims that cannot be verified. All stake-holders in development need to prioritize terrain transparency as an objective. Whereas transparency and good government is a rallying call of many of these institutions, their focus appears misplaced. It should not be transparency to donor and funding agencies only, but to all nationals, institutions and economic players – including NGOs. Otherwise, the already alienated governments use demands for transparency as scapegoats for the scrapping of any semblance of welfare programmes, such as education and health, which they had already run down and which should, in any case, have been funded from internally generated resources. Governments should be required, as a matter of course, to share as much of the data they collect as possible with alternative environment enabling institutions and agents, including commercial information vendors, NGOs, the spin-offs of the ICTs and the Web, and other interested organizations such as professional associations and chambers of commerce. The legal framework for data and information management such as statistical and disclosure legislation needs to be amended accordingly. Transparency for development should not be left to any one player.

In addition to such acts being in support of potentially new areas of employment and growth, enhanced transparency will make it possible for more economic agents to enter into productive ventures. As it is, opacity is prohibiting and ties resources to the secure, but less productive, sectors of real estate and land speculation. This weakens economic growth prospects.

There needs to be collective effort aimed at designing national information management policies. It has to be collective because there are many vested interests and beneficiaries in opacity. Rent-seeking activities such as influence-peddling depend on an opaque terrain. Transparency efforts must encompass donor and financial agencies, NGOs, and business consortia and syndicates. They are to the long-term good of everybody. A competitive location is attractive to local and foreign investment. An opaque terrain is uncompetitive and forbidding to dynamic organizations. The spin-off from a lack of competitiveness is evident in sub-Saharan Africa. Getting out of that vicious circle is in everybody's interest, including that of governments still suffering from afflictions of one-party Cold War dividends and non-accountable aid or grants. Such efforts need to begin over a wide participative framework. Exploiting the WWW and the Internet as well as seminars and workshops is one way. This is because many individuals and organizations will need to change their practices, and for this reason they need notice of what is forthcoming. Blueprints brought into national treasuries as public-sector retrenchments and privatization by World Bank/IMF experts can only have enclave impact, as has been the case with other blueprints.

Transparency is a comprehensive issue. It cannot be sectoral or enclave-focused. The fact that in countries with a higher tradition of transparency, such as Botswana, the activities of a credit bureau like the Information Trust Company can raise strong sentiments in Parliament[10] attests to what can be expected in an opaque culture like that of Kenya. This marks the seriousness with which the task involved in terrain transparency needs to be undertaken. Resources must, therefore, be up to the task.

For sub-Saharan Africa, fighting transparency could be highlighting something fundamental in prevailing attitudes to Western science, technology and productivity. Cultural differences in information management have been brought out in various past studies.[11] For Africa, these issues seem to run deeper. They appear to be underpinned by the uncomfortable juxtaposing of Western science to indigenous science without any effort at engineering an organic accommodation, as was witnessed in Japan and, later, in the Pacific Rim. This can partially explain why projects such as the ones studied here, which according to a Western scientific outlook (including financial management) would be considered dead, remain alive and exercise much emotion in Africa.[12]

There is a need for such disciplines as anthropology, sociology and information science to begin to address how this science can be acceptably and productively integrated into African life so that it can arbitrate over some of the social disruptions it brings in its wake. It is important that, in the tradition of the Pacific Rim, Africa finds its own accommodation with Western science and its rules of productivity, costs and competitiveness. The price of this unresolved arrangement is conflict that is making a murky terrain impossible to comprehend. Seeking innovative answers must include the search for ways of integrating Western science into African life. The assumption, prevalent since colonial times, that African science would wither away has proved false. However, it is Western science that continues to set the rules of global competitiveness. It needs to be harnessed and immersed into indigenous perceptions and approaches to productivity. The Botswana National Productivity Centre (BNPC)[13] is carrying out a study in that direction. Other African countries need to address it too. A harmonious national consensus in dealing with this reality is called for, but it needs to be conceived by Africa's centres of thinking. In this, a better understanding of how the Far East addressed this process is an important start. It is notable that this region has exercised little interest in these centres – until, of course, the Western institutions started looking in that direction. But these new studies will need a more localized centrism different from the Eurocentrism that colours current studies.

In these efforts, existing and potential infrastructures will be critical. In Nigeria, it is reported that a private consortium of educationists and business offered to upgrade the country's telecommunications infrastructure to take advantage of the competitiveness offered by the Internet.[14] The consortium considered itself disadvantaged compared to international competitors. This illustrates a growing convergence of opinion that ICTs are the determinants of future competitiveness. Even Africa's politicians, in general terms, have agreed.[15]

The infrastructure will need to be improved and enhanced if the development process is to take advantage of global pools of experience, information and knowledge on science, technologies and development. That infrastructure consists of hardware, regulatory and procedural, and the information human resources. The hardware infrastructure of telecommunications and communications is not of the required standard. There are efforts to improve on this, and a consensus on the need for improvement. Constructions like Africa One, the largest undersea fibre-optic cable network conceived, will improve on the Panaftel high-capacity microwave radios and the Rascom connectivity projects.[16] Infrastructures also include libraries, databases, archives and records centres, and newswire organizations, plus mass media and broadcasting. They include organizations that collect and disseminate data, information, news and productivity standards, and those responsible for coordinating and training human resources and creativity such as intellectual property managers. These organizations exist in both the public and the private sectors, and employ skills that range from database designing to records and library management to engineering infrastructure design and management. These are participants in what have been described as the information sectors of economies and the global knowledge industries.[17]

They have the common objective of enhancing terrain transparency in support of economic activities in the context of LDCs. This is the infrastructure that will come more into play in determining the new development agenda in this period of reconstruction. In terrain transparency efforts, the information human resources have a responsibility to bring into focus lessons from the past and from other parts of the world to inform the new development path and agenda.

This has education/training implications. But this is also a time of public-sector expenditure cutbacks – including in education and training. An immediate task is the pursuit of more multidisciplinary programmes in the information studies area. One reason is that these are cost-effective and in tune with the lean times. But the more important reason is the versatility the information studies area gives its products at a time of convergence of electronic, communications and information technologies and skills. Training programmes in this direction would include those addressing common training in mass media, communications, computing and information sciences with the concepts of environmental transparency in development as a common core. Such approaches are already coming on stream. For example, in Ethiopia, Kenya and Nigeria, archivists, librarians, publishers and editors, records and media specialists are already being trained on common degree programmes. Postgraduate conversion programmes as well as non-degree spin-offs are therefore possible. Infusing into such programmes more comprehensive elements of mass communication, development and project management will give the programmes the orientation needed to manage information as a development resource focused on terrain transparency as a necessity for the development process.

This could be stretched further. Project management could be made compulsory in the training fields expected to be called upon to manage projects. Included here are engineering, sciences, education, administration and business programmes. Projects are an integral part of the development process, and their basics need to be public knowledge to those with an interest in the development agenda and with the responsibility to enhance transparency and accountability in this area. This is critical in LDCs, where the culture of letting go of dead or failed projects needs to be nurtured. The political fall-out from a lack of this ability can be costly.

Information management in development is the way to the future. It is the avenue of hope into the next millennium. It is the means to bring into play participative governance in tune with the era of multi-party democracy that has dawned on most LDCs, although imperfectly in many. Exploiting ICTs to propagate symbols of commonness in diversity and competitiveness in the global village is possible only through this approach. It is the way in which current and potential conflict can be resolved through informed dialogue that marginalizes demagoguery.

NOTES

1 R. A. Onyango, 'Information, the nation-state and democracy: an African perspective', in C. Chen (ed.) *NIT '96: Proceedings of the 9th International Conference on New Information Technology*, MicroUse Information, West Newton, MA, 1996, pp. 187–97.

2 R. A. Onyango, 'Global information and Africa: on the crest of a mirage?', *http://www.mcb.co.uk/confhome.htm* 1996.

3 R. A. Onyango, 'New technology adaptations, SMMEs and reconstruction and development', paper read at the Conference on Science and Technology in Reconstruction and Development (STIRD), University of Natal, Pietermaritzburg, South Africa, 23–26 September 1996.

4 R. A. Onyango, 'The knowledge industries: aids to technological and industrial development in Africa', in B. Cronin and N. Tudor-Silovic (eds) *The Knowledge Industries: Levers of Economic and Social Development in the 1990s*, Aslib, London, 1990, pp. 1–29.

5 R. A. Onyango, 'New technology adaptations', op. cit.

6 O. Obayiuwana, 'Nigeria authorities determined to block Internet access', *Owner-Kenya-net@AfricaOnline.com*, 20 December 1996, pp. 1–2.
7 R. A. Onyango, 'Global information and Africa', op. cit.
8 T. Chitechi, 'Leaders are the problem', *Owner-Kenya-net@AfricaOnline.com*, 13 December 1996, p. 1; 'Non-governmental organisations: making changes?', *Owner-Kenya-net@AfricaOnline.com*, 12 December 1996, p. 6.
9 'Non-governmental organisations: making changes?', *Owner-Kenya-net@AfricaOnline.com*, 12 December 1996, p. 6.
10 'Motion on ITC receives support in Parliament', *Daily News*, 10 December 1996, p. 2.
11 R. L. Katz, *The Information Society: An International Perspective*, Praeger, New York, 1988; I. Paez-Urdaneta, 'Information in the Third World', *International Library Review*, vol. 21, 1989, pp. 177–91; R. Salinas, 'Forget the NWICO . . . and start all over again', *Information Development*, vol. 2, no. 3, July 1986, pp. 154–8; K. J. Mchombu, 'The cultural and political dimensions of information resources management in Africa', in N. Adeyemi (ed.) *Reader on Information Management Strategies for Africa's Development*, UNECA/PADIS, Addis Ababa, 1995, pp. 103–24.
12 'Raila's company loses bid for molasses plant', *Owner-Kenya-net@AfricaOnline.com*, 11 December 1996, p. 2.
13 BNPC, *Productivity Insights*, Botswana National Productivity Centre, Gaborone, 1996.
14 O. Obayiuwana, op. cit.
15 'Expert group develops Africa's Internet strategy', *Computers in Africa*, December 1995/January 1996, p. 36.
16 T. J. Afullo, 'Global information and Africa: the telecommunications infrastructure for cyberspace', Available e-mail: *Conference@mcb.co.uk* or HTTP: *http://www.mcb.co.uk.services/conferen/apr96/global_information/conhome.htm http://www.mcb.co.uk/confhome.htm*, 1996, p. 3.
17 B. Cronin and N. Tudor-Silovic (eds), op. cit.

INDEX